Stephen Crane in Transition
Centenary Essays

STEPHEN CRANE
IN TRANSITION

Centenary Essays

Edited, with an Introduction and Afterword, by

JOSEPH KATZ

Northern Illinois University Press

DEKALB

Library of Congress Cataloging in
Publication Data
Katz, Joseph.
    Stephen Crane in transition.

    Bibliography: p.
    1. Crane, Stephen, 1871-1900.   I. Title.
PS1449.C85Z69   818'.4'09   72-1390
ISBN 0-87580-032-7

First Printing 1972
Second Printing 1973

© 1972 by Northern Illinois University Press
Published by Northern Illinois University Press, DeKalb, Illinois 60115
Manufactured in the United States of America

Contents

Contents

Stephen Crane

He had the angle. The Crane slant of vision came into a scene or onto an action or a personality with terrible ironic penetration, and it came from a direction and a distance that no one could have suspected was there, much less have predicted. He came from nowhere, and is with us, bringing his peculiar and unforgettable kind of detached animism, sometimes frightening, sometimes ludicrous, the objects and people of the world all being seen as comments on or complements or qualities of each other, and none of them safe from this. War and poverty are Crane's best themes, and the needless suffering of animals. The cosmos is filled with the most stupifying fear about which, inexplicably, there is also something funny. After reading him, we ponder the possibility that we had better use more caution before we "rush out into the red universe any more."

James Dickey

Acknowledgments

For Vincent Starrett

I have assumed the privilege of dedicating this book to Vincent Starrett. We read Stephen Crane today largely because Starrett read him more than fifty years ago and talked about his work intelligently and enthusiastically at a time when few others were doing so. Ben Hecht has written about Starrett's infectious appreciation of Crane during the 1920s; I have been among those who have witnessed it at a later time. Founders deserve recognition. I am particularly happy to give it because he helped me when I began my work in Crane studies, at a time when kindness and the pleasure of sharing could have been his only motives. This book is his.

I am additionally grateful to Miss Sandra I. Anderson, my research assistant, and Mrs. Faye Grahl, my secretary, for help in preparing this book for publication. The Department of English of the University of South Carolina has been generous in providing time and other resources that have made the book possible, and graduate students enrolled in courses in the Department have aided with their responses to several ideas and judgments that follow.

J. K.

Introduction

"I go through the world unexplained," Stephen Crane once remarked, and so far that is still true. In the iconography of American literary history he continues to be the native Chatterton, the archetypical boy artist whose untutored genius produced a few superb things before he was crushed by a society hostile to what it could not understand. It is an illusion, of course, but this is the picture of Stephen Crane that developed in his own time and prevails in ours. There is no mystery about its sources. It began as a way to explain how a twenty-three year old who had no apparent background could write *The Red Badge of Courage* or even *Maggie: A Girl of the Streets*. William Dean Howells was one of the first to have used it when he introduced Crane at a party by saying "Here is a writer who has sprung into life fully armed." Seven years later, almost immediately after Crane's death, the misconception was complete in its essentials. The notion of a Chattertonian Crane was becoming useful on occasions when there was a need to lash the imperfections of American culture with a home-grown martyr to its art. Nearly a half century after Howells introduced Crane to his guests, it was the established view. An eminent historian of American literature protested that "the appearance of an original artist, springing without antecedent into life, is always illusion, but the sources of Crane's philosophy and art are as yet undeciphered."

Now, however, it seems that Stephen Crane is at last in transition from legendary figure to comprehendible author. Because attractive legends are difficult to dispel, the process has been slow. Nevertheless, the recovery of the facts of his career and the close reading of his texts are leading to a more reasonable explanation of Crane's place in American literature. The essays in this book, published to mark the one hundredth anniversary of Crane's birth, form an experiment in allowing Crane studies to reveal something of that transition. Although everything here was especially written for this collection, there has been no attempt to make it reflect an homogeneous point of view. To have done so—even were it possible—would have been to obscure the growing diversity in Crane scholarship and criticism that is essential to their future accomplishments. Coupled with a healthy regard for the directions of evidence, which legends always distort, this diversity will surely bring about a better understanding of Crane's life and work, and the significance of both to American culture.

There are some interesting results of this experiment in allowing Crane studies to reveal itself in the process of transition. One is that the following essays are oriented mainly towards Crane's achievement as a literary artist. This orientation implies seeing the variety of his career, instead of looking at *The Red Badge of Courage* as its pinnacle. The orthodox view has been to see everything before that novel as preparation, and everything afterwards as decline. Perhaps it is a judgment that will be proven correct; in the past it has been the assumption that towered above the need for proof. Because, in literary study as in everything else, heterodoxy is the only way to test orthodoxy, it is necessary to examine the entire corpus of a writer's work before anything valid about his achievement can be said. It is particularly necessary in the case of Stephen Crane because a concomitant of the vision of him as Chattertonian is a conclusion that he was a sport of American literary history, tied neither to the past nor the future—a phenomenon rather than a comprehensible, even in a developing tradition. Although the essays in this book imply disagreement on several specifics, all of them start from the assumption that Crane must be seen as a serious artist who drew from the tradition and contributed to it.

Another notable feature of these essays is that they open potentially valuable approaches to Crane's work, suggesting a variety of ways to look at his art and its influence. One trouble caused by a legend that dominates as long as the legend of Stephen Crane is that it encourages self-satisfied rigidity among some who manage to pierce it in a few places. That quality seems to be epitomized by the remark with which Crane's most recent biographer tried to close an argument over an event in Crane's life: "And that settles that." Saying the last word soothes the ego, of course, but the point of Crane studies now is a growing awareness that so far very little has been settled. It is a sign of maturation that Crane studies has arrived at the stage of realizing that there is a need to look at things with fresh eyes after evaluating what has been said and establishing what needs to be investigated. Signaling that stage is the willingness to try a variety of ways in the recognition that some of them will produce only tentative results. This is honesty, not uncertainty. It will improve the tone as well as the content of Crane studies.

Joseph Katz

Columbia, South Carolina

Stephen Crane in Transition

Centenary Essays

Bernard Weinstein

Stephen Crane: Journalist

It is relatively easy to outline Stephen Crane's career as a newspaperman. He began it early, probably in 1888, when he was seventeen. Around then he began working as an anonymous reporter for his brother Townley's New Jersey Coast News Bureau, which specialized in articles about the Jersey Shore. According to Willis Fletcher Johnson, day editor of the *New York Tribune* and a friend of the Crane family, Stephen's work was so unimportant that Townley paid him out of his own pocket and collected space-rate pay on it as for his own.[1] By 1890, however, Townley admitted to the *Tribune* that his "kid brother" was helping him. But Crane's introduction to the newspaper world must have taken place even earlier. Others of his family besides Townley were involved in it: when his father died in 1880, Stephen's mother supported herself and him partly by writing for several Methodist papers and the *Tribune,* and Wilbur Crane, another brother, also had been a short-term correspondent for that daily.[2] So it is understandable that Crane began to think of journalism as a career. He worked for his brother's agency until August 1892 when furor over his article on a parade of the Junior Order of

United American Mechanics compelled him to give up the job. Here began the pattern of confrontation that would continue throughout his newspaper career, encouraging the development of the themes, the style, and many of the incidents found in his major writings.

Immediately, however, survival became a struggle. In the fall of 1892, Crane went to New York City to find work on a paper, but he seems to have been only minimally successful. Although he probably did some journalistic work during the next two years, little of it can be identified. At last, while he was living in poverty, he made a newspaper connection with the *New York Press* which published two of his now-famous feature articles, "An Experiment in Misery" and "An Experiment in Luxury." He continued writing for the *Press* through the end of 1894, when it published "The Red Badge of Courage" in December.[3] That abbreviated version of his novel was being syndicated then by Bacheller, Johnson & Bacheller—he had been introduced to Irving Bacheller, the president, by Edward Marshall of the *Press*.

Now his career began to rise. Bacheller was taken by Crane's work and sent him out of the city as a traveling correspondent. In the first four months of 1895 Crane followed his own itinerary through the West and Mexico, writing only about what interested him.[4] When he returned to the East that spring, he did not resume newspaper work immediately. In the middle of 1896, however, he did a number of articles for the *New York Journal* and other papers about the Tenderloin, the area in New York's West Thirties known for saloons, brothels, and opium dens. This series eventually got him into trouble by involving him in a notorious altercation between a prostitute—Dora Clark—and a crooked policeman—Charles Becker—and drove him from New York with damage to his literary and personal reputations.

When he left New York in November 1896, he went to Jacksonville, Florida, the staging point for correspondents trying to cover the then raging Cuban insurrection. There he waited impatiently for passage on a filibustering boat that would carry guns, ammunition, and him to the insurgents. While he waited, he developed a relationship with Cora Taylor, proprietress of the Hotel de Dream, who later became his common-law wife. Finally, he sailed aboard the *Commodore* on 1 January 1897, but the ship suffered an engine-room explosion that night and sank the next morning. The thirty hours Crane spent in a ten-foot dinghy with three other men provided him with a front-page story about his experience and the germ of a short story about its significance: the newspaper report was "Stephen Crane's Own Story," as the *Press* headlined it on 7 January; and the short story, of course, was "The Open Boat."

Recovered from his physical strain and despaired of reaching Cuba, Crane took off to report the Greco-Turkish War that March. With him went Cora. Although the war lasted only a few weeks, Crane had the opportunity to write a number of battlefield accounts for the *New York Journal* and a series of clear, reflective, and compassionate essays for the *Westminster Gazette*. The war over, he and Cora went to England and settled at Ravensbrook, in Surrey. Barely a year later, however, he was off again as a correspondent, this time to cover the Spanish-American War. The *New York World* had cabled for his services, and since he was refused entrance into the United States Navy he followed the course of the Cuban campaign for Joseph Pulitzer. In Cuba, he fell ill, tropical fever aggravated by tuberculosis probably, and returned stateside to recuperate in July. When he returned to cover the Puerto Rican campaign, it was for William Randolph Hearst's *Journal* (Crane either had quit the *World* or was dismissed by it). The war ended quickly, but Crane stayed on, going underground in Havana to write articles and short stories about the Spanish-American War and a novel about the Greco-Turkish War.

Frantic Cora, who had heard nothing from him during that time, flushed him out and got him home. But he was a dying man, besieged at a borrowed Brede Place by creditors and spongers. He tried to rally his strength to cover the Boer War in January 1900, but all he

Bernard Weinstein

could do was write a few armchair accounts for the papers. There was no chance for him to go himself. By the time his last piece on that war was published, he was already dead.

I

Stephen Crane was far from an orthodox journalist. He was never completely at home in the newspaper world, although he wrote for major papers. In his early years his reporting was considered eccentric and overly subtle by editors and publishers. At the outset of his journalistic career, he had been influenced by a lecture given by Hamlin Garland on William Dean Howells in August 1891. In "Howells Discussed at Avon-by-the-Sea" (*New York Tribune*, 18 August) Crane reported Garland as saying that Howells "does not insist upon any special materials but only that the novelist be true to things as he sees them." (Later, Crane himself would write John Northern Hilliard, editor of the *Rochester Union and Advertiser*, that "A man is born into the world with his own pair of eyes and he is not at all responsible for his vision. He is merely responsible for the quality of his personal honesty." [5]) Crane took Howells's dictum, which was consistent with the literary doctrine of impressionism, as seriously in his journalism as he would in his fiction. One of his earliest attempts to carry it into practice may have been during a possible association with the *New York Herald*. "Youse Wants Petey, Youse Do" (*New York Herald*, 4 January 1892), a courtroom sketch, made up mostly of slum dialect, about three boys accused of stealing, may be his. Other pieces in the *Herald*—if it published anything of his at all—are unidentifiable.[6] The defiantly impressionistic accounts of an alderman who sat like "a rural soup tureen" and a horse who kicked "grey ice of the gutter into silvery angles that hurtled and clicked on frozen stone" that Thomas Beer mentions would hardly have pleased the whimsical and despotic *Herald* publisher, James Gordon Bennett, or the fact-hungry city editor, William C. Reick.[7]

Crane sometimes took risks in clashing with the newspaper establishment. In that notorious *Tribune* report of 28 August 1892, "On the

6

New Jersey Coast," Crane described the Labor Day Parade of the Junior Order of United American Mechanics: "The procession was composed of men, bronzed, slope-shouldered, uncouth and begrimed with dust. Their clothes fitted them illy, for the most part, and they had no idea of marching. They merely plodded along, not seeming quite to understand, stolid, unconcerned and, in a certain sense, dignified—a pace and a bearing emblematic of their lives." Crane intended to contrast the awkward, shuffling, ungainly marchers—"men who possessed principles"—with "the bona fide Asbury Parker," a member of the leisure class who produced nothing but assumed a superior air before his social inferiors. But he was already far too subtle and ironic, too subjective, for a newspaper representing even liberal traditions. The *Tribune* received countless irate letters attacking the anonymous young author for "slurring" the Mechanics on the manner in which they walked. Those whom he meant to attack seem not to have understood either. A question exists as to whether Willis Fletcher Johnson fired Crane for his indiscretion or whether Crane decided to leave Townley on his own. Whatever the case, he accepted Johnson's advice that news reporting was not a means for "subtle rhetorical devices."[8] Still, Crane may well have been bitter at the somewhat self-righteous way in which the *Tribune*, whose publisher, Whitelaw Reid, was the 1892 Republican vice-presidential candidate, defended itself—by publicly deploring and apologizing for "sentiments both foreign and repugnant to the *Tribune*." Arthur Oliver recalls that Crane seemed cheerful, almost proud, that the article had put Reid's opportunities in jeopardy. "You'd hardly think that an innocent little chap like me could have stirred up such a row in American politics. It shows what innocence can do if it has the opportunity!"[9] But one can hardly doubt that this absurd comedy of errors caused Crane to be more cynical than amused about the newspaper world.

If, in 1892, Crane indulged himself in playful nose-tweaking of the journalistic establishment, he was much more sober and serious in 1894 regarding the conflict between his personal ethics and journalistic expediency. Assigned by *McClure's Magazine* to write a piece on the Scranton coal mines, he contributed a gripping article about man's elemental struggle with nature underground: "In the Depths of a Coal Mine" (*McClure's*, 3 [August 1894]: 195–209). *McClure's* published the article as it stood except for the closing section which, thanks to the artist Corwin Knapp Linson who accompanied Crane on his trip to Scranton, remains part of the record. At the conclusion of the article, Crane had written an "excoriation" of "men who made neat livings by fiddling with the market":

> Relating the tale of a recent accident which had put a party of coal-brokers visiting the mines in peril of their lives, he concluded: "I confess to a dark and sinful glee at the description of their pangs; a delight at for once finding coal brokers associated in hardship and danger with the coal-miner. . . .
> If all men who stand uselessly and for their own extraordinary profit between the miner and the consumer were annually doomed to a certain period of danger and darkness in the mines, they might at last comprehend the misery and bitterness of men who toil for existence at these hopelessly grim tasks.[10]

Crane, seeing the article in print with its obvious omission, reacted scornfully, "The birds didn't want the truth after all. Why the hell did they send me up there then? Do they want the public to think the coal-mines gilded ball-rooms with the miners eating ice-cream in boiled shirt-fronts?" He undoubtedly equated this attempt at censorship with the general timorousness of editors and publishers he had already experienced. In all fairness, Crane may have ignored the fact that, at this time, *McClure's* was still struggling to exist and probably for that reason more than any other feared antagonizing business interests.[11]

It seemed inevitable that both Crane's love of truth and his journalistic idiosyncrasies would bring him into some conflict with the two newspaper "czars," William Randolph Hearst and Joseph Pulitzer, for whom he wrote during his latter days. In fact, when Crane, already a literary celebrity, went to work for the *Journal* in the middle of 1896, Hearst's aim was to capitalize on the literary talents of his young reporters like Julian Hawthorne, Alfred Henry Lewis, and Edward Townsend and to offer the public not synthetic attempts at objectivity but "news novelettes from real life; stories gathered from the live wires of the day and written in dramatic form."[12] Furthermore, both the *Journal* and the *World* obviously enjoyed exploiting Crane's name and reputation in headlines to his stories—"Asbury Park as Seen by Stephen Crane" (*Journal*, 23 May 1897), "Stephen Crane at the Front for the World" (*World*, 7 July 1898), "Stephen Crane Tells of War's Horrors" (*Journal*, 23 May 1897), "The Red Badge of Courage Was His Wig-Wag Flag" (*World*, 1 July 1898)—and encouraged him to write in the first person. Indeed, if one compares the pieces Crane sent from the Greek battlefield to the *Journal* with those he sent to the *Westminster Gazette*, the absence of "I," the over-all objectivity and artistic control of the *Gazette* sketches seem very pronounced.

Crane's distaste for the excesses of yellow journalism undoubtedly grew out of his 1896 encounter with the newspaper pieces about his defense of the prostitute Dora Clark. He had protected her from police brutality and later testified in court in her behalf, events which he himself reported in unemotional, even casual, tones in "Adventures of a Novelist" (*Journal*, 20 September). However, his sensitive and diffident nature must have smarted under the embarrassment and pain of journalistic notoriety. Although most New York papers praised his heroism lavishly, Crane could hardly have welcomed accounts, such as that in the New York *Sun*, of his standing in court "with the 'red badge of courage' flaming in his breast" ("Stephen Crane and Dora Clark," *Sun*, 17 September). He later took every opportunity to snipe at sensation-hungry newspapermen: in *Active Service* and "The Monster" these men distort truth and pander to the reader's morbid curiosity and taste for sensation; in war stories like "Death and the Child," "The Revenge of the Adolphus," and

"The Lone Charge of William B. Perkins," they appear shallow and childish nuisances alongside the seasoned, efficient soldiers. Crane sometimes turned his journalism itself against the excesses of the press, as he did in a Spanish-American War article, "Denies Mutilation of Bodies" (Philadelphia *Press*, 17 June 1898), where he asserted in the interest of honesty that the wounds of two American soldiers at Camp McCalla were the results of bullets, not bestial assaults by the Spaniards. Crane's later opinion was borne out by a medical inquiry.[13]

Upon his return from Cuba in July 1898, Crane left the employ of the *World* for unknown reasons. This seemed the only instance during the period of his literary fame when his newspaper employers made known any dissatisfaction with his reporting. Don C. Seitz, the *World*'s business manager at the time Crane left, made the rather preposterous charge in his biography of Joseph Pulitzer that Crane "sent only one dispatch of any merit, and that, accusing the Seventy-first New York Regiment of cowardice, imperiled the paper."[14] Crane actually contributed twenty articles to the *World*, many of very high quality. Furthermore, the article about the Seventy-first Regiment was filed from Port Antonio on 15 July, seven days after Crane had left Cuba for the United States. Yet, despite Seitz's unreasonable pique, the *World* may have been understandably antagonized by Crane's unorthodox style of newspaper work. He had frequently allowed a good deal of time—sometimes weeks—to elapse between an event and his published account of it, a fact that would have disturbed the most tolerant of editors and publishers. Furthermore, he had been conspicuously absent from decisive battles and victories; he had charged that the newspapers had given excessive coverage to the Rough Riders and ignored the steady, if unspectacular, regulars; he had taken a controversial stand against the army for supplying the American soldiers with black powder, thereby making them more conspicuous to enemy fire; and perhaps worst of all, he had filed the report of the wounded *Journal* newspaperman Edward Marshall, thereby missing the concluding action at the battle of Las Guasimas.

Crane had substituted loyalty to a friend for loyalty to an employer. His friendship with Marshall dated back to his early New York days when Marshall was the Sunday editor of the *Press* and published Crane's two "Experiments" in April 1894. At that time reporters thought "queer" the "occasional little article at $5 a column" he sold to the paper and thought Crane himself "aloof, 'stuck up,' arty, snooty and spoiled." [15] But if Crane felt isolated in 1894, he was much more familiar with fellow journalists by 1896 when he himself was famous, and when Hearst, who had taken over the *Journal* a year earlier, set a precedent by hiring literary "stars," men who were closer to Crane's temperament and sympathies than the hardened newsmen he knew vaguely on the *Press*. In 1895–1896 he was a member in good standing of a literary-journalistic fraternity called the Lantern (or Lanthorne) Club, and on 31 December 1895 he was tendered a dinner by the Society of Philistines, which numbered among its members several famous newsmen. The proud and pompous novelist-journalist Richard Harding Davis, who had been somewhat contemptuous and arrogant toward Crane in the Greco-Turkish War, became one of his most loyal champions during and after the Spanish-American War, when their acquaintance was renewed.[16] Other reporters marveled at Crane's casualness and daring in the face of war, and he became, to many, a subject of interest in himself. For example, John Bass, a famous *Journal* correspondent, described "How Novelist Crane Acts on the Battlefield" (*Journal*, 23 May 1897).

> Your correspondent sought shelter in a trench and cautiously watched the pale, thin face of the novelist as the latter seated himself on an ammunition box amid a shower of shells and casually lighted a cigarette.
>
> Stephen Crane did not appear surprised, but watched with a quiet expression the quick work of the artillerymen as they loaded,

fired and jumped to replace the small cannon overturned by the recoil.

I was curious to know what was passing in his mind, and said: "Crane, what impresses you most in this affair?"

The author of *The Red Badge of Courage* lighted another cigarette, pushed back his long hair out of his eyes with his hat and answered quickly:

"Between two great armies battling against each other the interesting thing is the mental attitude of the men."

Doubtless, Crane gradually inspired affection in much of the New York newspaper fraternity, although his relationships with editors and publishers remained generally uneasy, and he frequently expressed distaste for the field of journalism.

II

Crane did not live long enough to fulfill the promise of *Maggie*, *The Red Badge of Courage*, and "The Open Boat," and any speculation about his potential for growth had he lived beyond 1900 is purely academic. His last writings were frequently motivated by frantic attempts to repay debts and meet expenses, and it is difficult to determine whether, given more tranquil living conditions, he could have moved in new directions, philosophically and aesthetically. Yet his journalistic career, running parallel with his career as a writer of novels and short stories, reflects the several stages of his philosophical and artistic development and offers perhaps the best barometer of his attitude toward man and his place in the universe.

Crane subscribed to no one philosophical or social school of thought exclusively. The previous literary generation composed of such figures as Twain, Howells, James, and Adams had rebelled against the complacently optimistic and genteel values of middle-nineteenth-century America by flirting with Marxism, Darwinism, utopianism, and other doctrines or by retreating into the intellectual European past; but Crane was born into a world represented by his crusading, intellectual, yet fundamentalist parents, half-conservative and half-committed to social and intellectual change, and for him rebellion took the form of iconoclasm, of a rejection of systems altogether. "I was a Socialist for two weeks," he once said, "but when a couple of Socialists assured me I had no right to think differently from any other Socialist and then quarrelled with each other about what Socialism meant, I ran away."[17] What interested Crane was the integrity of his own vision.

But there is no doubt that Crane's parents, with their missionary zeal and their devotion to social causes, inspired him to think seriously about poverty, social inequity, and moral responsibility. His early journalism is both a rebellion against their bourgeois values and an affirmation of their ethics. From the beginning, Crane's newspaper tone was characterized by irreverence, such as that found in his Asbury Park pieces for the *Tribune*. If his mother, in her role as a correspondent and WCTU member, condemned alcoholism and prizefighting, Crane bragged that the fighter James Corbett, whose quiet and gentlemanly behavior had made him many friends, had arrived in Asbury Park ("Crowding into Asbury Park," *Tribune*, 3 July 1892), and he wrote frequently of frivolities and amusements calculated to antagonize the Methodists of Ocean Grove. Like H. L. Mencken a few decades later, he enjoyed his role as a "bourgeois-baiter." A favorite target was James Bradley, "founder" of the resort, who had a penchant for tacking moralistic signs over the entire area. But, generally, his barbs were directed against the self-important, complacent and frivolous vacationers—the "rather portly man, with a good watchchain and a business suit of clothes, a wife and about three children, a man whose pride and vanity made him the target of varied seaside fakirs and other entrepreneurs" ("On the Boardwalk," *Tribune*, 14 August 1892); the "summer girl"—Crane's name for the "flapper" of the New Jersey resort—who flirted and broke hearts outrageously ("The Seaside Hotel Hop," *Tribune*, 11 September 1892); the "summer youth," usually a vacation blade, who toiled the rest of the year at some non-descript clerical task ("On the Boardwalk"); and the "pseudo-scholars" who combined vacations with "worthwhile" pursuits and whose forays into scientific investigation consisted of "inspecting great glass jars filled with strange floating growths in the laboratory on the banks of the Shark River . . . . Microscopes and various instruments that resemble machine-guns and the entrails of alarm clocks are to them the world" ("Along the Shark River," *Tribune*, 15 August 1892). His central aims in his Asbury Park journalism seemed to be deflation of pomposity and satire, however mild, of the genteel tradition.

But Crane's skepticism, probably even as early as 1892, was based upon a deeper comprehension: the realization of the futility of posturing and pretentiousness. In the overtly comic *Sullivan County Sketches* which appeared in the *Tribune* from February to December 1892 he viewed man's egotism and vanity against a background of awesome nature where chance alone ruled. The hero of most of the sketches was aptly identified only as "the little man," a term of anonymity denoting his Lilliputian stature in a Brobdingnagian world. One cannot be certain whether Crane's inherent sense of fatality sprang up in natural rebellion against his parents' moral zealousness and sense of purpose, but it did help to give his journalism the same humanitarian impulse that motivated their own compassion toward the downtrodden and social outcasts. When he went to New York in the fall of 1892 and experienced poverty and discouragement himself, he became more conscious of the subservience of all men—even the rich—to "the eternal mystery of social condition." In "An Experiment in Misery" (*Tribune*, 22 April 1894), for example, and in "The Men in the Storm" (*Arena*, October 1894) he wrote gloomily of the demoralizing and dehumanizing struggle of derelicts and failures to survive in "a nation forcing its regal head into the clouds, throwing no downward glance; in the sublimity of its aspirations ignoring the wretches who may flounder at its feet." In "An Experiment in Luxury" (*Tribune*, 29 April 1894) he came to the realization that "nobody is responsible for anything," that the wealthy were as arbitrarily governed by nature's "incomprehensible machinery and system" which sent forth flowers in one field and denied them to another. Even in relatively light sketches, atmospheric pieces for the most part, Crane seriously contemplated man's precarious role in the universe and his feeble vanity. In "Coney Island's Failing Days" (*Press*, 14 October 1894), for example, he commented that "a mild quantity of egotism" is necessary for most people to survive in a world where "it is only the great philosophers who have the wisdom to be utterly miserable."

But, despite his cynicism, Crane could not altogether abandon his moral or ethical sense. While living in New York in 1894 he seemed convinced that one part of city life, symbolized by the Bowery at one extreme and the Fifth Avenue mansion at the other, was "a sort of cowardice" in which the poor allowed themselves to be trod underfoot and the rich abdicated their social responsibility. He later wrote to a friend, shortly after his return from the West: "Damn the east! I fell in love with the straight out-and-out, sometimes hideous, often braggart Westerners, because I thought them to be truer men and, by the living piper, we will see in fifty years what the west will do." [18] In the 1894 pieces for the *Press*, even in the Tenderloin articles for the *Journal* and other papers in 1896, he turned repeatedly to the theme of escape: to the barricades of wealth and social position, to frantic pleasure, to alcoholism and opium addiction, to a world of illusion where fictional and dramatic conventions served as a substitute for reality.

But when Crane traveled to Nebraska and the West he discovered the values he would affirm more fully in his war correspondence. In one of his most celebrated pieces of correspondence, "Nebraskans' Bitter Fight for Life" (Philadelphia *Press*, 24 February 1895) he wrote about man's heroic endurance in the face of nature, "the pitiless enemy." The Nebraskans were struggling through a terrible winter cold which had driven men from their homes and made the territory barren. However, despite the ordeal of the Nebraskans, which Crane had poignantly documented, the piece resounded with an optimism and confidence virtually non-existent in his earlier journalism. He noted, much to his wonderment, the capacity of these stricken people to survive and to help each other. The Nebraskan farmers were "not bended like the Eastern farmer, but erect and agile." Crane had lost little of his earlier fatalism while he was in Nebraska; but from this point on, the theme of endurance became a progressively stronger keynote of his journalistic writing. Even in the frantic and reckless world of the Tenderloin, which he observed after his return from the West, he marveled at the resiliency and vitality of the inhabitants.

Crane's experience in the open boat and his war correspondence bore out what he had discovered in Nebraska and the West: that in a seemingly indifferent or hostile universe man might still believe in himself and in the moral courage of his fellow human beings. Having been adrift for thirty hours in the ten-foot dinghy after the *Commodore* sank on 2 January 1897, Crane referred in "Stephen Crane's Own Story" (*Press*, 7 January) to the "splendid manhood of Captain Murphy and of William Higgins, the oiler." [19] In the journalism of the Greco-Turkish War and the Spanish-American War, he celebrated the solid and workmanlike achievements of the ordinary and unglamorous veteran soldiers. The idealized Greek soldiers, frequently ragged and wounded, are almost mystically stoic and superhuman, bridging the gap between nature's indifference and man's suffering, and depicting, as the Nebraskans did, the theme of the human struggle to survive in an absurd world.[20] Many of the images of the men in the war journalism are unforgettable: a wounded Greek soldier aboard a hospital ship using the bosom of his dead comrade as a pillow for his head ("Stephen Crane Tells of War's Horrors," *Journal*, 23 May 1897); a group of Greek soldiers praying before a shrine demolished by a shell ("Crane at Velestino," *Journal*, 11 May 1897); an American soldier in Cuba, calmly "wig-wagging" to signal an American ship while bullets whistle over his head ("The Red Badge of Courage Was His Wig-Wag Flag," *World*, 1 July 1898). In "Regulars Get No Glory" (*World*, 20 July 1898) he describes what for him might have been the archetypal soldier:

He goes into battle as if he had been fighting every day for three hundred years. If there is heavy firing ahead he does not even ask a question about it. He doesn't even ask whether the Americans are winning or losing. He agitates himself over no extraneous points. He attends exclusively to himself. . . .

After the battle, at leisure—if he gets any—the regular's talk is likely to be a complete essay on practical field operations. . . .

Then suddenly the regular becomes impenetrable, enigmatic. It is a question of Orders. When he hears the appointed voice raised in giving an Order, he is a changed being. When an Order comes he has no more to say; he simply displays as fine a form of unquestioning obedience as there is to be seen anywhere. It is his sacred thing, his fetish, his religion. Nothing now can stop him but a bullet.

The more Crane saw of war, the more disenchanted he became with causes and slogans and idealistic issues, and the more enraptured with the human verities revealed on the battlefield.

But, increasingly enamored as he was by the mystique of soldiership, it was almost inevitable that Crane would come to view the war in simplified terms, ignoring deeper moral issues. His rejection of causes was not like his earlier tough-minded skepticism, but, more likely, a hazily romantic adoration of the "strenuous life," bolstered perhaps by the philosophies of Theodore Roosevelt and Owen Wister.[21] Crane was little disturbed by growing uneasiness felt by many liberal Americans toward United States adventurism in the Caribbean and the Philippines. It is difficult to determine whether his attitude was merely a loyal response to his employers on the *World* and the *Journal*, who consistently generated jingoism and war fever (Crane's more personal reflections in "War Memories" are more temperate and more compassionate to the Spaniards in defeat), or whether he was simply blind to any fault in America's moral position, but his newspaper accounts from Cuba were almost as frequently self-righteous and chauvinistic as they were justifiably proud. For example, he jubilantly compared the offensive against the Spaniards at Cuzco to "a trap-shooting" and the figures of the Spaniards endeavoring to escape the American ambush to "pieces of white paper" ("The Red Badge of Courage Was His Wig-Wag Flag").[22] He concluded one lengthy sketch with an account of the taking of a covey of Spanish prisoners: "They were all of a lower class than one could find in any United States jail." He gloated complacently that the prisoners "expected to be butchered" but that "our great good motherly old country has only mercy, and nothing in her pockets but beef, hard-tack and coffee for all of them—lemon-colored refugee from Santiago, wild-eyed prisoner from the trenches, Spanish guerilla from out the thickets, half-naked insurgent from the mountains—all of them" ("Stephen Crane's Vivid Story of the Battle of San Juan," *World*, 14 July 1898). He was equally self-congratulating and chauvinistic in his attitude toward the civilian Spanish refugees at El Caney. On one hand, sympathetic to "the great gaunt assemblage" whose appearance reflected "the true horror of war," he could not resist chastizing Spain's "ignoble pride" and emphasizing with tiresome regularity American charity and patience.[23] Though he never ceased to admire the Cuban revolutionaries hiding out in the woods, his attitude toward the Santiago Cubans changed gradually from a feeling of admiration to one of contempt; the American soldiers, he wrote, "despise them. They came down here expecting to fight side by side with an ally, but this ally has done little but stay in the rear and eat army rations, manifesting an indifference to the cause of Cuban liberty which could not be exceeded by some one who had never heard of it" ("Vivid Story of the Battle of San Juan"). "The Cubans have not behaved well in the most prominent cases," he remarked retrospectively in "Mr. Stephen Crane on the New America" (*Outlook*, 3 [February 4, 1899]: 12–13).

In this latter piece, an interview he granted upon his return from Cuba, Crane denied any "direct American sense of Imperialism" in Cuba or the Philippines. But earlier, in "Crane Tells the Story of the

18

Disembarkment" (*World*, 7 July), he remarked that "our foot is firmly and formidably planted" in Cuba. He could criticize German imperialism in China and Spanish imperialism in Cuba, but he seemed to have been blind to empire-building by America or Britain. He was not unsympathetic, for example, toward British aims in South Africa during the Boer War. "One can conclude," he wrote in "The Talk of London" (*Journal*, 11 March 1900), "that an early British victory in the Transvaal would smite many political ambitions in Europe. Russia's clever and sly agents, France's waiting brigades in Algeria, would be very likely to stand in their tracks for some time to come." He was hostile to the many liberal Americans who had banded together to form the Anti-Imperialist League, even suggesting recklessly that these people, in their "Bostonese disapproval," were responsible for the deaths of American soldiers in the Philippines ("Stephen Crane Says Watson's Criticisms of England's War Are Not Unpatriotic," *Journal*, 25 July 1900).[24]

But notwithstanding Crane's indifference to, or oversimplification of, many political and moral issues, his journalism moved philosophically from a sense of youthful cynicism and pessimism to a complete celebration of courage, heroism, and sacrifice.

III

As Crane's journalism showed signs of philosophical change, it also showed change in literary style. The chief stylistic contrast in the early and late newspaper writing was between the self-conscious, elaborate prose of the former and the relative simplicity of the latter.

In a letter to Lily Brandon Munroe, probably written in 1894, Crane spoke of renouncing his "clever, Rudyard-Kipling style" after the last decisive summer at Asbury Park and referred to the "little creed of art" which he had developed for himself and whose chief ingredients were nature and truth. "It seemed to me that there must be something more in life than to sit and cudgel one's brains for clever and witty expedients."[25] By the summer of 1892, however, Crane had abandoned the idea of cleverness for its own sake which characterized the

19

irreverent but inconsequential pieces he wrote at Syracuse ("The King's Favor," Syracuse University *Herald,* 19 [May 1891]; "Great Bugs in Onondaga," *Tribune,* 11 June 1891). Several of his earlier pieces, including the New York sketches of 1894, frequently show a straining for effects that belied the relative unimportance of their subject matter. For example, "In a Park Row Restaurant' (*Press,* 28 October 1894) demonstrates Crane's fondness for imagery of battle and violence:

[The waiters] served customers with such speed and violence that it often resembled a personal assault. The crumbs from the previous diner were swept off with one fierce motion of a napkin. A waiter struck two blows at the table and left there a knife and a fork. And then came the viands in a volley, thumped down in haste, causing men to look sharp to see if their trousers were safe.

There was in the air an endless clatter of dishes, loud and bewilderingly rapid, like the gallop of a thousand horses. From afar back, at the places of communication to the kitchen, there came the sound of a continual roaring altercation, hoarse and vehement, like the cries of the officers of a regiment under attack. A mist of steam fluttered where the waiters crowded and jostled about the huge copper coffee urns. Over in one corner a man who toiled there like a foundryman was continually assailed by sharp cries. "Brown th' wheat!"

In the same manner, an earlier piece, "The Broken-Down Van" (*Tribune,* 10 July 1892), invoked a host of epic devices—similes, personifications, catalogues—to describe the collision of two furniture vans on a busy New York street.

But Crane's elaborate description and self-consciously literary style in these early writings were not altogether wasted. For example, in both the *Sullivan County Sketches* and in the pieces from Asbury Park, written during the same period in 1892, the very incongruity between subject and style furthered Crane's irony. In both sets of sketches the themes were egotism and vanity, and the heightened style only underscored the triviality and unimpressiveness of his characters. In the Asbury Park pieces Crane sometimes employed a mock-epic style to characterize idleness and pretentiousness in the middle-class world. In one sketch, the boardwalk became "the centre of the world of people . . . add but princes and gamblers and it would be what the world calls the world." About the effect of "the summer girl" Crane wrote, "She gives zest to life on the great boardwalk. Without her the men would perish from weariness or fall to fighting. . . . She absent, the bands would play charges and retreats and the soda-water fountains would run blood. Man is compelled by nature to be either a lover or a red-handed villain" ("On the Boardwalk"). In one of the *Sullivan County Sketches*, "The Octopush" (*Tribune*, 10 July 1892), Crane described a simple fishing scene in terms of swirling movement, dazzling imagery, and fierce combat; and in another, "The Black Dog" (*Tribune*, 24 July), he narrated a scene of anguish in a series of theatrical poses and exaggerated diction: "Four water-soaked men make their difficult ways through the drenched forest. The little man stopped and shook an angry finger at where night was stealthily following them. 'Cursed be fate and her children and her children's children! We are everlastingly lost!' he cried. The panting procession halted under some dripping, drooping locks and swore in wrathful astonishment." For a world where "heroism" was the product of chance, where ego counted for nothing, absurdly heroic diction proved an appropriately ironic descriptive device.

Crane's early journalism was almost always larger than life, and inanimate objects often took on an animate character, as if to overpower and devour man. In the *Sullivan County Sketches* Crane wrote hyperbolic descriptions of "baffled waters," "haggard tree trunks," and "vindictive weeds" ("The Octopush"). In "An Experiment in Misery," men are anonymously clustered together (as in *The Red Badge of Courage*) in "freights," "squads" and "a blend of black figures," while streetcars rumble ominously overhead "as if going upon a carpet stretched in the aisle made by the pillars of the elevated road"; buildings "lurk" in shadows; a saloon appears "voracious," its swinging doors "like ravenous lips" making "gratified smacks as if the saloon were gorging itself with plump men."[26] In "An Experiment in Luxury," the wealthy family lives in a house animated by a personality of its own: "broad, brown and stolid like the face of a peasant . . . a homely pile of stone, rugged, grimly self-reliant. . . . " Around them plants "lurk" and "a green luxuriant vine" dominates the windowless wall. The narrator finds himself disturbingly impressed with material objects, whose presence dwarfs the stature of the inhabitants. In Crane's Scranton account, "In the Depths of a Coal Mine," the machines are monsters and the atmosphere is wholly oppressive and destructive. The "breaker" becomes a "huge and hideous monster" whose "great teeth on revolving cylinders" chew huge lumps of coal into fragments, "grinding its mammoth jaws with unearthly and monotonous uproar." Even in his later sketches he sensed the irresistable power of machines and technology, symbols of man's capitulation before forces greater than he. At the beginning of the *Commodore* sketch he describes the boarding of the boat with ammunition and rifles: "Her hatch, like the mouth of a monster engulfed them. It might have been the feeding time of some legendary creature of the sea." In sketches like "When Everyone is Panic Stricken" (*Press*, 25 November 1894), not machines or inanimate objects but Nature itself, in the form of fire, emphasizes man's helplessness, feebleness, and awe before overpowering forces.

In fact, Nature gradually became man's chief adversary in Crane's later journalism. In "Nebraskans' Bitter Fight for Life," Nature appeared to be man's betrayer. "The imperial blue sky" of spring deceived man, leaving him helpless and unprepared for the hot wind that laid waste everything in its wake; the summer catastrophe gave over without warning to "its fierce counterpart," a winter frost that "came down like wolves of ice." If nature was not wholly malevolent, it was, as in *The Red Badge of Courage*, a symbol of a universe utterly oblivious to man's plight. Nature as a symbol dominated several of the pieces Crane wrote from Mexico and a good deal of his war journalism. One of his finest war accounts, "A Fragment of Velestino," began: "The sky was of a fair and quiet blue. In the radiantly bright atmosphere of the morning the distances among the hills were puzzling in the extreme. The Westerner could reflect that after all his eye was accustomed to using a tree as a standard of measure, but here there were no trees. The great bold hills were naked. The landscape was indeed one which we would understand as being Biblical. A tall lean shepherd was necessary in it." In the "Vivid Story of the Battle of San Juan" he described once again the deadly opening of hostilities against the paradoxical backdrop of placid nature: "At about 2500 yards in front of Grimes's position of El Paso arose the gentle green hills of San Juan, dotted not too plentifully with trees—hills that resembled the sloping orchards of Orange County in summer."

If Nature, malevolent or merely indifferent, seemed in Crane's later journalism a more cosmic and overpowering foe, man seemed proportionately more heroic, more suited to the struggle. Crane turned from the theme of man's entrapment to that of his participation in the act of survival, and consequently, the journalism grew increasingly less dependent upon artificial literary devices—less allusive, more concerned with telling the truth of existence, simply and resolutely. Indeed, the later journalism was characterized by the kind of writing that was unmistakably Crane's. As early as the Nebraska sketch, Crane was involved in writing about man's courageous assumption of responsibility for his fellow man, his own will to survive, and what Crane was later to call "pure, unsauced accomplishment." In the very style of the piece one notes an "unsauced" quality never before present in his journalism. He recounted simply and clearly the plight of a woman whose husband had left her and her child in order to seek work in the eastern part of the state.

The woman lived alone with her baby until the provisions were gone. She had received a despairing letter from her husband. He was still unable to get work. Everybody was searching for it; none had it to give. Meanwhile he had ventured a prodigious distance from home.

The nearest neighbor was three miles away. She put her baby in its little ramshackle carriage and traveled the three miles. The family there shared with her as long as they could—two or three days. Then she went on to the next house. There, too, with the quality of mercy which comes with incredible suffering they shared with her. From house to house she went pushing her baby-carriage She received a meal here, three meals there, and a bed here. The baby was a weak and puny child. ("Nebraskans' Bitter Fight for Life.")

In his war journalism Crane described the most harrowing of experiences with a matter-of-factness, a lean and stoic masculinity, a dearth of outward emotion suggestive of Hemingway. These qualities are demonstrated, for example, in the various interviews with Greek combat veterans that Crane wrote at the conclusion of the Greco-Turkish War:

"Which is harder—marching or fighting?"
"Marching."
"What impressed you in your first battle?"
"I was afraid of the shells."
"And in later battles?"
"I was still afraid of the shells."
"Did not the whistling of the bullets affect you more?"
"No."
"You have been under very heavy artillery fire?"
"Yes."
"Where?"
"At Domoko."
"Did you see anybody hurt by a shell?"
"Yes. A splinter laid open an officer's cheek."
"Was the infantry fire heavy on your front?"

"Not very heavy."
"What was the loss in your battalion from the Turkish infantry fire?"
"We lost twenty-eight men in killed and wounded."
"All from the infantry fire?"
"All but the officer who struck by a splinter."
"It strikes me that you would be about twenty-seven times more afraid of the bullets than of the shells."
"Yes, but then the shells are very loud."
"Do you want to fight any more?"
"Yes."
"Why?"
"Because Greece has not had a fair chance. She has been betrayed."
"By whom?"
"I cannot say. We think it was somebody high in command."
"How high in command?"
"Well—very high."
"Do your comrades also wish to fight more?"
"Yes."
"Do they also think Greece has been betrayed?"
"Yes."
"By whom?"
"They think as I think." [27]

It seems lamentable that despite the admirable restraint of Crane's war journalism, parodists should have seized upon his somewhat persistent use of the first person as an object of ridicule. For example, during the Greco-Turkish War the *Tribune* published an anonymous poem entitled "I Have Seen a Battle," burlesquing Crane's poetic style and interpreting his impressionism as egomania:

I have seen a battle.
I find it very like what

I wrote up before.
I congratulate myself that
I ever saw a battle.
I am pleased with the sound of war.
I think it is beautiful.
I thought it would be.
I am sure of my nose for battle.
I did not see any war correspondent while
I was watching the battle except
I.

Still, Crane's growing objectivity and the relative unpretentiousness of his later journalism provide us with an insight into his maturation and into the salutary effects experience had upon his brilliant imagination.

IV

Thomas Gullason states that Stephen Crane's writing a social novel like *Maggie* was inevitable because of his parents' background and interests; the social crusaders and preachers he had heard throughout childhood and young manhood, the influence of Garland, Howells, and Jacob Riis; and the drive during the early Nineties for a reform movement; but Gullason also points out that the novel grew out of Crane's visit to New York in 1891.[28] In fact, with the possible exception of *The Red Badge of Courage*, Crane's fiction was grounded in personal experience as well as documentary evidence. Many similarities existed between Crane's early newspaper pieces and *Maggie*, *The Red Badge of Courage*, and *George's Mother*: the ironic view that deflated the illusion of romance and heroism, the symbols of entrapment and animality, the over-all sense of nihilism and despair.

But not until Crane's 1895 trip westward did the fiction grow directly out of the journalism and out of experiences he had had as a journalist. "Horses—One Dash," "A Man and Some Others," and "The Five White Mice," for example, were inspired by Crane's encounter with a bandit named Ramon Colorado in a small Mexican village. "The Bride Comes to Yellow Sky," with its ritual duel and its observation of the peculiar decorum of the frontier, was suggested by his real-life attempt in Nebraska to stop a barroom fight in which a big man was pummeling a smaller one, and Crane's consequent offense to a local custom. "The Blue Hotel" seems to have grown out of an incident, possibly seen by Crane, concerning a loud-mouthed, comic gun-fighter who ranted at an unidentified opponent from inside a stationary freight-car but who was later killed in a saloon ("Caged With a Wild Man," Philadelphia *Press*, 19 April 1896). In several Western stories, the setting mirrors the central character's isolation, providing a poignant suggestion of man's insignificance in vast, alien surroundings; but, consequently, in each case the character is forced to make his own destiny. Without the conventional heroic trappings, Crane's fictional Westerners, like the Nebraskans and the Westerners whom he had met in his travels, are placed in elemental situations, frequently of life and death proportions, and are forced to act decisively, thereby gaining an heroic stature lost to such young men as Pete, Jimmie Johnson, and George Kelcey.

The experience aboard the *Commodore* provided Crane directly with two stories: "The Open Boat" and "Flanagan and His Short Filibustering Adventure." In "Stephen Crane's Own Story" he had made no mention of the ordeal in the dinghy that followed the sinking of the filibustering boat, and one can think that the idea for "The Open Boat" was already perking in his mind at the time. Both "Flanagan" and "The Open Boat" dealt with man's struggle for survival and his capacity for heroism in a terrifying and inexplicable universe. In "Flanagan," unlike the real-life situation, the filibustering boat *Foundling* sinks in a squall after it has already accomplished its purpose of delivering arms to the Cuban insurgents; ironically, what was thought to be the chief danger was over. Flanagan, the captain, weeps and swears as he watches the boat sink, but he acts in a manly and heroic way to save his men. The short disclaimer that closes the story provides the final irony: "The expedition of the *Foundling* will never be historic." But the confrontation between man and nature and the struggle between life and death are in reality, as they were for Crane, cosmic in their implications. In "The Open Boat," as in the newspaper sketch, the chief "voice" of the story is that of the correspondent, and it is he who rails, as does Crane in the newspaper account, at the irony of fate: "If I'm going to be drowned—if I'm going to be drowned, why in the name of the seven mad gods who rule the sea, was I allowed to come thus far and contemplate sand and trees?" Finally, in both the newspaper sketch and "The Open Boat," Crane describes the sense of interdependence of men suffering a common calamity. In "Stephen Crane's Own Story" the young correspondent observes the cooperation among the bailers in the engine room, among the men atop the slippery deckhouse wrestling with lifeboats that "weighed as much as a Broadway cable car," among the men aboard the doomed *Commodore* facing a common fate, among the four in the dinghy, making their way to shore under the leadership of Captain Murphy. In "The Open Boat," the need for interdependence becomes the only "logical" explanation for the death of the oiler. When the boat turns over in the icy water, the oiler swims ahead "strongly and rapidly" but drowns within reach of land, while the others cling to some remnant of the boat: a life jacket, a piece of life belt, a section of the boat itself. At the same time that the oiler is dying in symbolic isolation, a man comes running into the water, stripping off his clothing and dragging ashore the survivors. "He was naked," Crane writes, "naked as a tree in winter; but a halo was about his head and he shone like a saint."

Finally, Crane's war journalism served as a direct antecedent for a novel and several short stories. Two fictional pieces, the story "Death and the Child" and the novel *Active Service*, came out of the Greco-Turkish War. "Death and the Child" served multiple purposes: to trace the awakening of an innocent journalist, somewhat like Crane, to the realities of battle; to demonstrate Crane's admiration for the professional soldier; to demonstrate Crane's preference for the straightforward, unimaginative, even insensitive, attitude toward war over the reflective, intellectualized one. Unlike such earlier war fiction as *The Red Badge of Courage*, in which a thoughtful young recruit's initiation into the mysteries of warfare were treated sympathetically, "Death and the Child" ridicules the journalist Peza's illusions and leaves him not much more enlightened than it found him. *Active Service*, too, served to deflate the correspondent's overglamorized view of war and to ridicule yellow journalism. The hero, newspaperman Coleman, who becomes a war correspondent, loses his cynicism in Greece and gains a sense of involvement and concern and even thinks positively about the function of the news correspondent. He reasons that his role is to act as "a sort of cheap telescope" with which the reading public back home can view the common soldier and appreciate his efforts.

Coleman deemed it proven that the common man and many uncommon men, when they go away to the fighting ground, out of sight, out of the hearing of the world known to them, and are eager to perform feats of war in her place, they feel an absolute longing for the spectator. It is indeed the venerable coronation of the world. There is not too much vanity of the street in this desire of men to have some disinterested fellow perceive their deeds. It is merely that a man doing his best in the middle of a sea of war longs to have people see him doing his best.

If Crane had gone to war originally to see if *The Red Badge of Courage* "was all right," to feel the bullets whistling overhead, and to know the meaning of fear, he sensed in Cuba, as he had sensed in Greece, that the intellectualization of battle was meaningless and pretentious, even an affront to the brave. In the Cuban stories, eventually collected in *Wounds in the Rain*, he saw the curious sensation-seeking correspondent as the direct antithesis of the fighting man. In stories like "The Lone Charge of William B. Perkins," "The Revenge of the Adolphus," "God Rest Ye Merry Gentlemen," and "Virtue in War" he elevated and idealized the soldiers at the expense of the silly, self-important journalists. Only one correspondent is drawn completely sympathetically: Little Nell of "God Rest Ye Merry Gentlemen," who resembles Crane in every attitude. Little Nell is skeptical of and bewildered by the frantic opportunism of his managing editor and fellow reporters, and he possesses "the virtue of a correspondent to recognize the great moment in any disguise," seeing "greatness" in the commonplace and unspectacular. In "This Majestic Lie," Crane comments on the strangeness that "men of sense can go aslant at the bidding of other men of sense and combine to contribute to the general mess of exaggeration and bombast." Not only the journalists but even the soldiers themselves are sometimes rendered ineffectual by excessive imagination, as in "The Sergeant's Private Madhouse," or by self-interested glory-seeking, as in "The Second Generation."

The key to virtue, if not always to survival, in Crane's war stories as in the journalism, is the matter-of-fact performance of a singular duty. This alone was the "mystique" of soldiership, the strength of Private Nolan in "The Price of the Harness" and the professional soldier Gates in "Virtue in War." The realization and affirmation of this carried Crane through the frantic and uncertain last years of his life.

V

Crane's journalism may be faulted for its many shortcomings: he frequently scorned the conventions of reporting; he described trivial subjects with sometimes unnecessary artistic flourishes, gaining only gradually the terseness and simplicity that gave his war dispatches their power; he wavered between the tough-minded but humanitarian realism of Howells, Garland, and Riis and the neo-romanticism of Roosevelt, Wister, and Frederick Remington which glorified courage and the strenuous life and helped to lead America into internationalism and world power; his political views were frequently simplistic and self-righteous—though, in justice, one might say that he had to accommodate himself to yellow journalism in order to earn a living, and that he nevertheless tried, whenever possible, to speak for responsible journalism.

Stephen Crane: Journalist

But the strengths of Crane's journalism far overshadow its weaknesses: highly personalized observation and selectivity of detail; concern and compassion that embraced both the poor and the weak and that, in war time, enabled him to sacrifice views of major strategies in order to write personal observations of soldiers in the field—a characteristic of such a celebrated World War II correspondent as Ernie Pyle; most importantly, a pattern of thought, moving from despair about man's helplessness to an existential view that all men are to a degree responsible for themselves and their fellows and that the tests of life are courage and endurance. And, of course, Crane's journalism helps to trace the pattern of his thought and to throw new light on his literary work.

NOTES

1. Not much has been written about Stephen Crane's newspaper work. Among the important accounts by those who knew him are Willis Fletcher Johnson, "The Launching of Stephen Crane," *Literary Digest International Book Review* 3 (April 1914): 494–506; Edward Marshall, "Stories of Stephen Crane," *Literary Life*, N.S. No. 24 (December 1900): 71–72; Irving Bacheller, *Coming Up the Road* (Indianapolis: Bobbs-Merrill, 1928); Richard Harding Davis, "Our War Correspondents in Cuba and Puerto Rico," *Harper's* 98 (May 1899): 938–48.

Among the important examinations are Don C. Seitz, "Stephen Crane, War Correspondent," *Bookman* 76 (February 1933): 137–40; Ames W. Williams, "Stephen Crane: War Correspondent," *New Colophon* 1 (April 1948): 113–23; Victor A. Elconin, "Stephen Crane at Asbury Park," *American Literature* 20 (November 948): 275–89; Joseph J. Kwiatt, "The Newspaper Experience: Crane, Norris and Dreiser," *Nineteenth-Century Fiction* 8 (September 1953): 99–117; Scott C. Osborn, "The 'Rivalry-Chivalry' of Richard Harding Davis and Stephen Crane," *American Literature* 28 (March 1956): 50–61; E. R. Hagemann, " 'Correspondents Three' in the Greco-Turkish War," *American Literature* 30 (November 1958): 339–44; William Linnemann, "Stephen Crane's Contributions to Truth," *American Literature* 31 (March 1959): 196–97; Thomas A. Gullason, "Stephen Crane's Private War on Yellow Journalism," *Huntington Library Quarterly* 22 (May 1959): 201–8; Olov W. Fryckstedt, "Stephen Crane in the Tender-

31

Bernard Weinstein

loin," *Studia Neophilologica* 34 (November 1962): 135–63; Joseph Katz, "An Editor's Recollection of 'The Red Badge of Courage,'" *Stephen Crane Newsletter* 2 (September 1968): 3–6; Bernice Slote, "Stephen Crane in the Nebraska *State Journal* 1894–1896," *Stephen Crane Newsletter* 3 (Summer 1969): 4–5; Joseph Katz, "Frank Norris and 'The Newspaper Experience,'" *American Literary Realism* 4 (Winter 1971): 73–77.

2. In addition, the Rev. Jonathan Townley Crane—Stephen's father—wrote for the *Methodist Quarterly Review* and the *Christian Advocate* on the evils of popular amusements, smoking, alcoholism, and drug addiction. Like his wife and sons, the Rev. Crane had the economy of a journalist and the eloquence of a preacher. Crane's maternal grandfather, George Peck, edited the *Review* and the *Advocate*, in addition to writing books.

3. A study of this newspaper publication of the novel—its first—and a preliminary examination of Crane's relationship with Bacheller, Johnson & Bacheller can be found in Joseph Katz, *"The Red Badge of Courage"* (Gainesville: Scholars' Facsimiles & Reprints, 1967).

4. This is treated in detail in Joseph Katz, *Stephen Crane in the West and Mexico* (Kent, Ohio: Kent State University Press, 1970).

5. John Northern Hilliard, "Stephen Crane," *New York Times*, 14 July 1900, p. 466; reprinted in R. W. Stallman and Lillian Gilkes, eds., *Stephen Crane: Letters* (New York: New York University Press, 1960), pp. 108–10.

6. John Berryman, *Stephen Crane* (New York: William Sloane Associates, 1950), p. 34, was the first to suggest that this piece "may be" Crane's. By a curious transformation, R. W. Stallman, *Stephen Crane* (New York: George Braziller, 1968), p. 68, has it *as* Crane's. The suggestion that Crane worked for the *New York Herald* at all is in Thomas Beer, *Stephen Crane* (New York: Alfred A. Knopf, 1923), p. 82, in a quotation from a letter: "The *Herald* fired me last week."

7. Beer, *Stephen Crane*, p. 82.

8. Johnson, "The Launching of Stephen Crane," p. 290.

9. Arthur Oliver, "Jersey Memories—Stephen Crane," *New Jersey Historical Society Proceedings*, N. S. 16 (October 1931): 459–60. See also Johnson, "The Launching of Stephen Crane," and Elconin, "Stephen Crane at Asbury Park."

10. Corwin Knapp Linson, *My Stephen Crane*, ed. Edwin H. Cady (Syracuse: Syracuse University Press, 1958), p. 70.

11. Linson, *My Stephen Crane*, p. 70, tells how he lent Crane $50 because *McClure's* could not yet make advance payments to reporters. See also Katz, *"The Red Badge of Courage,"* pp. 21, 24, for a summary of the reasons for this. In "Stephen Crane: Muckraker," *Columbia Library Columns* 17 (February 1968): 3–7, Joseph Katz points out that this situation was not so simple as Linson suggests: "Down in A Coal Mine" is the version of Crane's piece distributed by the

S. S. McClure Syndicate for publication a month before the *McClure's Magazine* appearance, and it is about as tough a job of muckraking as the manuscript (now in the Alderman Library, University of Virginia) Linson saw. One piece of irony Katz notes is "that the muck Crane raked up was in a large sense his own": his mother's family had invested in Scranton mines, and on her death Stephen inherited a block of her stock—with which he paid for the first edition of *Maggie*.

12. John K. Winkler, *William Randolph Hearst* (New York: Hastings House, 1955), p. 72.

13. See Gullason, "Stephen Crane's Private War on Yellow Journalism." Pertinent also is "A Newspaper is a Collection of Half-Injustices," from *War Is Kind* (Joseph Katz, *The Poems of Stephen Crane* [New York: Cooper Square Publishers, 1966], Poem 87).

14. Don C. Seitz, *Joseph Pulitzer: His Life and Letters* (New York: Simon and Schuster, 1924), p. 241.

15. Curtis Brown, *Contacts* (London: Cassell & Co., 1935), p. 222; Edwin H. Cady, *Stephen Crane* (New York: Twayne Publishers, 1962), p. 33.

16. Osborn, "The 'Rivalry-Chivalry' of Richard Harding Davis and Stephen Crane."

17. Beer, *Stephen Crane*, pp. 205–6.

18. To Willis Brooks Hawkins, "about November 5, 1895," in Stallman and Gilkes, *Letters*, p. 70. See also Katz, *Stephen Crane in the West and Mexico.*

19. It is possible to suspect that Crane wanted to see heroism in an essentially unheroic situation. His praise of Murphy and adulation of the men's courage and matter-of-fact determination may have overstated the truth. See Cady, *Stephen Crane*, p. 54; and Cyrus Day, "Stephen Crane and the Ten-Foot Dinghy," *Boston University Studies in English* 3 (1957): 193–213. In "The Open Boat," however, Crane depicted the oiler as having violated the "community" of the boat by swimming ahead toward land, dying tragically in the surf as a result.

20. For a study of the poem "The Blue Battalions" (*Poems of Stephen Crane*, Poem 74) as rooted in Crane's Greco-Turkish War experiences, see Joseph Katz, " 'The Blue Battalions' and the Uses of Experience," *Studia Neophilologica* 37 (1965): 107–16.

21. See Edwin H. Cady, "Stephen Crane and the Strenuous Life," *Journal of English Literary History* 28 (December 1961): 376–82.

22. Still, in "War Memories" (*Anglo Saxon Review* 3 [December 1899]: 16–38), Crane wrote of the Spaniards: "Our enemies? Yes—perhaps—I suppose so. Leave that to the people in the streets at home. They know and cry against the public enemy, but when they go into actual battle not one man in a thousand concerns himself with an animus against the men who face him. The great desire is to beat them, beat them whoever they are, as a matter, first, of personal safety; second, of personal glory."

23. In "War Memories," however, he views with considerable sympathy the Old World vanity and ineffectuality of the Spanish civilians, and he admires them generally for being "wondrously casual" amid the carnage and suffering.

24. Much of the journalism contradicts Thomas A. Gullason's view ("Stephen Crane: Anti-Imperialist," *American Literature*, 30 [May 1958]: 237–41) that Crane was consistently anti-imperialistic.

25. Crane to Lily Brandon Munroe, [March 1894?], in Stallman and Gilkes, *Letters*, pp. 31–32.

26. There is a similar description in *George's Mother:* "a little glass-fronted saloon that sat blinking jovially at the crowds. It engulfed them with a gleeful motion of its two widely smiling lips." See Joseph Katz, *The Portable Stephen Crane* (New York: Viking Press, 1969), p. 90.

27. Compare this with Hemingway's "A New Kind of War," his interview with an American volunteer in the Spanish Civil War, whose face had been shot away. Despite this he speaks with pride and spirit, inspiring the correspondent's compassion. See William White, *By-Line: Ernest Hemingway* (New York: Charles Scribner's Sons, 1967), pp. 264–66.

28. *The Complete Novels of Stephen Crane*, ed. Thomas A. Gullason (Garden City, New York: Doubleday & Co., 1967), pp. 55–56.

Marston LaFrance

George's Mother and the Other Half of Maggie

Elsewhere, I have tried to argue that Stephen Crane's *Maggie: A Girl of the Streets* cannot profitably be read as literary naturalism if this critical term is to signify philosophic determinism.[1] Maggie's fate is in no way determined by either heredity or environment, but—like the slum environment itself—it results primarily from the moral cowardice and personal dishonesty of the other characters, principally Mrs. Johnson, Pete, and Jimmie; and the willful dishonesty of none of Crane's characters can legitimately be excused by any appeal to philosophic determinism. Maggie's personal story actually occupies slightly more than half the novel, only ten chapters of the nineteen. As much the study of a journey to awareness as is Henry Fleming's story, it begins in chapter 5 with Maggie's illusory notions of Pete's character, and its climax occurs in chapter 14 when finally she becomes aware of what Pete really is as she watches him succumb to Nell. Even the most case-hardened naturalistic critic, it seems to me, would be hard put to find any philosophic determinism in this half of the novel. Because Maggie's progression to an awareness of the reality of Pete is not primarily a moral struggle (her seduction, which occurs off-stage between chapters 9 and 12, is only incidental to her personal progress), because the real center of this half of the book *has* to be

Maggie's awareness which is far too weak to bear such a burden and because the structure of the novel requires her to begin her journey at an unreasonably low level of awareness—well below even that of Pete, Jimmie, and Mrs. Johnson—the other nine chapters (1 through 4, 10, 11, 13, 18, 19), given to Mrs. Johnson, Pete, and most importantly to Jimmie, fulfill two vital requirements: they embody, in Jimmy, the most significant moral struggle in the novel, and they divert the reader's attention from Maggie's unbelievably dense innocence.

George's Mother is best read as a compendium of the materials and setting from *Maggie,* the plot from "An Experiment in Misery," and the narrative technique from *The Red Badge of Courage.* When the novel is considered in this fashion, its traditional companion-piece relationship with *Maggie* disintegrates the moment one probes beneath the surface concerns of materials and setting. The plot of *Maggie*—or at least of the ten chapters containing Maggie's personal story—is the protagonist's progression to an awareness of a reality which, when this psychological journey begins, does not lie within the scope of her experience—a flawed, fumbling, but recognizable version of the plot which I believe is found, in one form or another, in every important Crane story from "The Mesmeric Mountain" to "The Upturned Face." But the plot of *George's Mother*—George's degeneration from manhood to professional pauperism—is a moral struggle which the protagonist, like the assassin of "An Experiment in Misery," obviously loses. Although the centers of both stories lie within the minds of the respective protagonists, these minds differ violently from each other. Maggie is personally honest in that she acts sincerely upon the basis of what she perceives. She has the force of will necessary for moral commitment, and she is neither vain nor lazy. However, her perception is extremely poor; and the resulting distortion is abetted by adolescent love, by the sentimental Bowery theater, by her reasonable desire to escape from the world of her mother, and by an unvoiced fear that she may be compelled to become a prostitute. George's perception, however, is entirely adequate to his needs—he always knows what he is doing. He is both vain and lazy, and he lacks the force of will necessary to do that which he perceives is right for himself. (He is quite willing to be good if only someone will make it easy for him.) Thus, unlike Maggie, George is personally dishonest.

In the other half of *Maggie*, however, Jimmie's story traces a moral struggle which the protagonist loses, and thus there is an important relationship between this half of *Maggie* and *George's Mother*. So far unexplored, this relationship deserves close examination because it implies, once again, that neither novel offers its reader any philosophic determinism.

It must be admitted, however, that the first four chapters of *Maggie*, particularly at first glance, certainly give the opposite impression. Surely all this—the street fighting, the drunken and brawling parents, the squalid tenement, the casual brutality, the wild scenes of violence which Crane piles on with a vengeance in these chapters—*must* be philosophic determinism. Jimmie has the starring role in these chapters, and there is no suggestion either that Maggie will be the principal protagonist or that her psychological progression to awareness of Pete's character will be the foundation of the main plot. Instead, these chapters imply the typical naturalistic tale of another rough lout from the slums, a first impression which, once established, apparently lingers on well after Maggie's story finally gets under way in chapter 5. Nevertheless, Crane cuts the ground from beneath this impression immediately, beginning with the brief eighth paragraph concerning the street fight between rival gangs of little boys:

> From a window of an apartment house that upreared its form
> from amid squat, ignorant stables, there leaned a curious woman.
> Some laborers, unloading a scow at a dock at the river, paused for
> a moment and regarded the fight. The engineer of a passive tugboat
> hung lazily to a railing and watched. (P. 4.) [2]

This passage presents a basic image which, in one form or another, is repeated almost ad nauseam throughout both halves of the novel.

Marston LaFrance

Appearance here belies reality. These onlookers are not helpless victims of overwhelming economic forces, immobilized by their despair. Their apparent inertia is deliberate simply because they are enjoying themselves. The fight between the gangs of urchins—in which "a stone had smashed into Jimmie's mouth. Blood was bubbling over his chin and . . . his thin legs had begun to tremble and turn weak, causing his small body to reel"—is no more than a source of momentary amusement to them, as Maggie is to Pete, as "two women in different parts of the city" are to grown-up Jimmie, as unbroken furniture is to Mrs. Johnson. The reality of their enjoyment is openly presented when Pete enters the story: " 'Gee!' he murmured with interest, 'a scrap, Gee!' " It is repeated more emphatically when, after the gang fight, Jimmie and Blue Billie clinch in a kind of encore: " 'Smash 'im, Jimmie, kick deh damn guts out of 'im,' yelled Pete, the lad with the chronic sneer, in tones of delight" (p. 6). The whole audience's entertainment is stopped, finally, by Jimmie's father who is returning from work and obviously hoping to eat as soon as he gets home. In chapter 2 we find that little Maggie, alone out of all the people met thus far, is sincerely troubled by the fact of Jimmie's fighting—and for good reason: she knows what will happen as soon as they get within reach of their mother.

Mrs. Johnson, easily the most monstrous character in Crane's entire canon, has two never-failing sources of delight: one is brutality and destruction—either of her husband and children or of inanimate things such as the furniture—and the other is sentimental self-pity. Her enjoyment of either pastime increases in proportion to her degree of drunkenness at the time it is indulged. A comparatively calm merging of both activities is presented in chapter 8:

It seems that the world had treated this woman very badly, and she took a deep revenge upon such portions of it as came within her reach. She broke furniture as if she were at last getting her rights. She swelled with virtuous indignation as she carried the lighter articles of household use, one by one, under the shadows

38

of the three gilt balls where Hebrews chained them with chains of interest. (P.32.)

Crane's giving these two particular sources of amusement to Mrs. Johnson is a clever bit of business because they complement each other to fix the character of this drunken hypocrite in a stasis which offers no hope of change: if her economic condition were improved to the point where she could no longer feel sorry for herself, she would smash everything into a chaotic mess until self-pity again became possible. This woman is no unfortunate soul downtrodden by environmental forces over which she has no control; she is a moral monster who absolutely creates her own environment herself. We see her in the act of creating it every time she comes on stage.

When her family enters the flat the first thing Mrs. Johnson does is to grab Jimmie and go to work upon him as if he were a piece of furniture. Then, when her husband objects to the screams of his son, she seizes the opportunity to go after him. This quarrel ends when her husband rushes from the room "determined upon a vengeful drunk"—no great victory for Mrs. Johnson, really, because her husband also enjoys drunkenness and self-pity. (His drinking as vengeance duplicates the "reasoning" behind his wife's trips to the pawnshop; his telling everyone in the bar what a hell his home is anticipates his wife's telling the police justices, in chapter 13, of her daughter's downfall.) His real enjoyment is presented when he steals the pail of beer from Jimmie: "The man caught his breath and laughed. He hit his son on the head with the empty pail" (p. 13). Mrs. Johnson then proceeds to drink herself through the maudlin stage of self-pity— "shedding tears and crooning miserably to the two children about their 'poor mother' and 'yer fader, damn 'is soul' " (p. 11)—to the point of drunken rage, whereupon Maggie's breaking a plate gives her the excuse to thrash her daughter. The night climaxes with a drunken battle between both parents which, apparently, ends in a draw that leaves the children huddled pathetically in a corner until dawn breaks—huddled not because of their economic plight, but because of their fear that their mother may regain consciousness before the alcohol has worn off. As the novel moves forward we find that Mrs. Johnson and Pete differ from the passive spectators at the street fight principally in that they are always *actively* destructive. And given a world in which the active people act only to destroy, in which the others look upon social evil or human suffering only as a means for their own momentary amusement, there would not seem to be much hope for it, no matter how much grocery money becomes available.

That Crane's Bowery is densely populated with such people, if the evidence of both *Maggie* and *George's Mother* seems inadequate, is amply shown by the Bowery sketches. At one extreme are the destroy-ers, the denizens of "Minetta Lane," the executed convicts of "The Devil's Acre"—men "who died black souled, whose glances in life fled sidewise with a kind of ferocity, a cowardice and a hatred that could perhaps embrace the entire world."[3] At the other extreme are the professional paupers, those who have followed passivity to its logical limit to make a career of doing absolutely nothing, the tramps such as Billie Atkins of "Billy Atkins Went to Omaha" and more importantly the "assassin" of "An Experiment in Misery" who believe that flophouse life, no matter how disgusting, is "livin' like kings" because they avoid work. Pauperism, as defined by Jacob Riis, can be confused with poverty at the surface level of appearance because an honest man can be temporarily reduced to the pauper's economic status; but no man can be simultaneously honest and a professional pauper because pauperism is a *moral* disease as contagious as small-pox: "A moral distemper, like crime . . . where once it has taken root it is harder to dislodge than the most virulent of physical dis-eases."[4] Crane shows, in "The Men in the Storm," how easily this disease is caught by decent men: paupers and honest men, carefully distinguished at the beginning of this sketch, together wait to be let into a flophouse, but by the end of the piece, when the door opens, this distinction has vanished and one jeering, struggling mob files inside. (Although there are plenty of paupers in *George's Mother*, there is only one in *Maggie*—the gnarled old woman with the music box—and she is not a particularly good example because the presence of Mrs. Johnson in the same novel makes her seem quite decent by comparison, as when she offers her room to Maggie as a refuge.) Between the two extremes are the average cowards such as the audience at the street fight. Neither paupers—because they work—nor black-souled destroyers—because they are not actively vicious like Mrs. Johnson—they are primarily onlookers who enjoy what they see. When an Italian collapses in the street they become the "dodging, pushing, peering group . . . satisfied that there was a horror to be seen and apparently insane to get a view of it." [5] They are the spectators who have "come for curiosity's sweet sake" to the police court where they sit comfortably and wait for "a cry of anguish, some loud painful protestation that would bring the proper thrill to their jaded, world-weary nerves." [6] Spectators who look upon human misery only as a source of amusement are not absolved from responsibility in Crane's world, and no confusion of moral values with physical or economic forces will excuse their apparent inertia: the failure to act in such a context is itself a cowardly action, merely a less violent form of the active destructiveness of Pete and Mrs. Johnson. Maggie, who "blossomed in a mud puddle," is uncontaminated by her slum environment; but she is seduced by Pete who *willfully* takes advantage of her innocence; after her seduction she is neither a prostitute nor a suicide until she is *willfully* repudiated by her own mother; and, of course, once she is turned out onto the street the spectators of the Bowery world *willfully* refuse to help her. Maggie thus becomes a temporary amusement to everyone: to Pete she is a sexual object, to her mother a means to unlimited sentimentality and self-pity, to the onlooker an entertaining exhibition of misery. In the world of this novel the only character, besides Maggie herself, who is endowed with at least the capability of transcending this moral mess is Jimmie.

Presumably no one, with the possible exception of David Fitelson,[7] would wish to argue that Mr. and Mrs. Johnson have reasonably fulfilled their responsibilities as parents. Chapter 4, devoted to Jimmie's growing up in this moral cesspool, shows that, as should be expected, he has to begin from nothing. "He studied human nature in the gutter, and found it no worse than he thought he had reason to believe it. He never conceived a respect for the world, because he had begun with no idols that it had smashed." From this beginning he soon develops the attributes of the executed convicts—"sullen," "dreaming blood-red dreams," "a belligerent attitude," a sneer that "turned its glare upon all things. He became so sharp that he believed in nothing." He also reveals the "logic" and attitudes of his mother: his belief that he occupies a downtrodden position has, for him, "a private but distinct element of grandeur." Thus, "*in revenge*, he resolved never to move out of the way of anything" (italics added). He does worship the superior force of a charging fire engine, but the connotations of this image—the engine splitting a tangle of trucks into fragments "as a blow annihilates a cake of ice"—are as destructive as the actions of his mother and Pete. Hence, Jimmie's tendencies do not offer much hope. Yet there is something in him. As Crane says at the end of this chapter, "Nevertheless, he had, on a certain star-lit evening, said wonderingly and quite reverently: 'Deh moon looks like hell, don't it?'" (pp. 19–20).

What Jimmie has is sufficient awareness to perceive his moral responsibility and sufficient conscience to be troubled by it. Mrs. Johnson and Pete also realize that they act dishonestly—or else Crane's intense irony in their presentation has to be gratuitous, Mrs. Johnson's wallowing in her exquisite session of self-pity at the end of the novel has to be taken strictly at face value, and Pete's drunken purification rite before his hired audience of prostitutes (chapter 18) has to be considered merely a Bowery version of good clean fun—but their conscience has atrophied to the point at which it no longer directs the will toward any action which may conflict with their own pleasure.[8] Jimmie, in chapter 10, has not yet sunk to this depth. His realization that it is not "common courtesy for a friend to come to one's home and ruin one's sister" leads him—precisely as it should—straight to a consideration of his own dishonest sexual adventures. "It occurred to him to vaguely wonder, for an instant, if some of the women of his acquaintance had brothers. . . . He was trying to formulate a theory that he had always unconsciously held, that all sisters, excepting his own, could advisedly be ruined." Thus, Jimmie is aware of his moral duty in this crisis; he realizes that "what is wrong for Pete cannot be right for him." [9] If he is to be honest with himself he will have to show compassion for his sister, face up to the responsibility of his own actions with those two women in different parts of the city, and refrain from such seductions in the future. The price of such personal honesty for Jimmie, obviously, would be the curtailment of his own sensual pleasures. Because he is not man enough to pay this price, he falls. He channels the energy aroused by this crisis into the substitute outlet of anger, and thus he willfully becomes—as chapter 4 fore-shadowed he would—the destructive peer of Pete and his mother. His destructiveness is first shown in the excellent fight in Pete's saloon (chapter 11). Logically irrelevant to the moral issue, this action merely provides a cheap release from the tension evoked by his con-science, and the complete pointlessness of this fight is implied by the comment which closes both chapters 10 and 11: "what deh hell?"

However, Jimmie's moral struggle is not yet over. It is presented again, in chapter 13, in a conversation between himself and his mother. And this time his inner troubles are not relieved by a fist-fight: this time Crane specifically presents Jimmie's acquiescence to Mrs. Johnson. When his mother speaks, Jimmie nods in agreement. At his suggestion of bringing Maggie home, his mother's obvious en-joyment, even in anticipating this great opportunity for wreaking de-struction, shows what Jimmie's moral promptings are pitted against: "The mother's eyes gloated on a scene her imagination could call before her. Her lips were set in a vindictive smile." Jimmie is not man enough to oppose both this vicious hypocrisy in his mother and his own urges toward irresponsible relations with women. Thus, he finally falls. He damns his sister and thus accepts the point of view of the destroyer, a moral failure which is entirely a failure of the will. From this point onward Jimmie is just one more moral coward, as personally dishonest as his mother and Pete and therefore morally indistinguishable from them during the remainder of the novel.

Chapters 18 and 19 are given respectively to Pete and Mrs. Johnson as they enjoy themselves before their selected audiences of sycophants. The word "Bowery" in Crane's day, as Julian Ralph observed, functioned locally as an adjective as well as a noun: "Whatever has the Bowery stamp is not merely an imitation, but it is a loud and offensive falsity." [10] And if ever this loud and offensive falsity were illustrated in fiction, Crane portrayed it in these two closing chapters of *Maggie*. It is worth noting that Jimmie also is given a brief opportunity to perform before an audience, but he muffs it—possibly because at this point in the novel he has not yet finally committed himself. At the end of chapter 10, as he goes out to beat up Pete, he passes through a group of tenement harpies who have already gathered in the hall to enjoy the misery of his sister's destruction, but they are so intent upon their gossip about Maggie that they pay no attention to him. Far more worthy of note is the fact that the enjoyment of both the destroyers and the onlookers has at least one justification, bitterly ironic though it is: in such a *moral* climate the existence of an undestroyed honest person such as Maggie is a continuous reproach to the dishonest. The very presence of the quiet and true is an implicit curse upon the loud and offensively false.

Crane's best-known comment about the Bowery—specifically offered to prompt an intelligent reading of *Maggie*—will bear one more repetition because its focus is squarely upon the moral reality of the inhabitants, that which lies within their own power of control, and because it ignores all external forces beyond the individual's power of control:

I do not think that much can be done with the Bowery as long as the [*word blurred*] are in their present state of conceit. A person who thinks himself superior to the rest of us because he has no job and no pride and no clean clothes is as badly conceited as

Lillian Russell. In a story of mine called "An Experiment in Misery" I tried to make plain that the root of Bowery life is a sort of cowardice. Perhaps I mean a lack of ambition or to willingly be knocked flat and accept the licking. . . . I had no other purpose in writing "Maggie" than to show people to people as they seem to me.[11]

Both halves of *Maggie*, it seems to me, support this statement with a vengeance.[12]

George's Mother, compared with *Maggie*, is much less shrill in tone and in several ways a better piece of work, even though it is less important than the earlier novel is to the sequence of Crane's development. The plot is simple and straightforward—the gradual decline of an honest man to pauperism. The book cannot be divided into halves as *Maggie* can because, beginning with chapter 6, George Kelcey's degeneration is seen consistently from the third-person limited point of view within his own mind, and the use of this narrative technique implies that George, like Henry Fleming but unlike Maggie, has sufficient mind to bear this burden. The wavering of the point of view in the first five chapters—1 and 4 are given to George, 2 shows his mother at home, 3 and 5 are shared about equally between George and his mother—implies that this novel, as most scholars believe, was begun before *The Red Badge of Courage*, laid aside, and finished after the much greater book had been completed. Although Crane's irony is as omnipresent as it is in *Maggie*, there is far less use of the parallel scene, and the flicks of the whip—even in the first five chapters—are more subtle: "He *should have seen* a grinning face with a rather pink nose" (chapter 1); "Two children, *being in the proper yard*, picked up the bits of broken glass and began to fondle them as new toys" (chapter 2); "Kelcey was proud that the prominent character of the place talked *at* him" (chapter 4).[13] The heavy artillery of Crane's irony in this novel is trained upon George as a person because, again unlike Maggie, George is dishonest. This novel is not based upon any progression to awareness because George is always aware of the reality he is too lazy to face; instead, as both Max R. Westbrook and James B. Colvert have noted, George's story is the same as the assassin's in "An Experiment in Misery" because both characters, through their own moral cowardice, fall to the "utter depths of degradation."[14]

The assassin of the "Experiment," having arrived at the bottom level of pauperism long before he is introduced to the reader, illustrates a *fait accompli*, and the aesthetic center of this sketch is the mind of the young man who conducts the experiment and thereby gains awareness of the professional tramp's "point of view," the moral posture which has led the assassin to pauperism. But George begins his story as an honest man: he is morally upright and he holds a steady job because he has accepted the responsibility of supporting himself and his mother. Thus, in terms of the Bowery world of *Maggie*, he is neither a pauper, an onlooker, nor a destroyer. And because he is his widowed mother's sole means of support—Crane implies that George's brothers have died—he is well aware of his duties in life. Moreover, his subsequent failure cannot be excused by any appeal to philosophic determinism. He may live in the same tenement as the Johnsons, but his flat is clean and neat; he has a parent who loves him and does her best to see to his needs as she perceives them; and the opening chapters make it clear that he has been able to keep the wolf from the door. George's struggle, like Jimmie's, is a moral one which takes place within his own mind; his failure, like the assassin's, like Jimmie's, is a failure of the will. The principal distinction of George's fall is that he faces no single moment of decision as climactic as Jimmie's. George's gradual descent from virtue—in that part of the book, from chapter 6 onward, which seems to have been written after *The Red Badge of Courage*—goes through three fairly definite stages, each of which is signaled by Crane's having him openly defy his mother.

George's first appearance, however, shows him solidly—if a bit uncomfortably—a part of life. He is walking home from work, a part of the

endless processions of people, mighty hosts, with umbrellas
waving, banner-like, over them. Horse-cars, aglitter with new
paint, rumbled in steady array between the pillars that supported
the elevated railroad. The whole street resounded with the tinkle
of bells, the roar of iron-shod wheels on the cobbles, the ceaseless
trample of the hundreds of feet. Above all, too, could be heard the
loud screams of the tiny newsboys, who scurried in all directions.
(P. 89.)

This montage of purposive movement symbolizes the reality, the life,
of the city in this novel just as similar images do in "An Experiment
in Misery." This is the reality of honest men in which the professional
paupers choose not to participate. Crane ends his paragraph with a
view of the onlooker, the audience to all this action. "Upon the cor-
ners, standing in from the dripping eaves, were many loungers,
descended from the world that used to prostrate itself before pag-
eantry." As George comes down the street, holding his lunch-pail
"under his arm in a manner that was evidently uncomfortable," one
of these loungers grabs his hand and pulls him out of the procession.
George immediately puts his lunch-pail on the ground. Then he and
Jones enter the "little glass-fronted saloon that sat blinking jovially
at the crowds" as if it, too, were one of the onlookers. It receives
them, much as Jones received George, "with a gleeful motion of its
two widely smiling lips." Later the same night, while his mother goes
to *her* saloon—the prayer meeting—George returns to meet the "fine
fellows" headed by Bleecker, gets mildly drunk, and returns home
feeling that "he had spent the most delightful evening of his life."
Yet alcohol is not to be George's undoing; he has enjoyed himself
because of his kinship with the state of mind of Bleecker and the
other onlookers. By chapter 6, when Crane begins to probe into
George's mind, the stage has been set and all the external properties
for George to use in his fall have been assembled.

Chapters 6 and 7 explain why George is vulnerable to the onlooker's point of view. Emotionally he is still a little boy with a boy's

47

conceit and laziness. When Maggie goes out with Pete—George being too timid even to speak to her—his ego is so battered that, with "reasoning" worthy of Mrs. Johnson herself, he vows "to taste the delicious revenge of a partial self-destruction. The universe would regret its position [not being grateful for his presence in it] when it saw him drunk" (chapter 8). George's willingness to act on the basis of such logic as this is his first step down from virtue, and one must insist that it stems from the conceit Crane identified as the root of Bowery life. George believes that "his life was to be fine and heroic, else he would not have been born . . . that the common-place lot was the sentence, the doom of certain people who did not know how to feel . . . that the usual should fall to others whose nerves were of lead." Thus, for him, "the world was *obliged* to turn gold in time" (chapter 7, italics added). When the universe fails to honor its obligations, this boy fights back by willfully debauching himself.

His next step down, of course, is Bleecker's party at which George gets horribly drunk. The first half of chapter 10, George's bitter awakening the morning after, specifically insists upon his awareness of what he is doing: he feels "utter woe, regret and loathing" at his perception of the "futility of a red existence"; he knows this sort of dissipation is a "calamitous retrogression" from reality, but he cannot face up to his duty as he perceives it. "He was aghast at the prospect of the old routine. It was impossible." His moment of truth comes with a sentence which would fit Jimmie every bit as well as it does George: "Upon reflection, he saw, therefore, that he was perfectly willing to be virtuous if somebody would come and make it easy for him." George simply wants to have his cake and eat it, too. Thus, he staggers home, lies to his mother and to his foreman, and, after a temporary reformation while the memory of his hangover lingers, he takes the final step down.

George reaches the bottom, the logical result of the moral flaws exhibited in chapters 6 and 7, when he joins his peers, the street-corner louts who are "all too clever to work":

Their feeling for contemporaneous life was one of contempt. Their philosophy taught that in a large part the whole thing was idle and a great bore. With fine scorn they sneered at the futility of it. Work was done by men who had not the courage to stand still and let the skies clap together if they willed. (P. 132.)

These professional paupers are, of course, onlookers; but their tendencies are more destructive than those of Bleecker's drunkards. They also believe that the universe is obliged to drop pots of gold in their laps, but they are obviously ready to help the obligation along by violence: "They longed dimly for a time when they could run through decorous streets with the crash and roar of war, an army of revenge for pleasures long possessed by others, a wild sweeping compensation for their years without crystal and gilt, women and wine." In brief, the paupers look upon normal people, those who work for their women and wine, as their legitimate prey because paupers are superior to the "common-place lot." Therefore, George finally has found his own moral level. Shortly thereafter he gets fired from his job, and when his mother asks him what he is going to do he answers truthfully: "Oh, nothin'!" When the death of his mother removes his last external responsibility, George presumably is left free to live the life he has chosen, that of the professional pauper. As Gullason argues, his final "collapse is conveyed when, in the end, he stares at the wallpaper whose patterns suddenly feel 'like hideous crabs crawling upon his brain.'" [15]

The defiances of his mother which accompany George's steps downward to this moral pit become progressively more serious until, with the final one, the imagery associated with him leaves little doubt of what he has become. The first one occurs right after Maggie leaves with Pete and Mrs. Kelcey asks her little boy to hang up his coat: "He turned toward his mother a face red, seamed, hard with hate and rage" (chapter 7). The second one comes after Bleecker's party when his mother asks, "Whatever am I goin' t' do with yeh?" " 'I don't

49

know,' he said with calmness. 'What are yeh?' He had traced her emotions and seen her fear of his rebellion. He thrust out his legs in the easy scorn of a rapier-bravo. 'What are yeh?' " (chapter 11). Finally, when his mother rebukes him for swearing after he has joined the professional paupers, he slowly walks up to her and speaks deliberately at point-blank range: " 'Whatter yeh goin' t' do 'bout it?' He regarded her then with an unaltering scowl, albeit his mien was as dark and cowering as that of a condemned criminal" (chapter 14). The implication of criminality, of moral guilt, reappears in "An Experiment in Misery": "His head was a fuddle of bushy hair and whiskers, from which his eyes peered with a guilty slant. In a close scrutiny it was possible to distinguish the cruel lines of a mouth, which looked as if its lips had just closed with satisfaction over some tender and piteous morsel. He appeared like an assassin steeped in crimes performed awkwardly."[16] And at the end, when the youth understands his companion's frame of mind, he tries to imitate it: "He confessed himself an outcast, and his eyes from under the lowered rim of his hat began to glance guiltily, wearing the criminal expression that comes with certain convictions."[17] It appears again in "The Men in the Storm": "the mob chuckled ferociously like ogres who had just devoured something";[18] and, of course, its ultimate example is the black-souled convict with his ferocity, cowardice, and hatred for the whole world of honest men.

It is worth noting that defiance of Mrs. Kelcey is not entirely unjustified, even from such a moral coward as George, because she is not much more honest than he is. The church in this novel is as useless as it is in *Maggie,* and Crane obviously associates it with the saloon as an equally futile retreat from reality. The chapel to which Mrs. Kelcey resorts is "little," like her son's saloon. It sits in a side street squeezed between gigantic apartment houses. The roar of purposive movement "emblematic of the life of the city" (chapter 11) will eventually overwhelm it, and Crane suggests that it will then be "pierced" to die with scorn for its slayers. (Crane's use of "pierced" is not meant to imply any analogy with Christ—who did not scorn his slayers. This word is Crane's favorite term for expressing what reality inevitably does to an illusion.) Mrs. Kelcey devotes herself to an empty ritual as fatuous as the rituals practiced by Bleecker's crowd. Thus, her constant nagging to get George to go to prayer meeting is quite pointless: the imagery implies that he might just as well go to the saloon.[19] Just as George sees his mother from the point of view of his saloon—"She never understood the advanced things in life. He felt the hopelessness of ever making her comprehend. His mother was not modern" (chapter 13)—so his mother sees him from the point of view of pulpit clichés: he will "become a white and looming king among men" if only she can make him follow the Horatio Alger myth —hang up his coat, work hard, refrain from alcohol and profanity, and go regularly to prayer meeting.[20] And she has a vanity of her own. If she can succeed in running her son's life for him she will be "fêted as the mother of this enormous man." Thus, Mrs. Kelcey's day-dreams about George are almost as silly as his are about his ideal woman; and she refuses to give them up, in spite of the evidence of what she sees daily, because to do so would be to admit her failure. Still, Mrs. Kelcey's actions are somewhat more excusable than those of her son, partly because of her age and what she has already suffered, partly because if George goes to the bad there will be nothing left for her but despair. But George is a young man with all life before him, and he chooses to ruin it just as Jimmie does because he is too cowardly to live as an honest man.

I can find no evidence of philosophic determinism in either of these novels or the Bowery sketches. In Crane's work, poverty, the external physical or economic environment, does not stultify or destroy human beings *morally*, in spite of the claims of much naturalistic criticism and modern sociological theory. The ruination of Maggie, the dishonesty of Pete, Jimmie, and George, the moral exhaustion of the assassin, the executed convict or Fidsey Corcoran, the monstrous hypocrisy of Mrs. Johnson are all "inevitable only under the precondition of human irresponsibility."[21] Crane's Bowery writings portray human irresponsibility in action. Crane's constant irony proclaims

that, to him, such irresponsibility is never inevitable, never determined by anything other than the willful dishonesty of human beings.

NOTES

1. My treatment of *Maggie, George's Mother*, and the Bowery sketches can be
found in *A Reading of Stephen Crane* (Oxford: Clarendon Press, 1971), chapter
2. In that chapter I also argue the essential futility of attempting to define literary naturalism on the basis of characteristics other than philosophic determinism.
In order to avoid repeating this argument here, I will try to demonstrate merely
that these novels contain no such determinism—and let others decide whether a
work without determinism in it can properly be classified as naturalism.

2. For the "more than three hundred variants" between the 1893 and 1896 edi-
tions, see Joseph Katz, "The *Maggie* Nobody Knows," *Modern Fiction Studies* 12
(Summer 1966): 200–212. My quotations are from the 1893 text in Joseph Katz,
ed., *The Portable Stephen Crane* (New York: Viking Press, 1969), pp. 3–74. For
the importance of the passage quoted and the general role of the audience in
Maggie, see Joseph X. Brennan, "Ironic and Symbolic Structure in Crane's
Maggie," *Nineteenth-Century Fiction* 16 (March 1962): 310; and Maurice Kramer,
"Crane's *Maggie*: A Girl of the Streets," *Explicator* 22 (February 1964), item 49.

3. Olov W. Fryckstedt, *Stephen Crane: Uncollected Writings* (Uppsala: University of Uppsala Press, 1963), p. 210.

4. *How the Other Half Lives* (New York, Charles Scribner's Sons, 1890),
chapter 21.

5. "When Man Falls A Crowd Gathers," *The New York City Sketches of
Stephen Crane and Related Pieces*, ed. R. W. Stallman and E. R. Hagemann (New
York: New York University Press, 1966), pp. 107–9.

6. "An Eloquence of Grief," in Stallman and Hagemann, eds., *New York City
Sketches*, p. 262.

7. See "Stephen Crane's *Maggie* and Darwinism," *American Quarterly* 16
(Summer 1964): 189.

8. See Donald Pizer, "Stephen Crane's 'Maggie' and American Naturalism,"
Criticism 7 (Spring 1965): 173–74.

9. Max R. Westbrook, "Stephen Crane's Social Ethic," *American Quarterly* 14
(Winter 1962): 590.

10. "The Bowery," *Century* 43 (December 1891): 234.

11. Thomas Beer, *Stephen Crane* (New York: Alfred A. Knopf, 1923), pp.
140–41.

12. There are several excellent essays on *Maggie* besides those by Brennan, Pizer, and Westbrook. Crane's sources are discussed by Marcus Cunliffe, "Stephen Crane and the American Background of *Maggie*," *American Quarterly* 7 (Spring 1955): 31–44; and by Thomas A. Gullason, "The Sources of Stephen Crane's *Maggie*," *Philological Quarterly* 38 (October 1959): 497–502. Gullason also points out the resemblance of Maggie to George Kelcey and Henry Fleming in "Thematic Patterns in Stephen Crane's Early Novels," *Nineteenth-Century Fiction* 16 (June 1961): 59–67. Janet Overmyer, like Brennan, notes Crane's use of parallel scenes in "The Structure of Crane's *Maggie*," *University of Kansas City Review* 29 (October 1962): 71–72. James B. Colvert's excellent "Structure and Theme in Stephen Crane's Fiction," *Modern Fiction Studies* 5 (Autumn 1959): 199–208, has important comments on *Maggie*. Good recent essays which argue against a naturalistic reading are William T. Lenehan, "The Failure of Naturalistic Techniques in Stephen Crane's *Maggie*," in *Stephen Crane's Maggie: Text and Context*, ed. Maurice Bassan (Belmont, California: Wadsworth, 1966), pp. 166–73; and Milne Holton, "The Sparrow's Fall and the Sparrow's Eye: Crane's *Maggie*," *Studia Neophilologica* 41 (1969): 115–29. See also W. B. Stein, "New Testament Inversions in Crane's *Maggie*," *Modern Language Notes* 73 (April 1958): 268–72; Eric Solomon, *Stephen Crane: From Parody to Realism* (Cambridge, Mass.: Harvard University Press, 1966), pp. 23–44. *George's Mother*, by contrast, has received very little critical attention. A convenient collection is Stanley Wertheim's *Merrill Studies in "Maggie" and "George's Mother"* (Columbus: Charles E. Merrill, 1971).

13. Italics added. My quotations are from Katz, *The Portable Stephen Crane*, pp. 89–146.

14. See James B. Colvert, "Stephen Crane: The Development of His Art" (Ph.D. dissertation, Louisiana State University, 1953), p. 65; and Max R. Westbrook, "Stephen Crane and the Revolt-Search Motif" (Ph.D. dissertation, University of Texas, Austin, 1960), p. 112.

15. Gullason, "Thematic Patterns in Crane's Early Novels," p. 62.

16. Katz, *The Portable Stephen Crane*, p. 157.

17. Katz, *The Portable Stephen Crane*, p. 165.

18. Katz, *The Portable Stephen Crane*, p. 152.

19. Cf. Joseph X. Brennan, "The Imagery and Art of *George's Mother*," *C L A Journal* 4 (December 1960): 106, 115.

20. See Solomon, *Parody to Realism*, pp. 49–67.

21. Max R. Westbrook, "Stephen Crane: The Pattern of Affirmation," *Nineteenth-Century Fiction* 14 (December 1959): 220–21.

Jean Cazemajou

The Red Badge of Courage: The "Religion of Peace" and the War Archetype

All Nature so calm in itself, the early summer grass so rich, and foliage of the trees . . . but fierce savage demons fighting there . . . rapid-filing phantoms through the woods.—Walt Whitman, "A Night Battle over a Week Since," notes dated 12 May 1863, in *Specimen Days* (1882).

Any examination of Stephen Crane's mental processes ought to begin by referring to his "irony of soul," a term he himself used in "This Majestic Lie," a story in *Wounds in the Rain*. He rejected one-sided views on human problems, for even if his dominant voice was one of dissent, he never fell into the trap of nihilistic iconoclasm. Irony often serves as a vehicle for a veiled but deeply-felt sense of justice; Crane's irony is of that kind.[1] What he seems to strive for in his work is the projection of a mental image to convey his personal conception of truth. Moving as he does in the sphere of abstractions and unresolved polarities, he often reduces his characters to a single feature in order to sketch their psychological progress along allegorical lines. This mythic approach to reality is a constant in his work: such primordial ideas as Mother, Child, Sin, Rebirth, War, and Peace operate in his writings as archetypal antagonists which evoke a dialectical tension.

54

One consequence of this semantic structure is that in his writings no process of individualization is ever sufficiently complete to fill out the image of any character, even in Crane's most deeply wrought character studies. His artistic orientation precluded a sense of obligation to make his pictures picturesque or his characters thoroughly defined. That is one element of his comment on the genesis of *The Red Badge of Courage*: "It was essential that I should make my battle a type and name no names. . . ."[2]

Notions of war and peace in such a stylized and strangely constricted vision of the world—because of their recurring presence and their permanent influence on Crane's metaphoric fancy—provide the critic with two valuable tools for studying the writer's creative processes. Metaphoric war is notable in whatever topic Crane treated, whether it was urban life, adventure, or domestic relationships, because he always saw human existence in terms of conflict. In a coal mine near Scranton, Pennsylvania, miners at work are described as if they were waging some subterranean war:

> The place always resounds with the shouts of mule-boys, and there can always be heard the noise of approaching coal-cars, beginning in mild rumble and then swelling down upon one in a tempest of sound. . . . There is booming and banging and crashing, until one wonders why the tremendous walls are not wrenched by the force of this uproar. . . . It is war. It is the most savage part of all in the endless battle between man and nature.[3]

And the threat of death in "The Open Boat," hovering around the dinghy in the form of an omnipresent shark, is objectified as a bullet—"a gigantic and keen projectile." No matter where he may be, Crane is faithful to his idea that "the sense of a city is battle"—prefiguring in this central metaphor Edward Albee's vision of the city in *The Zoo Story*.[4] And domestic conflicts, especially those between mother and son, are projected as a version of war: in "An Experiment in Luxury" the mother is called "a spearswoman of the Philistines," and in

George's Mother Mrs. Kelcey wields her broom like a lance when she cleans her apartment (p. 93).[5] Even the conduct of Whilomville's children, patterned on that of fictional heroes, is warlike in character. But in all these writings there always lurks a shadow of peace, dreamlike or nostalgic, in contrast to the figures of war. In most of Crane's works the two are linked together. In *The Red Badge of Courage* war and peace function simultaneously as factual realities and archetypal values.

The descriptive force of Crane's style may lead one to read that novel as if it were an introduction to the sound and fury of real combat. Specific details of camp life, preparations for attacks, charges and countercharges, captures of prisoners, and seizures of enemy flags serve to convey the illusion of verisimilitude. Indeed, these details sufficiently parallel reality to allow one scholar to argue convincingly that Crane had the Battle of Chancellorsville in mind when he wrote *The Red Badge of Courage*.[6] But the picture of battle given in the novel is blurred and limited in scope. It is not "war," but only war seen through the eyes of one raw recruit, a "youth." For him battle is chaos and confusion.

That is, however, only one possible view of war. The novel balances it with another, in which a world at peace continually intrudes on the smoke and destruction. Again, it is through the eyes of the youth that this antidote to war is visualized. He associates peace with images of rural harmony. Simultaneously frightened and fascinated by violence, Henry displays ambivalent tendencies. Tired of the routine of farm life, he is a dreamer soon carried away by the war hysteria that sweeps the land and reaches him first through the sound of a church bell ringing "the twisted news of a great battle" (p. 193). It makes him decide to escape from the monotony of chores by plunging into adventure. Soon after enlisting, however, he decides that endless drilling in camp is no better than "endless rounds from the house to the barn." And as the story unfolds a small number of flashbacks evoke the memory of peace, sharp and bright against the blurred image of battle: the warm farewell scenes of chapter 1, the crisp, gay circus parade of chapter 5, the cosy family meals and cool swimming parties of chapter 12—all introduce a universe in which everything is familiar and where a refreshing harmony of man with Nature prevails. These vignettes remind us of Whitman's glorification of life and the rebirth of Nature in his notes on the same battle.

Despite Crane's famous accuracy of detail, war and peace in *The Red Badge of Courage* function to a greater degree as archetypes than as realities. The novel invests both with the attributes of religious significance. For example, in a minute and highly evocative description of battle sounds, Crane introduces a reference to a war very different from the War between the States: "This uproar explained a celestial battle; it was tumbling hordes a-struggle in the air" (p. 237). Sketching the other side of the diptych: "This landscape gave him assurance. A fair field holding life. It was the religion of peace" (p. 234). In this way war and peace are cut off from ordinary experience and are raised to the level of primordial image.

This elevation is increased through the use of two emblematic figures borrowed from the farm: the cow and the horse. These two animals fulfill two opposing functions in Crane's symbology. The placid cow is associated with peace; the fierce horse is made representative of war. When in *The Red Badge of Courage* the peace archetype is centered around the image of "a fair field holding life," the gilded pageant of Henry's memory makes the cows on his farm appear with "a halo of happiness about each of their heads" (p. 206). Although this sanctification has its humorous connotations, it is not merely an occasional metaphor. In another passage, Crane identifies Henry with his quondam charges: "He developed the acute exasperation of a pestered animal, a well-meaning cow worried by dogs" (p. 223). This strange metaphor in fact becomes a structural device in the novel, serving both to represent peace and to group together pine forests, vast green fields, and cows as symbols of peace (p. 210).

Thus, one is tempted to say that Nature is simply a haven of peace in Crane's vision of the world, and many passages in *The Red Badge of Courage* seem to support this conclusion. Nature provides a wonderful backdrop for the hero's romantic regression into the bosom of the Mother of the Universe while he waits for his first battle to begin: "The moon had been lighted and was hung in a treetop. The liquid stillness of the night enveloping him made him feel vast pity for himself. There was a caress in the soft winds; and the whole mood of the darkness, he thought, was one of sympathy for himself in his distress" (p. 206). In the chapel-like forest, which welcomes Henry after he has made his "separate peace" in chapter 7, he projects "Nature to be a woman with a deep aversion to tragedy" (p. 234), and a religious serenity pervades this secluded place: "The trees began softly to sing a hymn of twilight. The sun sank until slanted bronze rays struck the forest. There was a lull in the noises of insects as if they had bowed their beaks and were making a devotional pause. There was silence save for the chanted chorus of the trees" (p. 236). But the forest is at best an ambiguous reality in this novel. Far from always being a haven of peace, it sometimes bristles with threatening fingers and vibrates with accusing voices: "He was obliged to force his way with much noise. The creepers, catching against his legs, cried out harshly as their sprays were torn from the barks of the trees. The swishing saplings tried to make known his presence to the world. He could not conciliate the forest" (p. 234).

Instead of being a specific setting, located precisely in space and time, this forest appears rather as a symbolic place reminiscent of the one in Genesis where Adam takes refuge after his fall and tries to hide behind trees in his flight from the face of God (Genesis, 3:8). Henry's Edenic vision which concludes the book is also fraught with Biblical overtones in which can be heard echoes of The Song of Songs: "He turned now with a lover's thirst to images of tranquil skies, fresh meadows, cool brooks—an existence of soft and eternal peace" (p. 318).

On the other hand, the horse remains central to Crane's concept of war: pilfering a horse (p. 205) is presented—ironically—as a typical act of war. The animal that one critic regards as the main symbol of aggressiveness in Crane's work appears invested with complex threats in *The Red Badge of Courage.*[7] At the beginning of the novel it appears in the centaurian image of "the gigantic figure of the colonel on a gigantic horse" (p. 203) as a means of announcing the impending holocaust. Epitomizing the potential danger of an annihilating onslaught, the simile of the "mad horse" conveys the fury of sudden attack (p. 312). Most of the time, the author refers to the eyes—or, rather, the "orbs"—of horses, or "dragons," advancing in battle formation (p. 203). But there is also elevation to abstract symbolism here, and war gradually becomes "the red animal . . . the blood-swollen god" (p. 213).

In this way the expressionistic quality of the novel brings into play an ancient world in which two abstract figures are opposed—the war-god, representing the animalism of bloody conflict, and the radiant goddess, the "anima" of Jung symbolized by the flag, which operates as a unifying and sheltering force in the chaos of battle. In chapter 19 the flag is endowed with feminine attributes, attracting as a maiden and protecting as a mother:

> It was a goddess, radiant, that bended its form with an imperious gesture to him. It was a woman, red and white, hating and loving that called to him with the voice of his hopes. Because no harm could come to it he endowed it with power. He kept near, as if it could be a saver of lives, and an imploring cry went from his mind. (P. 294.)

But whereas the flag never loses caste and always retains its godly virtues, even when reduced to shreds, the animalistic side of war occasionally loses all connection with a presumed deity. The "blood-swollen god" of war topples from his majestic throne into inferno where his very image is blurred by those of "savage demons" of the netherworld and "to the youth the fighters resemble[d] animals tossed for a death struggle into a dark pit" (p. 282). Seen through the eyes of a Methodist consciousness, this pit literally teems with reptilian menace. Crane once confessed that "priests who paint hell well, fill it with snakes instead of fire."[8] Only Melville's barren, solitary, withered wasteland in "The Encantadas"—also overrun with reptiles—surpasses *The Red Badge of Courage* in offering one of the most nightmarishly infernal pictures in American literature. Crane's war novel mentions serpents early, and they never really disappear from the scene. Thus on the morning of the first day of battle, the landscape appears to be soiled and violated by an ugly, ominous presence stretched across the belly of the earth: "When the sunrays at last struck full and mellowingly upon the earth, the youth saw that the landscape was streaked with two long, thin, black columns which disappeared on the brow of a hill in front and rearward vanished in a wood. They were like two serpents crawling from the cavern of the night" (p. 204).

That same simile reappears several times. It acquires its most fantastic significance when battle fury reaches a peak: "The blue smoke-swallowed line curled and writhed like a snake stepped upon. It swung its ends to and fro in an agony of fear and rage" (p. 282). But although snakes predominate, the teratology of *The Red Badge of Courage* includes monsters of divers kinds. Snakes easily turn into dragons, and Henry's adventure truly is a kind of dragon-hunt, a frenzied chase of "the beast that ascendeth out of the bottomless pit" in Revelation, (11:7). Shells are like "storm banshees" or seem to have "rows of cruel teeth" (pp. 218, 230). Still more frightening are the "smoke phantoms" that stifle the soldiers, restrict their vision, and bury them in a fuliginous world in which every object assumes grotesque shapes and where life itself becomes meaningless (pp. 216, 223). This chamber-of-horrors atmosphere is introduced even before the beginning of the battle, when the youth lies in his hut, torn by doubts and misgivings, tormented by the fear of a faceless monster: "In the darkness he saw visions of a thousand-tongued fear that would babble at his back and cause him to flee, while others were going coolly about their country's business. He admitted that he would not be able to cope with this monster" (p. 208).

But Crane's originality is not centered upon his handling of the horrible in war. That had been even more fully exploited by his contemporary, Ambrose Bierce, whose battle pictures are closer still to the Gothic tradition. Where *The Red Badge of Courage* goes the extra step is in pointing to the co-existence of the banal with the gruesome, not hesitating to undercut the significance of death on the battlefield with a simile such as "The men dropped here and there like bundles" (p. 224). While Crane tries his hand at a tale of initiation and demands that the hero defeat some fantastic monsters, he simultaneously applies the debunking lever of irony to challenge traditional concepts of heroism. Henry's qualifications for that kind of authentic bravery are indeed questionable. Appearing to his comrades as an admirable and almost inimitable "jimhickey" (p. 304), he has led the final charge, taken the bright colors to the front, and even participated in the conquest of the enemy flag. But deep down in the recesses of his soul he knows that he is closer to being an impostor than a jimhickey. At the very end of his ordeal the successive stages of his spiritual journey return to his mind, spelling shame more often than glory. The circular shape of this journey, which takes him back to the point at which he started, seems a parody of *The Pilgrim's Progress,* a series of trials in which the protagonist often makes wrong decisions.

At the beginning of his adventure, although he had plunged into the maelstrom of war on his own accord, Henry is deeply afraid of violence. This fear leads him to his panic and desertion in chapter 6. Then a series of encounters in no man's land serve to throw his instinctive flight into a moral perspective. Remorse sets in. Henry's meeting with mortally wounded Jim Conklin, who dies under his eyes, his rejection of the "tattered man," and his providential meeting with "the man of the cheerful voice" who takes him back to his regiment leave his conscience buffeted and sore. Then, a second time, the ambivalent force of violence plunges him into action. Swept by "the winds of battle," he is "not conscious that he [is] erect upon his feet"—and he fights like a "barbarian," a "beast" (pp. 282, 283, 284).

In *The Red Badge of Courage,* war is not the splendid and generous crusade that many Northern writers wanted their readers to see in the Civil War; nor is it the last stand for a lost cause that Southern writers glorified. Crane differs from most nineteenth-century authors of war stories in not offering Manichaean pictures of battlefields. In his book war is nothing but the outward manifestation of a dark force buried in the collective unconscious of man, "the throat-grappling instinct." That view of the Civil War as a catastrophe caused by a deep-lying flaw in human nature is very close to the one Melville offers in *Battle Pieces.* In this light the concluding episode of chapter 9 gives new significance to its final line, "The sun was pasted in the sky like a wafer" (p. 246).The redness of the wafer is indeed a sign of sacrifice, but it does not point—as some critics believe—to the redemptive self-sacrifice of a Christ-figure.[9] It refers, intuitively rather than deductively, to the common archetypal image which is part and parcel of Aztec culture: the occasional need to sacrifice the life of a young man to the sun in order to preserve its life and brilliance.[10] This reference is reinforced by the ritual-like quality of many furious battle scenes in the novel, especially in such similes as "In front of the colors the three men began to bawl: 'Come on! come on!' They danced and gyrated like tortured savages" (p. 294).

Thus Crane, by depriving war of all of the conceptual adornments with which traditional religion and contemporary myth invest it, prepared the ground for a reassessment of its sociological significance. He did so, however, with no sense of carrying out a sociological inquiry. In the process of clarifying the personal drama of an isolated consciousness, he stumbled upon the dark impulses with which the collective unconscious had struggled for ages. It is in the constant swing from macabre war scenes to peaceful visions that *The Red Badge of Courage* develops its fundamental set of polarities; and they climax in the circus metaphor at the beginning of chapter 5, when the parade through the village street—a colorful vignette seen in retrospect—is followed by the infernal and spectacular fireworks of the circus of war:

There were moments of waiting. The youth thought of the village street at home before the arrival of the circus parade on a day in the spring. He remembered how he had stood, a small, thrillful boy, prepared to follow the dingy lady upon the white horse, or the band in its faded chariot. He saw the yellow road, the lines of expectant people, and the sober houses. He particularly remembered an old fellow who used to sit upon a cracker box in front of the store and feign to despise such exhibitions. A thousand details of color and form surged in his mind. The old fellow upon the cracker box appeared in middle prominence.
Some one cried, "Here they come!"
There was a rustling and muttering among the men. . . .
Across the smoke-infested fields came a brown swarm of running men who were giving shrill yells. They came on, stooping and swinging their rifles at all angles. A flag, tilted forward, sped near the front. (Pp. 220–221.)

The contrast between those two scenes is achieved mostly in terms of painting, through a shift from a bright impressionistic tableau to a blurred and confused panorama pierced by touches of expressionism. A fundamental image takes shape here, the one that will transform Henry into an invisible man: "In the battle blur his face would, in a way be hidden, like the face of a cowled man" (p. 252). This expressionistic distortion of appearance reaches its own climax as Crane follows pictures of close combat with a bewitched world that oscillates between the fantastic and the grotesque: "They in blue showed their teeth; their eyes shone all white. They launched themselves at the throats of those who stood resisting" (p. 312).
The archetypal war described in *The Red Badge of Courage* was fought against a "composite monster" (p. 220) that kept recurring in his work afterwards—a fire-spitting, dragon-like monster containing Biblical and primitive characteristics both, a Moloch that could not be laid by the sheer force of arms. Thus, in war, true heroism is the result of spiritual and not physical prowess and derives its might from

effacement rather than affirmation of self. So, although Henry failed at Chancellorsville, as an old veteran in Whilomville he redeemed himself by plunging into his burning barn to rescue his horses, dying amidst the purifying flames.[11]

But *The Red Badge of Courage* is not Crane's definitive statement on war. The way he realized his hypotheses was by going from dream to experience, and until he had felt what war really was like he could not be satisfied. Like one of the protagonists in his Spanish-American War fiction, William B. Perkins—Ralph D. Paine in actual life—he came out of his first battle giddy and bruised but "with his hat not able to fit his head for the bumps of wisdom that were on it."[12] From then on, the prosaic side of war introduced in *The Red Badge of Courage* began to predominate in his work, replacing much of the glamor in his own early imaginings. With a terseness that characterizes his most famous poems, he eventually coined this aphorism: "War is death, and a plague of the lack of small things, and toil."[13] Crane never could attain the serenity and detachment needed to define Peace. This concept he had to be content with relegating to the remote and mysterious status of a fable—a "religion."

NOTES

1. Vladimir Jankélévitch, *L'Ironie* (Paris: Flammarion, 1964), p. 39: "Ironiser c'est choisir la justice."

2. Crane to John S. Phillips, 30 December [1895], in R. W. Stallman and Lillian Gilkes, eds., *Stephen Crane: Letters* (New York: New York University Press, 1960), p. 84.

3. "In the Depths of a Coal-Mine," *McClure's Magazine* 2 (August 1894): 195–209.

4. "Mr. Binks' Day Off," *New York Press*, 8 July 1894.

5. References in parentheses are to Joseph Katz, *The Portable Stephen Crane* (New York: The Viking Press, 1969).

6. Harold A. Hungerford, " 'That Was at Chancellorsville': The Factual Framework of *The Red Badge of Courage*," *American Literature* 34 (January 1963): 520–31.

7. Daniel G. Hoffman, *The Poetry of Stephen Crane* (New York: Columbia University Press, 1957), p. 110.

8. "The Snake," *Pocket Magazine* 2 (August 1896): 125–32.

9. See, for example, various writings of R. W. Stallman beginning with his introduction to *The Red Badge of Courage* (New York: Modern Library, 1951); and Daniel Hoffman's introduction to the same novel (New York: Harper & Brothers, 1959).

10. This myth is particularly well analyzed in Georges Bataille, *La Part maudite* (Paris: Editions de Minuit, 1967), pp. 103–4.

11. "The Veteran," *McClure's Magazine* 7 (August 1896): 222–24.

12. "War Memories," *Anglo-Saxon Review* 3 (December 1899): 10–38.

13. "War Memories," p. 19.

E. R. Hagemann

"Sadder than the End":
Another Look at "The Open Boat"

I

Toward the end of "Stephen Crane's Own Story," a newspaper account of the sinking of the filibustering S.S. *Commodore*, the newspaperman says:

> The history of life in an open boat for thirty hours would no doubt be instructive for the young, but none is to be told here now. For my part I would prefer to tell the story at once, because from it would shine the splendid manhood of Captain Edward Murphy and of William Higgins, the oiler, but let it suffice at this time to say that when we were swamped in the surf and making the best of our way toward the shore the captain gave orders amid the wildness of the breakers as clearly as if he had been on the quarter deck of a battleship.[1]

Undoubtedly, Crane was already planning his fictional version—he says he "would prefer to tell the story at once." Furthermore, he included the title within the first sentence, i.e., "The Open Boat." He also knew enough not to put too much into a story for the papers; knew enough not to waste what he had to say, or wanted to say, on that most uncomprehending of all readers, the reader of the newspaper. What was "instructive" would be the focus of the story, for after thirty hours in a small boat in the open Atlantic, he was an interpreter of many things. So were his two surviving companions, but Crane was the artist among them; and although he may have wanted to tell the story at once, it takes time to become an interpreter in an artistic or creative sense. Obviously it is significant that Crane did not attempt "at once" to write of and publish his open boat experiences.[2]

In the epigraph to "The Open Boat," laid out like subheads in a news column, there is an important idea—"A Tale Intended to be after the Fact,"—in which Crane established the tie between the *New York Press* story and the finished short story. This tie cannot be stressed too strongly, and its importance will emerge in this analysis. Questions arise from these cryptic words, "A Tale Intended to be after the Fact." The "Tale" is "The Open Boat." "Intended" indicates that Crane proposed or designed. But why the quasi-legal language, "after the Fact"? What in *fact* is the "Fact"? Is it the adventure of the open boat, a ten-foot dinghy? Or is it the sinking of the *Commodore* in the early morning hours of 2 January 1897? Then "after" offers ambiguities. Does this suggest "later" or "afterward"; i.e., subsequent to the thirty-hour ordeal at sea; "in search of"; "in pursuit of"; "in the manner of"; "in honor of"; "concerning"? All are dictionary definitions, but as questions they are central to the meaning of "The Open Boat."

I do not wish to appear bizarre by saying that one possible aid here is a legal dictionary. So close in terminology are "a Tale . . . after the Fact" and "accessory after the fact" that one wonders. In common law, states *Ballentine's Law Dictionary*, an accessory is "a person who, knowing a felony to have been committed, receives, relieves, comforts, or assists the felon, or in any manner aids him to escape arrest."[3] Contemporary accounts and recent scholarship on the problem of the *Commodore's* sinking do not indicate treachery from the Spanish (or

Cuban) passengers. There was a leak, but the tiny *Commodore* had twice run aground (once in a fog on the St. Johns River, thereby damaging her seams) before setting out to sea under the aegis of the decrepit tub, the revenue cutter *George S. Boutwell.*[4] No apparent felony therefore, not in the matter of the leak; and no accessory, per se, according to accepted standards. However, there had been professional misconduct. The pumps failed to work properly because the coal had been washed down and the sediment choked them. Asked directly if there had been treachery, Captain William Murphy said, "No, I don't think so. It was neglect, more than anything else."[5] Such an allegation cannot be lightly tossed aside. Negligence on the part of an officer in the maritime service is a serious offense, and can be a felony. Simply put, what had occurred on board the *Commodore* was culpable negligence on the part of Chief Engineer James Redigan, who drowned. Had Redigan survived, there may have been grounds for a trial in courts of admiralty.[6] Crane was faced, as we are faced, with an aberration—namely Redigan's negligence, however drily Crane tells the story in the newspaper—and aberration is the center of any culpable act, any act of criminality. Seven men had drowned when the *Commodore* went down, an injustice in an unjust world.[7]

The sinking of the *Commodore* is the fact to commence with. The "Tale" that is "The Open Boat" is after the fact in point of time, i.e., *post factum*, after the event. The tale "after the Fact" does not in any manner relieve, comfort, or assist the felon in any legal sense; however, it does relieve, comfort, and assist the reader (after the reader understands it) in an artistic sense—and that most disturbingly so. There is also a sense of *ex post facto* (ignoring the various legal complexities for the moment), specifically and adjectively: "done or made after a thing but retroacting upon it; retroactive, as, an *ex post facto* argument."[8] And "argument" suggests, by its Latin root, evidence or proof; thus, the story written by Crane as he looks back (retrospection). In his unfolding of the tale, Crane reveals other facts—the drowning of Billy Higgins, the oiler, in the surf near Daytona Beach; the survival of Crane, Murphy, and Montgomery (the cook)—and, in the true function of the artist, maneuvers the reader into position *post* these facts and prompts his (the reader's) retrospection.[9]

Finally, to close this discussion of the epigraph to the story, there are the words: "Being the Experience of Four Men from the Sunk Steamer *Commodore*," emphasizing the newspaper-like tone and the notion that the *fact* is the sinking of the ship. Naturally, one's attention is directed to the word "experience," and rightly so, for it is the formative principle of the tale; that is, if this word is understood, then form and character (a necessity in art) can be arrived at. So: Crane has gained "direct personal knowledge" and is one of a company of "interpreters," to quote the last word of "The Open Boat." But an interpreter of what? To answer this is the purpose of the remainder of this essay.

II

Precisely mid-point in the story (in section 4), there occurs among the four occupants of the ten-foot dinghy a spirited conversation concerning a dimly apprehended man on the beach.

> "Look at the fellow with the flag. Maybe he ain't waving it!"
> "That ain't a flag, is it? That's his coat. Why, certainly, that's his coat."
> "So it is; it's his coat. He's taken it off and is waving it around his head. But would you look at him swing it!" (P. 372.)

Metaphorically, the man has a message for the four men, incomprehensible to them at that moment, although it should not have been for, after all, they had been previously forced to take the boat back out to sea. The signalman also has a message for the reader, incomprehensible as it is at this moment despite the foreshadowings given by Crane.

The appearance of the signalman mid-way in the story indicates its careful construction. His frantic, if not demonic, waving is the climax. Before sighting him, the four men—pained by the rowing,

69

discomfited by the waves, and chilled by the cold—were confident, despite an unsuccessful attempt to run through the surf, that they would ultimately make it without undue difficulty. They should not have been; their circumstances warranted no such confidence.

Three times in the first paragraph, fourteen times in all in section 1, Crane mentions or alludes to the waves, beyond and through which these men must go to gain the shore—that beautiful, macadam-hard, gently-inclined stretch of sand just south of Daytona. Looking out from the boat, there are always the waves; the horizon narrows and widens, dips and rises; "at all times its edge . . . jagged with waves that [seem] thrust up in points like rocks"; each wave-top is "a problem in small boat navigation." Nature, at her most unpleasant, allows the men a glimpse of the shore, reminds them of her indifferent strength as if they needed to be reminded. For they have escaped, in the "greys of dawn," the fate of seven of their shipmates as "a stump of a top-mast with a white ball on it" slashed at the waves and then went "low and lower, and down."

As already stated, the sinking of the luckless S.S. *Commodore* is the fact, and I suggest that Crane indicates this by alluding to it so soon in the story. Now these four men are *after the fact*, on one level of meaning, and they must get to shore before they are bested by "these problems in white water" and "the snarling of the crests." The correspondent and the cook argue about the difference between a life-saving station and house of refuge. The cook insists that a crew from the house of refuge will pick them up as soon as they are sighted.[10] The correspondent insists that a house of refuge does not have a crew. He is correct.[11]

Abruptly, Billy Higgins, the oiler, says, "Well, we're not there yet, anyhow." Indeed they are not; the cook shifts his argument; the oiler repeats, "We're not there yet" (p. 362). What the oiler says is true in several ways: they have not gained the shore—far from it; nor have they garnered the "direct personal knowledge" to be able to say, "I've been there," which implies experience and thereby allows them to become interpreters. Billy's words foreshadow his own end and make all the more ironic a third level of meaning—not one of them has met Death. They had seen Him in the "greys of dawn," though, and seen His attribute, "the white ball" on the mast, in that carefully arranged canvas Crane paints for the reader.

In section 2, the occupants in the "freighted" boat (figuratively laden with death and violence) oscillate between hope and despair with Crane carefully introducing each element. The cook mentions the on-shore wind—they wouldn't have a "show" without it; the oiler and the correspondent heartily agree. Captain Murphy laughs away their optimism; his "crew" is silent: "the ethics of their condition was decidedly against any open suggestion of hopelessness." Then Murphy soothes them, saying, "Oh well, . . . we'll get ashore all right." Immediately, the oiler agrees, but only if the wind holds; the cook agrees, but only if they don't catch "hell in the surf" (p. 363).

Nature is toying with them; Crane is toying with the reader. "Canton-flannel" gulls, ordinarily a welcome sight to the sailor, fly about the men or ride the waves. The gulls come close and stare "with black, bead-like eyes . . . uncanny and sinister in their unblinking scrutiny" (p. 363). One gull perches on the captain's head! Seated in the bow of the dinghy, that smallest of all boats that puts to sea, the Captain with the gull atop him is a perfect duplication of the image seen when the *Commodore* went down: "a stump of a topmast with a white ball on it" (p. 361). In this masterful bit of ambiguous foreshadowing, Murphy is the mast and the gull is the ball; the men in the "freighted" craft sense Death because the sea bird strikes them somehow as "gruesome and ominous." They breathe easier when the Captain waves it away, and they set to rowing and rowing and rowing and oscillate to a feeling of optimism, as adjacent "brown mats" of seaweed inform them they are "making progress slowly toward the land."

Their optimism increases when the Mosquito Inlet lighthouse appears like "a small still thing on the edge of the swaying horizon," having the dimensions and forcefulness of "the point of a pin." That they could see the light, 159 feet above mean high water, was cause

71

for hope: probably they were no more than fifteen or sixteen nautical miles from shore.[12] Will they make it, is the question. "If this wind [an on-shore wind] holds and the boat don't swamp [in the surf], we can't do much else" says the Captain (p. 365). Crane skillfully balances the wind and the surf against the lighthouse. Hope is strong aboard the "wee thing" wallowing "at the mercy of five oceans."

"Bail her, cook," said the captain, serenely.
"All right, Captain," said the cheerful cook. (P. 365.)

They have overlooked the gull. They have been *gulled*!
    Captain Murphy wishes for a sail (section 3), and almost magically his overcoat is rigged to an oar and the little boat makes "good way" as the oiler steers and sculls with the other oar, such good way that the lighthouse becomes "an upright shadow on the sky" and the land seems "a long black shadow on the sea," adumbrations of the ultimate tragedy. This stretch of shore is not a welcoming and verdant shore. Crane renders this ironically apparent when the cook suggests that they should be opposite New Smyrna, Florida. Surely the sounding of this New World name (almost a cognomen for a town of about 500 souls) conjurs a vision of the flourishing seaport of the old Ottoman Empire.[13] Even the life-saving station seems to have been recently abandoned, and the cook so informs the Captain who merely says, "Did they?" The wind slowly dies, Crane briefly alludes to the foundering of the *Commodore*, and the crew take to the oars. They make good progress; they cannot be concerned with irony. They make out a house on the shore—the house of refuge for the homeless and destitute of the sea. The lighthouse rears high; "slowly and beautifully" the land looms out of the Atlantic.
    Nevertheless, there are discords: the sound of the surf and the veering of the wind to the southeast. They cannot make the lighthouse now. They are not discouraged—far from it. They swing the dinghy "a little more north" and watch the shore grow. They are quietly cheerful. "In an hour, perhaps, they would be ashore." That simple!

A relatively easy matter of a few hours at sea! The correspondent passes out cigars, and the "four waifs" puff away and ride "impudently" in their little boat, forgetful of the earlier argument over a life-saving station and a house of refuge. They willingly pin their hopes on the latter; forgetful, if they in fact knew, that they are "waifs"; blown by the wind, wanderers, discarded human goods from a sunk ship, owner unknown.

Captain Murphy reminds them, remarking to the cook that "there don't seem to be any signs of life about your house of refuge" (p. 368).The surf's roar is plain to hear; everyone is suddenly positive they will swamp. In what amounts to a parenthetical aside, Crane says that "there was not a life-saving station within twenty miles in either direction." [14] Understandably, their "light-heartedness of a former time" has "completely faded." No boat is seen pulling to succor them. They had better make a run through the surf; the oiler turns the boat "straight for the shore," amidst some "admonitions" and "reflections" with a "good deal of rage" in them.

> "If I am going to be drowned—if I am going to be drowned—if I am going to be drowned, why, in the name of the seven mad gods who rule the sea, was I allowed to come thus far and contemplate sand and trees? Was I brought here merely to have my nose dragged away as I was about to nibble the sacred cheese of life? It is preposterous!" (P. 369.)

It *is*, no one will deny, seemingly preposterous to be so close. But they are not *there* yet, to recall the oiler's words; and to have made it through the surf on the first run was not to be their lot. Fate, Clotho, Lachesis (I cannot suppress the thought that Crane has constructed a pun with "sacred cheese"), and Atropos have other plans, namely, interpretation. Aware now that they wouldn't last three minutes in such a surf, they take the dinghy to sea again. Wind, wave, and tide fight for possession of the craft; it gains a little northward. They spot a man, a "little black figure," running on the shore. He

73

waves; they tie a bath towel to a stick and wave back. Another man appears; he, too, waves. A resort hotel omnibus appears, and yet another man stands on the steps and waves. And we are brought to mid-point of the story, the signaling episode, the climax, told by Crane from the point of view of the four "waifs" in the dinghy in two full pages of dialogue, without tag lines, description, or exposition, to point up the irony.

"What's that idiot with the coat mean? What's he signaling, any-how?" demands one waif (p. 372). A perfectly marvelous question. The answers are various: he is telling them to go north; he thinks the waifs are fishing and is giving them "a merry hand." Another waif says, "He don't mean anything. He's just playing." That, most assuredly, he is not doing. As I interpret it, what he is telling them is this: *you can't come in yet; you can't get through so easily; you stay outside there and suffer; when your time comes, you can come through; sorry, but that is the way it is.* In the growing dusk, the four men helplessly sit in the boat. When the spray hits them, they swear "like men who were being branded" (p. 373). They row and they row and they row. The lighthouse disappears from the southern horizon. And again the "if I am going to be drowned" motif enters this section (p. 374), stressing the structure within the section and within the story and stressing the meaning. (See figure 1.) In this reappearance of "if I am going to be drowned," Crane pointedly, yet subtly, omits the statement "It is preposterous" and all that follows relative to Fate. Their situation is no *longer* preposterous in the "freighted" dinghy, and they see a glimmer of what is in store for them. A different mood is among them, and Crane employs appro-priate language: the captain is "patient" when he issues orders; the crew's voices are "weary" and "low" in reply; the evening is "quiet"—a prelude to the morning to come; and all but the oarsman lie "heavily and listlessly" in the dinghy.

Figure 1 schematizes the arch-like construction in the story (this is more fully detailed in figure 2)—the action and mood in section 5 simultaneously balances and offsets the action and mood in section 3.

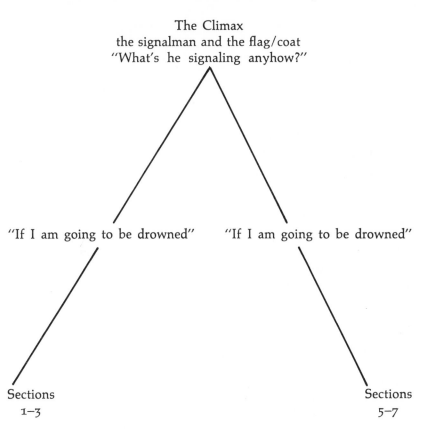

The Climax
the signalman and the flag/coat
"What's he signaling anyhow?"

"If I am going to be drowned"   "If I am going to be drowned"

Sections   Sections
1–3   5–7

Figure 1. Situation in Section 4.

What was buoyant optimism and hope in the earlier part is now a long
night "on the sea in an open boat." Two lights, one to the north (one
is tempted to think it is the St. Augustine Lighthouse) and the other
to the south (Mosquito Inlet Lighthouse), are "the furniture of the
world" and remind us of the argument about the house of refuge and
the life-saving station.[15] Only the man at the oars is awake; the

75

others are sleeping, a word that Crane used, naturally enough, time and again with variations in this passage; for now, having attained a dim perception of what is in store for them, they need the preparatory sleep.

The correspondent keeps the boat headed and regards the sleeping oiler and cook, arms wrapped about each other, there in the bottom: "babes of the sea." This womb image, shortly to be repeated, wryly recalls the jauntily oblivious "waifs" in section 3 as they "impudently" rode the waves. Such a difference now. Writes Crane: "The wind had a voice as it came over the waves, and it was sadder than the end" (p. 376). Nothing could be more felicitous at this point in the story. The end, of course, is Death for all of us (and them, too), and this is sad; sadder yet is to remember what we did not know we knew, as Robert Frost says; sadder yet is to become "interpreters" before Death and to carry this burden and tell of its meaning to the uninitiated. This sentence also sums up the ordeal of the correspondent and the oiler as they meekly and steadily spell each other at the oars throughout the night. No arguments or petulant comments; rather compassion and contriteness if a wave but splashes into the boat. Dim as their perception of the ways of existence may be, "the subtle brotherhood" of men at sea, spoken of by Crane in section 3, indicates obedience and grace of conduct as they approach what is "sadder than the end."

Suddenly there appears the predatory shark, the largest fish of all, swishing through the water "like blue flame," speeding "like a shadow" ahead or astern, port or starboard. Its fin, knifing the water, leaving "a gleaming trail of phosphorescence," literally draws a magic circle around the dinghy. The waifs must stay in the boat, perform, carry on. This particular shark is not a predator—it will not plunder; it is, Crane says, a "biding thing," and the correspondent, without horror, simply looks "dully" at the sea and swears "in an undertone." He is not vindictive; he merely wishes he were not alone "with the thing." But his companions are sleeping their preparatory sleep (pp. 376–77).

The final iteration of the "if I am going to be drowned" motif opens section 6 (p. 377). This seems a normal thought on the part of the lonely correspondent and directs the reader to compare this third repetition with the previous two. The first expressed the collective emotions of the four waifs; the second (more a refrain than anything else and assigned to no one waif) expressed the mood of the moment; the third expresses the meditations of the correspondent and expands them into a fear of drowning, "an abominable injustice" to a man who has worked "so hard, so hard." He wants so to live, to survive. To drown would be "a crime most unnatural." To this point in his life, apparently, the correspondent, unlike his creator and his counterpart, has not given time and effort to wrestling with the idea of an unjust, i.e., unlawful universe. Only in the physical realms, in the sciences (for example, astronomy), is the universe lawful; here lies what Thomas Paine once called the "true theology" of man.

Injustice is not for the correspondent. He wishes for recognition of himself as an entity. But:

> When it occurs to a man that nature does not regard him as important, and that she feels she would not maim the universe by disposing of him, he at first wishes to throw bricks at the temple, and he hates deeply the fact that there are no bricks and no temples. Any visible expression of nature would surely be pelleted with his jeers. (P. 377.)

Crane at last has tentatively stated the theme of the story: the indifference of nature to man's struggles. If there be "no tangible thing to hoot," muses the correspondent, at least he wishes to confront "a personification" and plead, "Yes, but I love myself." The reply is the symbolic "high cold star," and the correspondent knows "the pathos of his situation": to be faced by an indifferent but ever-watchful Nature. A vagrant ditty from his childhood about "A soldier of the Legion" who is dying in Algiers—where there are also sand and trees (to recall the motif)—enters the correspondent's memory and

E. R. Hagemann

enforces the delineation of the theme. As a child, he had never regarded this death as important, notwithstanding that it was dinned
into his boyish mind by "myriads of his school-fellows" (p. 378). He
had been indifferent to such a death; it was something less important
to him than "the breaking of a pencil's point." Now, at the oars with
the "cold star" above him, he is very sorry "for the soldier of the
Legion." Crane's irony is subtle: the correspondent's dinning in the
presence of Nature has produced indifference; the schoolboys' dinning
the song in his presence had produced indifference. However, in
his desert ordeal the soldier had had a comrade to hold his hand; of
this small boon the correspondent on the morrow cannot be sure.

Captain Murphy and the correspondent briefly discuss the shark,
who has departed the vicinity, evidently "bored at the delay." The
oiler and the correspondent spell each other at the oars; the cook
lends a hand and works the dinghy farther out to sea, only to be
driven back. The shark returns. The correspondent assumes the
thwart and works the dinghy outward. Then this cogent close to the
section:

At last there was a short conversation.
"Billie! . . . Billie, will you spell me?"
"Sure," said the oiler. (Pp. 380–81.)

There is much more here than a simple question-and-answer;
present are foreshadowing and irony and a signpost planted by
Crane to direct the reader to the violent finish of the story. What the
correspondent (who "loves" himself and feels "sorry" for the dying
soldier) has really asked the oiler is for Billie to serve in his place, to
replace him, when the dinghy makes its ultimate run through the
surf and when "the old ninny-woman Fate" (in three persons) decides
finally the destiny of these four humans who have been wallowing
in the sea under the "cold star." There is something disconcerting
about the oiler's prompt affirmative.

It is time for the final journey through the combers, after which

78

they will be *there*. The preparations are over. Crane opens the section with the same gray cast that was present in the first paragraph of the story. On the dunes appear "many little black cottages" and "a tall white windmill" which rears above them as they plunge for the beach; these provide the focus for Crane's specific statement of the theme of "The Open Boat."

This tower was a giant, standing with its back to the plight of the ants. It represented in a degree, to the correspondent, the serenity of nature amid the struggles of the individual—nature in the wind, and nature in the vision of men. She did not seem cruel to him then, nor beneficent, nor treacherous, nor wise. But she was indifferent, flatly indifferent. It is, perhaps, plausible that a man in this situation, impressed with the unconcern of the universe, should see the innumerable flaws of his life . . . . (P. 381.)

The Captain orders, "don't jump until she swamps sure" (p. 382); the oiler (as he had in section 1) has the oars, and he backs in toward "the lonely and indifferent shore." The correspondent's thoughts touch briefly on the drowning motif (what "a shame" it would be) just before the first comber smashes them; they survive this as they do the second crest. The third wave, "huge, furious, implacable . . . fairly swallows" them, and the men go into the icy water: the oiler swimming strongly in the lead, the cook using the life-belt, the Captain clinging to the overturned dinghy. Three times Crane describes the shore, the representational *there* to these waifs—representational to them as having "a certain immovable quality," as being set before them like "a bit of scenery on a stage," and as "a picture" in "a gallery," a scene from Algiers perhaps (pp. 383–84). The thought of the dying legionnaire haunts the correspondent as does the thought of drowning. "Can it be possible? Can it be possible? Can it be possible?" echo and balance his previous cadence, "If I am going to be drowned." A perverse observation adds, "perhaps an individual must consider his own death to be the final phenomenon of nature."

79

The four waifs struggle mightily there in the surf. Finally an actor appears on the stage-like shore: a man running, undressing rapidly as he runs. Miraculously the surf flings the correspondent over the dangerous, overturned boat and into shallow water. He is not safely *there* yet; now he fights the undertow. The naked man-actor comes into the water, rescues the cook, and wades toward the correspondent who sees "a halo about his head." He shines "like a saint." There is something suggestively comic about the rescue here as the man heaves and tugs at the correspondent, but the comedy fades when the man points "a swift finger" and runs at the correspondent's command. "In the shallows, face downward, lay the oiler. His forehead touched sand that was periodically, between each wave, clear of the sea" (p. 385).

Billy Higgins, oiler aboard the S.S. *Commodore*, who had earlier implacably said, "We're not there yet," has arrived *there*, not as an interpreter, but as "a still and dripping shape" being carried to the grave in the midst of "the welcome of the land" (the people with restoratives and blankets). The survivors are *there;* indifferent Nature is transformed into benevolent Nature, and now "the old ninny-woman Fate" has extracted her toll.

> When it came night,the white waves paced to and fro in the moonlight, and the wind brought the sound of the great sea's voice to the men on shore, and they felt that they could then be interpreters. (P. 386.)

III

The "voice" here—a coda surely—sounds the notes of the other wind (in section 5) which was "sadder than the end." And we are brought to the final word, "interpreters." Of what are these men, no longer waifs, interpreters? The necessity was to struggle against an indifferent nature. But also much more than that, for this seems almost absurd in its simplicity. We must return to the epigraph, "A TALE INTENDED TO BE AFTER THE FACT: BEING THE / EXPE-RIENCE OF FOUR MEN FROM THE SUNK STEAMER / COM-

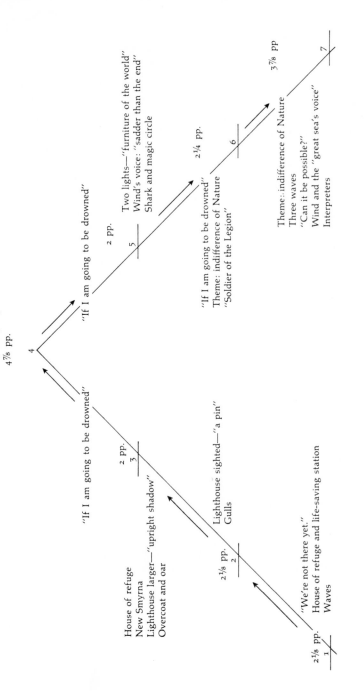

The Signalman and Flag—Message
"What's he signaling anyhow?"
4⅞ pp.

4

"If I am going to be drowned"

"If I am going to be drowned"

2 pp.
3

House of refuge
New Smyrna
Lighthouse larger—"upright shadow"
Overcoat and oar

Lighthouse sighted—"a pin"
Gulls

2⅛ pp.
2

"We're not there yet."
House of refuge and life-saving station
Waves

2⅛ pp.
1

2 pp.
5

Two lights—"furniture of the world"
Wind's voice: "sadder than the end"
Shark and magic circle

2¼ pp.

"If I am going to be drowned"
Theme: indifference of Nature
"Soldier of the Legion"

6

3⅞ pp.

7

Theme: indifference of Nature
Three waves
"Can it be possible?"
Wind and the "great sea's voice"
Interpreters

Figure 2. Structure of "The Open Boat."

E. R. Hagemann

MODORE," and to the discussion early in this paper to glean the many complexities involved.[16] Crane in this story is seeking the universal fact of existence subsequent to the particular fact of the sinking of the *Commodore*. "The Open Boat" is his retrospection (*ex post facto*) and, as I have said, the reader's, too. From this retrospection emerges his (and the reader's) personal knowledge which makes plain the ultimate meaning of experience. Made plain, too, is the form or structure. (See figure 2.) Significantly, Crane in the epigraph speaks of the experience of four men; so Billy Higgins is included. To sum up, the totality of experience for the living and the dead is: existence. These three men have become brothers to Henry Fleming whose journey to the other side is so brilliantly explicated in the final paragraphs of *The Red Badge of Courage*. Captain Murphy, the cook, and the correspondent, in their journey from "the greys of dawn" to the "welcome of the land," went on yet another journey—a private one to another land of There. The length of that journey, the time consumed is of little import. Within its duration, they learned a little bit, gained an "accidental education" (to use Henry Adams's doctrine, which in the final analysis is a goodly amount) in and about courage. Not heroism and all its ritualistically empty gestures, but *courage*. They have returned to the same unjust but nevertheless welcome world that so outrageously allowed the S.S. *Commodore* to sink, but now they view it with a "fresh pair of eyes."

Indeed, to be an "interpreter" is "sadder than the end." Another allusion to Henry Adams is fitting: the correspondent's education began and ended in the open boat; what he has learned and communicated in "The Open Boat" is no doubt "instructive for the young."

NOTES

1. Joseph Katz, *The Portable Stephen Crane* (New York: Viking Press, 1969), p. 342; reprinted from the *New York Press*, 7 January 1897, p. 1. At this point, I wish to express my appreciation to Prof. R. W. Stallman for his remarks on

"Sadder than the End": Another Look at "The Open Boat"

"The Open Boat" (*Stephen Crane: An Omnibus* [New York: Alfred A. Knopf, 1952], pp. 415–20); they are very suggestive. In some ways, but certainly not all, my essay is a commentary on those remarks.

2. "The Open Boat" was originally published in *Scribner's Magazine* 21 (June 1897): 728–40. Quotations are cited from Katz, *The Portable Stephen Crane*, pp. 360–86.

3. Rochester, N.Y., 1948 ed.

4. Built in 1873, the 151–ton cutter was named for the feckless Secretary of the Treasury (1869–1873), during Grant's first administration.

S.S. *Commodore* was built in 1882 in Philadelphia; she had a gross tonnage of 178.25; net, 99.25; length 122.5 feet; breadth, 21 feet; depth, 9 feet (cf. *Twenty-Eighth Annual List of Merchant Vessels of the United States* . . . , 54th Cong., 2d Sess., H. R. Doc. 38. [Washington, 1896], p. 228). These data are deduced from the fact that this ship, Official Number 126017, does not appear in the *Twenty-Ninth Annual List* (Washington, 1897). *Commodore's* estimated value was $20,000 (see *Report of the Chief of Division of Revenue Cutter Service, 1897*, Treasury Department Document No. 1993 [Washington, 1897], p. 49).

Some of the technical information herein is also to be found in Cyrus Day, "Stephen Crane and the Ten-Foot Dinghy," *Boston University Studies in English* 3 (Winter 1957): 193–213; but I preferred to seek and to find my own.

5. Stallman, *Omnibus*, p. 460. Professor William Randel, "The Cook in 'The Open Boat,'" *American Literature* 34 (November 1962): 406, states that "almost all the crew, including the captain, were recruited and given their instructions in less than thirty hours . . . ." Randel further states that "neither the chief engineer . . . nor the second engineer . . . had an intimate knowledge of her machinery" (p. 408).

6. In the United States, initial jurisdiction is vested in the federal courts. Sr. Paul Rojo, one of the Cuban leaders aboard the *Commodore*, openly charged Redigan with being drunk on duty. There were also various charges hurled about by the steward (cook), Charles R. Montgomery; each one of which was examined by Randel in his article and dismissed as untrue. One Horatio Rubens, a lawyer, conducted a private inquiry into the sinking; reporters were barred.

My interpretation of the cause of the tragedy differs from Prof. Day; he places much of the blame on Captain Murphy and just barely refrains from convicting the skipper of dereliction of duty. Day also has some upleasant things to say about Crane himself (see Day, "Stephen Crane and the Ten-Foot Dinghy," pp. 204–8).

7. The ship was apparently engaged in illegal business, running guns and ammunition to Cuba; in this instance the cargo had an estimated value of $5,000. This was in seeming violation of United States neutrality laws. I say "apparently" and "seeming" deliberately, for Secretary of the Treasury John G. Carlisle,

E. R. Hagemann

on 30 December 1896, "granted permission for a cargo [*Commodore*] destined
for a foreign port [Cienfuegos, Cuba], the same kind of routine clearance given
for any shipment of goods abroad, and left it to the Customs men in Jacksonville
to decide whether neutrality regulations were properly observed" (Randel, "The
Cook in 'The Open Boat,' " p. 408).

It is still not clear why the *Boutwell* did not apprehend the *Commodore*. Prof.
Randel believes that Treasury's clearance reflects an opinion from Attorney-
General Judson Harmon, 10 December 1895, in response to a request from Secretary of State Richard Olney on the matter of international law and the Cuban
insurrection. Three of Harmon's major points can be summarized: (1) "International law takes no account of a mere insurrection . . . which has not been protracted or successful enough to secure for those engaged in it recognition as
belligerents by their own government [Spain] or by foreign governments [e.g.,
the United States]. . . . No state of war is acknowledged by Spain and . . . no
blockade has been declared. . . . It follows, therefore, that the rules of international law with respect to belligerent and neutral rights do not apply to the
present case." (2) "The mere sale or shipment of arms and munitions of war by
persons in the United States to persons in Cuba is not a violation of international
law, however strong a suspicion there may be that they are to be used in an
insurrection against the Spanish government." (3) "If, however, the persons supplying or carrying arms and munitions from a place in the United States are in
any wise parties to a design that force shall be employed against the Spanish
authorities . . . the enterprise is not commercial, but military, and is in violation
of international law and of our own statutes." See *Official Opinions of The
Attorneys-General of the United States* 21 (Washington, 1898): 269–71.

Attorney-General Harmon's views may account for a somewhat cryptic statement in the *Report of the Chief of Division of Revenue Cutter Service, 1897,*
p. 22: "Some question having arisen as to the validity of seizures made by
vessels of the Revenue Cutter Service in enforcing the neutrality laws, a duty
performed by this Service in strict accordance with law upon numerous occasions
running through the more than one hundred years of its existence, two of them
[cutters], the *Boutwell* and *Colfax*, were placed in cooperation with the Navy by
the President, under the provisions of Section 2757, Revised Statutes [Revenue
officers to co-operate with the Navy], and so remained from April 8 until May
31, 1897."

8. *Webster's New International Dictionary,* 2nd ed. (1934).

9. *Ballentine's Law Dictionary* defines *ex post facto* as "after the thing is done;
after the act is committed"; *post facto* as "after the fact; after the commission
of the crime." Of course, such definitions urge the reader into even more complexities, but this is not the place for them.

10. Maintained by the United States Life-Saving Service, this house of refuge

84

"Sadder than the End": Another Look at "The Open Boat"

is on the beach outside Mosquito Lagoon, just north of Mosquito Inlet Light (known as Ponce de Leon Light on present-day charts). In 1897, this house was in the 7th District, United States Life-Saving Service.

11. The Life-Saving Service then maintained three types of installations: life-saving stations, which had a crew and life-saving appliances of all kinds; houses of refuge, supplied with boats, provisions, etc., in the charge of keepers but without crews; and life-boat stations.

12. The light at Mosquito Inlet was fixed white, used oil as an illuminant, and was visible at night to a maximum of 18¾ nautical miles. The tower was red brick and conical in shape; there were three brick dwellings near it. Established in 1887 and given Number 1059, the tower was about one mile to the north and west of the entrance to Mosquito Inlet and 52 miles SSE from the St. Augustine Lighthouse (*List of Lights and Fog Signals on the Atlantic and Gulf Coasts . . . to . . . March 1, 1907* [Washington, 1907], pp. 206–7).

13. About 13 miles SSE of Daytona Beach; the name was changed to New Smyrna Beach in 1937.

14. As a matter of fact, there was no life-saving station in the area at all. The next house of refuge north was at Smiths Creek, 20 miles south of Matanzas Inlet; south, at Chester Shoal, 11 miles north of Cape Kennedy. See *Annual Report of the Operations of the United States Life-Saving Service for . . . 1897*, Treasury Department Document No. 1996 (Washington, 1898), p. 369.

15. It is unlikely that the correspondent saw the St. Augustine Light; what he saw was probably a light in Daytona Beach or possibly north of the town. The tower of the St. Augustine Light was 161 feet high with a fixed white light, varied by a white flash every three minutes. It was visible for 18¾ nautical miles.

16. As originally printed in *Scribner's Magazine* in 1897.

Max Westbrook

Whilomville: The Coherence of Radical Language

Warner Berthoff is right when he concludes that there is a "Crane problem," something akin to the long-running effort of critics to account for the power of Dreiser's art. With Crane, it is an effort to discover his coherence, the unity of language and story. According to Berthoff, there is "a gap between the story and the concrete demonstration." The language invokes meanings the story cannot accommodate. Berthoff wants to mitigate the flaw, for he believes that the integrity of Crane's art is beyond structural coherence. Crane is a "visionary writer," and his "particular gestures or moments of consciousness are given a dream-like autonomy." Berthoff refers to "certain free-floating images" and a "passivity of observation," but he concludes that the "serenity and intactness of dream images," in "The Monster" for example, "draw what force they have" from a "strange" and "self-animating" quality—that is, from the imagery itself. Unity and structure, or what Kenneth Burke calls qualitative progression, are absent from Crane's art. Still, Berthoff concludes, there is merit in Crane's "puzzlingly inconclusive power," for certain passages "come to life as they manage to convey the sense of some self-contained and irreversible apprehension."[1]

86

Jay Martin holds a comparable position: "The world of Stephen Crane is conveyed by general or fragmentary impressions"; and any standard that could help one relate the particular to the general "is wholly absent from his work." Crane "uses successive impressions," and he "insistently offers only a blurred world." [2]

So Berthoff and Martin have called into question the very legitimacy of Crane's art, and their strictures are surprisingly common in writings about an author who is so frequently the object of critical analysis. One critic has focused on critical strictures in a book-length study of Crane, introductions in anthologies have been used to discuss Crane's limitations, and many of the articles in scholarly journals illustrate further the "Crane problem." [3] With *The Red Badge of Courage*, critical debate has centered around the concluding announcement that Henry Fleming has become a man. Is the maturation contained dramatically within the novel, is it a tack-on ending, or is it intended by the author as merely another illusion on the part of Fleming? With "The Blue Hotel," critics have debated the structural relevance of the concluding discussion between the Easterner and the cowboy; Maggie Johnson's fall into prostitution is said to lack structural demonstration; and the oiler's death in "The Open Boat" has a disputed relation to his courage and endurance. With "The Monster" the problem of structural integrity is located not in a climactic scene but in the story itself, in its entirety.

When critics decide that Crane's art is coherent, they often run to exotic interpretations, with the result that Crane seems convicted rather than cleared of the charge of "fragmentary impressions." James Hafley, for example, proposes that "The Monster" is a story based on the theme of saving face: the man who loses his face saves it; the man who saves his face loses it. [4] Hafley discovers an amazing quantity of "face imagery," and he makes intelligent insights into the story; but the accumulation of image patterns does not produce a context that will accommodate Dr. Trescott's moral courage. Hafley is left with the awkward decision of calling Henry Johnson a figurative God; and yet Johnson is an unsatisfactory vehicle for ultimate values. As a sane man, he was a rather innocuous bully of small boys, a harmless dandy; and, in his one time of heroism, his genuine interest in Jimmie's welfare is undercut by a frenetic desperation, the same quality which characterizes the melodramatic and momentary heroism of volunteer firemen and the self-righteousness of the mob which later stones the helpless man.

And thus, in a variety of ways, the Crane problem: his imagery seems to constitute value judgments, but who are we to believe is making those judgments, and with what authority, with what relevance to the story? Does his art consist of dazzling images that are "self-contained," unrelated to any standard and offering "only a blurred world"? I believe that Crane's most characteristic and most troublesome imagery—certainly not all of it—is written from a dualistic viewpoint and that neither viewpoint, by itself, represents the authorial voice.

Typically, Crane writes through the viewpoint of his characters, individually and severally, and sometimes through the eyes of a group. If the reader tries to judge the validity of a given individual viewpoint, say in terms of the events of the story, he will flounder; for Crane's protagonists are often men of a sensibility alien to the author's. Even when the hero is, as is typical of Hemingway, a novitiate in the intimate values of the author, the hero's apprenticeship is that of the recalcitrant. Jake Barnes and Frederic Henry err in dedication; Henry Fleming and the correspondent err in philosophy. The challenge to a Hemingway hero is to do his duty well enough; the Crane hero needs to figure out what that duty is. And when a Crane hero progresses from alienation to an alignment with reality, the style suddenly changes; the radical irony is dropped, as in "The Open Boat," or adjusted to the rationality of the character on stage, as in "The Monster."

The other possibility, for critics like Berthoff and Martin, is that the authorial voice is represented by the radical language used to admonish errant characters for their improper reactions to events; but this too is misleading, for Crane shifts his admonition to suit the individual character. Crane's imagery is dualistic, I think, in that it represents an ironic expression of the further implications of the *character's* reactions. Thus neither the bare content of a character's response nor the ironic expression of that response is representative of Crane's viewpoint. A Crane character lives, typically, in a "personal atmosphere" which he himself creates, the atmosphere implied by his actions.[5] He is seldom aware of his personal atmosphere, but it is a powerful force in his life and, often, in the lives of others. It is only by learning to read the coherent pattern of ironic interpretations, I think, that we can realize the structural integrity of a deceptively straight-forward story like "The Monster."

I

Shortly before the end of the story, Jimmie Trescott returns from his rest-cure in Connecticut. Henry Johnson, the Negro hostler who had saved Jimmie's life when the Trescott house caught fire, is now faceless and mindless—a harmless type of idiot it is true, yet a sight too horrible for eyes to behold. Jimmie at first is "much afraid of the monster," but his fear slowly passes "under the influence of a weird fascination" (p. 495).[6] With the cruelty of childhood, Jimmie displays this freak and saviour to the neighboring children and seems "to reap all the joys of the owner and exhibitor of one of the world's marvels" (p. 496).

The visiting children remain "at a distance—awed and entranced, fearful and envious" (p. 496). One, a slightly older child accustomed to first rank in the pecking order, cannot bear Jimmie's "new social elevation" (p. 496). He finds it "revolutionary," and he is desperate. Dares are exchanged as the children begin to play a game that might be called "touching the monster." This game is the central image of the story, and it represents an instance of the dualistic technique that is essential to the still-puzzling art of Stephen Crane.

Part of the problem is that the social criticism of such a scene seems only too clear: the children are an example of that jealousy, false pride, and cruelty to others which characterize the adult world. The reader will find the story interesting, for Crane is a good craftsman and can make his characters come alive; but there is the feeling that the theme is obvious and the story predictable. The structure seems an illustration of what Kenneth Burke calls repetitive form: the multiplication of incidents illustrating a single and rather static theme, quantitative art as distinguished from qualitative art. I am arguing, obviously, for an opposite conclusion.

As it happens, in this case, fear of social ridicule proves stronger than fear of the monster, and the two boys are driven to the heroics of touching a faceless man, whereupon their fear is replaced by a hypocritical show of boredom—the better to embarrass the other children—and the antagonists become buddies and veterans, bragging as if "they had been decorated for courage on twelve battle-fields" (p. 498). One little waif makes a feeble attempt at glory but panics before getting close enough to touch the monster, and the scene closes with a comment on his pathetic frustrations, "his attempts to reach the front rank and become of some importance, dodging this way and that way, and always piping out his little claim to glory" (p. 500).

The image of "twelve battle-fields" does not represent Jimmie's viewpoint, for the image does not represent his language; nor does the image represent an authorial denouncement of Jimmie, for the boy is not being consciously or willfully cruel. The boasting of the boys is a projection, a personal atmosphere, for which they bear a mitigated responsibility; and it is for this reason that motivation is the most important single principle in Crane's values. Herein, also, is a presentational quality basic to the unity of the story: the guilt of the boys is mitigated by a power in their environment, by the reprehensible presence of the same quality in adults. It is personal atmosphere that blinds Judge Hagenthorpe and his like to Whilomville's ethical duty to Henry Johnson. The boys, in play, cannot see that they are turning an instance of pathos into a game of heroics. The Judge, with more guilt, blinds himself to ethical duty. Trescott, by contrast, is ethical. Thus his final insight, lacking the personal hyperbole of battlefields and rationalization, is recorded by the author in language that is straight and flat: "Trescott found himself occasionally trying to count the cups. There were fifteen of them" (p. 508).

Crane's characteristic stance is neither the "view from the balcony" (that of the removed and ironic observer) nor the "view from the boat" (that of the intimate and sympathetic observer). He does write from these two points of view, but essential to the Crane style is the use of both at once, telescoped into a presentation of personal atmospheres. The ironic refrain in "The Open Boat"—"seven mad gods who rule the sea"—is an objective rendering of subjective feelings, and yet it represents neither Crane's values nor, fully, those of the men in the boat. The irony is a distortion appropriate to men who wrongly feel they must choose between a world in which nature pays them personal attention and a world of madness. When the men progress toward Crane's values and learn that brotherhood is a real value even though nature is indifferent, the style suddenly changes. The alignment between hero and author is then like that of Hemingway and his heroes, and the style is clearly suggestive of Hemingway:

> When it came night, the white waves paced to and fro in the moonlight, and the wind brought the sound of the great sea's voice to the men on the shore, and they felt that they could then be interpreters. (P. 386.)

The values of the authorial voice are directly sympathetic with those of the characters, an alignment which is found in a variety of styles. When Nick Carraway says, at the beginning of *The Great Gatsby*, that he came back from the East wanting the world to be at "a sort of moral attention forever," we know how to read the metaphor, how to read the irony, for the story is over. It is being written— and this is characteristic of Hemingway too—after the fact, and with the result that the narrator or viewpoint character is, in one form or another, to one degree or another, a persona of the author. Crane's typical protagonists, by contrast, have not yet lived the story. Since Crane rejected overt signs for his readers ("preaching is fatal to art"),[7] his imagery has been found by some to be "fragmentary," "self-contained."

In a curious way, the dualism I am describing bears comparison with the generic distinction Hawthorne makes in his preface to *The House of the Seven Gables*. Hawthorne explains that the author of a romance, when he finds it suitable, "may so manage his atmospherical medium as to bring out or mellow the lights and deepen and enrich the shadows of the picture." The deepening, however, is not a sign of mere subjectivity. Hawthorne states that his tale fits the definition of romance *because* of its "attempt to connect a bygone time with the very present that is flitting away from us." In short, he takes latitude in presenting an objective reality which is not literal. Crane's radical imagery is dualistic, takes latitude for the same purpose: he wants to establish a connection between human complaint and the unconscious implications of that complaint.

When Jimmie Trescott exhibits his monster to neighboring children, he does not himself think that he is reaping "all the joys of the owner and exhibitor of one of the world's marvels." If he becomes a moral adult, he may one day develop perspective and learn to see what he has done, as old Henry Fleming in "The Veteran" has developed a dualistic understanding of courage and cowardice. Jimmie, as a child, is unaware. His experience is being presented in immediacy, not in reflection. Thus, if we take the image of the "owner and exhibitor" as representing Jimmie's viewpoint, we misread; for Jimmie, of course, is not consciously cruel. If we read the image as representing Crane's viewpoint, we misread in a different way, creating in ourselves the expectation that Crane's world view will be grounded in a negativism that does not permit the moral heroism Dr. Trescott is obviously intended to achieve. To read the image as an "atmospherical medium," however, to read it as an ironic and authorial implementation of a meaning implied but not felt by Jimmie, is to see that Crane is being at once ironic and sympathetic. The guide to such distinctions, of course, is the context.

In the scene that follows, Trescott calls on Sadie Winter, the little girl who was frightened by the sudden appearance of the monster at a window. Jake Winter, the girl's father, is rude, sullen, and clearly does not want Trescott to attend his daughter. Trescott sees the intent, suggests with dignity that Winter see a physician soon, and calmly leaves. With Trescott at a safe distance, Winter explodes in petty wrath. He stands on the porch yelling at the doctor's back. Jake Winter is "like a little dog" (p. 502).

Such an image is customarily read in a unilateral fashion, assuming a direct relation between "dog" and Crane's definition of man, with the result that Crane is read as a deterministic naturalist, perhaps as a naturalist whose story aims at a moral courage not connected with the fragments of animal imagery. But the two scenes, it seems to me, share a common emphasis on the sin of social bravado and the importance of motive. Jimmie and his little friends are driven by their childish ambitions to appear brave before their fellows. And Winter, though having the greater responsibility of an adult, is driven by the same ambition. He is not an animal in the sense that an animal is without moral responsibility, else Crane would not deftly castigate him with language, would not allow Trescott to appear so much the better man, would not write so as to make the reader admire Trescott for his character and blame Winter for his vicious cowardice.

In the next scene, the structural parallel is even stronger. Carrie, Martha, and Kate—three gossips—play their version of "touching the monster." Martha snorts in contempt at the report of Winter's supposed triumph over Trescott and bluntly denies the seriousness of Sadie Winter's illness, pointing out that the little girl goes regularly to school. As Jimmie's friend had felt chagrined before the monster, as Jake Winter had felt chagrined before the doctor, so do the gossips Carrie and Kate feel chagrined before Martha; and now they too play "touch the monster" in a desperate effort to recoup their social loss. In terror, Jimmie's friend touches the monster and flees; in cowardice, Jake Winter waits on the porch and then screams at Trescott's back; Kate and Carrie bait Martha, claiming her talk suggests she would not be afraid of the monster. A childish argument ensues:

93

Carrie was grinning. "You've never seen him, have you?" she asked, seductively.

"No," admitted Martha.

"Well, then, how do you know that you wouldn't be scared?" Martha confronted her. "Have you ever seen him? No? Well, then, how do you know you *would* be scared?" (P. 504.)

Typically, for Crane, the bravado is undercut by the anti-climactic, the irrelevant, which is the structurally appropriate fate for a personal atmosphere out of touch with reality. The children have been disrupted in their game by the entrance of Trescott; Winter waits until Trescott's back is turned and then barks, after the proper moment; and the gossips are interrupted in their game by the entrance of a trivial question about the Hannigans' move to a new house. The Whilomville story called "The Fight," at least half the chapters in "The Monster," and almost all of the Sullivan County sketches employ the same tactic.

Far from being a "blurred world," Crane's fiction is remarkably clear—perhaps too clear. He has not the stature of a Melville or a Faulkner, but he is coherent. In the first chapter of "The Monster," for example, Crane establishes the obverse of the cowardice that will be shown later. When Jimmie accidentally breaks the flower, Trescott is required to "go forward alone" to view the destruction. This is a humorous variant on "touching the monster." The scene is not related to Johnson's injuries in a quantitative way, as critics have assumed; for Jimmie is responsible for breaking the flower (he was going too fast), whereas no one is responsible for the fire. No cause is assigned (there is no hint that Trescott is at fault for having chemicals in his laboratory) and that is precisely Crane's point: he is concerned with moral duty undergoing trial by the indifferent event.

The doctor is said to be "shaving this lawn as if it were a priest's chin" (p. 449). As Jimmie is intent on his business (playing train), so is the doctor. Later, Johnson prepares to go calling on his sweetheart and he is "like a priest arraying himself for some parade of the church" (p. 453). Returning home from a visit to a patient, the doctor is so intent on business he thinks at first the fire alarm signals a district other than his own. Similarly, the bandmaster, intent on his business, is caught short by the fire alarm, his arms left suspended in the air. Similarly, in *The Red Badge of Courage*, a Negro trooper dancing a jig is suddenly deserted by his audience: "He sat mournfully down" (p. 191). The technique is central to Crane's art, and what he is saying with his ironic extrapolation has to do with man's capacity to act when caught by the trivial, the accidental, the horrible. In the context of such a test, how well does a man perform? Are his values confirmed or undercut?

The answer, expressed by a coherent pattern of imagery, depends largely on the integrity of a man's motives. Jimmie's concentration in play is a mixture of the innocence and cruelty of childhood; the doctor, a Crane hero, shows a consistent moral courage. He is aware of what his business is, and his honesty enables him to maintain his perspective. Thus he can move to meet the situation without panic. He can "go forward alone." The small-town bandmaster, by contrast, is playing concert-orchestra director, as Jimmie is "for the time" not a boy but "engine Number 36" (p. 449). When the game is innocent, Crane's irony is good-humored. When the game is vicious, Crane's irony is devastating. The standard, always, is honesty of will—Crane's most fundamental value.

Having assumed that Crane is using a quantitative language, critics conclude that the purpose of the first chapter is to establish an analogy between the broken peony and the broken Henry Johnson. Such a reading does make the language "self-contained" and "fragmentary," for the quantitative content of chapter 1 would suggest that accidental destruction is the lower layer of reality. Trescott's moral courage would be left suspended, bearing no relation to the language of the story, and the radical imagery would then be judged "visionary," a flash for the sake of a flash. To recognize the dualistic nature of Crane's viewpoint, however, is to see that Crane's subject is guilt and responsibility. The irony is directed at honesty and dishonesty in response to moral duty. Jimmie does mumble and finally get out a confession. And the doctor delivers a reasonable judgment, suggesting that Jimmie "not play train any more to-day" (p. 450).

It is Jimmie who feels "some kind of desire to efface himself" (p. 451), and Crane, by turning to radical language, gives us the deeper significance of that feeling: "Whenever Jimmie became the victim of an eclipse he went to the stable to solace himself with Henry's crimes. Henry . . . could usually provide a sin to place himself on a footing with the disgraced one" (p. 451). The irony here does not represent Crane's objective values, the judgment of Trescott, or the language of the culprits. Jimmie merely feels "some kind of desire to efface himself." But he, like Johnson, considers the doctor "the moon," their demi-god, and their childish dependence is being shown in coherent perspective. It is only from their viewpoint, as expressed in terms of objective implications, that "an eclipse" has occurred.

The subsequent language—"shame," "abominations," "gory from unspeakable deeds," "dwelt for a time in sackcloth"—is an integral part of the structure of "The Monster"; for it is just this type of subjective distortion which makes a mindless and faceless man into a monster to be ridden out of town. And it is just this type of atmosphere, in its pillar-of-the-community form, which leads to the pseudo-reason of Twelve and his committee.

The unity of the story, in fact, is a marvel. Johnson pretends to have warned Jimmie against playing with the flowers: "As a matter of fact, Henry had never mentioned flowers to the boy" (p. 452). This statement, in flat language, is not needed to uncover the role-playing of others: the young men at the band concert, who make remarks merely because one is supposed to say that type of thing; the Twain-like braggart, who explains how the fire started, gets it all wrong, and pompously announces that "they'll die sure" (p. 469); and the town generally, with false stories in the newspaper and false reports, for example, of how Mrs. Farragut broke her leg.

Crane is writing, then, of man's own image-making capacity, showing it in its actual and distorted form.[8] This capacity, furthermore, is what makes it impossible for weak men to live with the monster. To "touch the monster" would be to come into direct and physical contact with an unpleasant fact, one not covered by role-playing. And this is why Henry Johnson is pictured as a dandy, the opposite of a faceless monster, and this, in turn, is why Jimmie and the hostler and almost all the characters in the story have a "moon," a demi-god to worship, a cane to stroke, some prop to save them from actual facts and responsibilities. Johnson assumes "all the dignity of a man whose duty it was to protect Jimmie from a splashing" (p. 452). Similar postures of protectiveness are shown by Twelve and his committee, by Jake Winter for his daughter, and finally (when it saves itself from the monster) by Whilomville itself.

One's public performance is, of course, essential to role-playing; and even the Farragut family and their gentleman caller put up a great show of manners, of imitation, "the most tremendous civilities" (p. 456), as if "they had been the occupants of the most gorgeous salon in the world" (p. 457). The young ladies who attend the band concert gather "preferably in threes, in the curious public dependence upon one another which was their inheritance" (p. 457). And even a dog, prowling the Trescotts' lawn, imagines "himself a formidable beast" (p. 461). Griscom, the lawyer, remarks on Johnson "to the parliament" (p. 454), and the young boys of Whilomville brag that the fire company from their district is the best fire company. At the fire, "each man in this stretcher party had gained a reflected majesty" (p. 470). Men who live in the atmosphere of reflections cannot meet the moral challenge of the monster, nor can they understand a fire as a fire.

Berthoff has said that Crane's radical language is "self-contained," is not related to the social and moral themes of the story; but language and theme in "The Monster," it seems, are successfully unified. Crane gives but one overt signal:

After a moment the window brightened as if the four panes of it had been stained with blood, and a quick ear might have been led to imagine the fire-imps calling and calling, clan joining clan, gathering to the colors. (P. 461.)

The hypothetical "quick ear" is the sign of Crane's dualism. We are not being told how the fire looked to Crane, nor are we being given the language that would be used by any of its witnesses. Crane is describing how the fire would look to those accustomed to exaggerating their own prowess *if* they had the capacity to see the full and absurd meaning of their own distortions. Jimmie exaggerates his own importance as "engine Number 36" and the seriousness of his sin in breaking the flower. Johnson exaggerates his role as protector of Jimmie and his role as the gorgeous lover. Alek Williams imagines himself a salaried provider. And the tragedy is that men who live on the assumption of such pictures, lacking the honesty to see the absurdity of their posing, exaggerate also the supposed purposefulness of the fire, the heroism of the firemen, the "deaths" of the three victims, the broken leg of Mrs. Farragut; and thus, finally, they are ill-equipped to understand the unaffected courage of Dr. Trescott. Modern psychology has paid considerable attention to the importance of our images of ourselves; Crane, in his time, realized that reality is not unilateral, not confined to observer and observed. There is an image in between, one which most of us realize but dimly. The monster, lacking a face, short-circuits that third factor and forces the issue.

Events are so arranged, then, that Trescott, as a moral man, can do nothing else, can only suffer for doing what he had to do. An unrealistic image-maker, the Judge for example, can suggest that saving Johnson is one of "the blunders of virtue" (p. 473). But Trescott, who has a good pair of eyes, will tolerate no dim and absurd image obscuring his vision: "Well, what would you do? Would you kill him?" (p. 474). And the question, like the monster himself, shatters the pretensions of morality found in the Judge and in almost all of Whilomville, including the victim himself. A doctor of less courage would have seized the Judge's meaning: of course you do not kill the man who saved your son's life. You do not even say the word. You do everything you can for the man, within reason; and then, despite your fine efforts, the man dies. You lead the mourning, and then the world of pretensions is safe to go forward, safe again for the playing of games.

But Trescott is the man who refuses to play, and the sign of a sudden penetration of the mask is Crane's characteristic shift to a style that is at once both flat and powerful: "he now had no face" (p. 471); "Trescott found himself occasionally trying to count the cups. There were fifteen of them" (p. 508). This is what is, with the personal atmospheres left out. This is what a man like Trescott has the courage to see and not to lie about: "Well, what would you do? Would you kill him?" And this is why sights and sounds from above, Crane's images of an impersonal backdrop for our petty human drama of pretensions, loom in such cold fashion: the clanging bells, the sky, the ominous lights. When Johnson escapes from Alek Williams, Williams runs "wildly through the fields" (p. 487) yelling for Trescott: "It was as if Trescott was poised in the contemplative sky over the running negro, and could heed this reaching voice—'Docteh Trescott!' " (p. 487). Trescott, the "moon," is an adult, and Williams is like the child who hits the front door hollering, as if parents permeated the house and could be spirited forth upon need. When the false projections of adults are cracked, they too panic, gather in committees, boycott friends, and fight again for the comfort of their world of atmospheres.

Beneath this world are the unspeakables—the minor ones like the Judge's opinion of his sister; the mysterious ones like the Judge's secret need for his gold-headed cane; the perverse ones like the strange in-law and earth-mother role of Martha; and most importantly the monstrous ones which Johnson's sacrifice reveals in us all.

II

These structures of meaning give to the *Whilomville Stories*, the companion volume to "The Monster," a unity much more fundamental than the recurrence of the protagonist, Jimmie Trescott, the common setting, and the recurrence of street-names and characters. Several of the stories, "The Angel Child" for example, are admittedly minor and efforts to bolster their repute with critical ingenuity does a disservice to Crane, who can survive on honest criticism. "The Knife" is a credible study in character, relevant also for information connecting "The Monster" to the *Whilomville Stories:* Henry Johnson is now the late Henry Johnson, and Alek Williams, who has a tribe of "pickaninnies" in "The Monster," now has a seventeen-year-old daughter, though Jimmie himself seems only slightly older.[9] "Making an Orator" contains a minor error in plotting,[10] but it is a delightful tale, a good choice to read aloud to children. Crane was writing rapidly, desperately, for money; and, in any case, one need not apologize for his having written some enjoyable stories.

Still, most of the stories, in subtle ways, achieve a significant power. "His New Mittens," for example, is an excellent story with a striking relevance to "The Monster." Little Horace has been told to come straight home from school and to be especially careful of his new mittens. He must not soil them. But Horace encounters some friends, who torment him, urging him to come and join their snowball fight. When he hesitates, they sense, with animal cunning, the reason for his reluctance: "A-fray-ed of his mit-tens! A-fray-ed of his mit-tens" (p. 509).

As in "The Monster," adults are shown to have a civilized version of the elemental cruelty of children—"chanting cannibals" (p. 510), Crane calls them. But this time the role of the honest man is taken by a child, Horace; and the story is structured, typically, by dualistic language. The oft-quoted last line of the story—"We make it ourselves"—has been taken as a reference not just to homemade root beer but to life.[11] The reading leads us again to the Crane problem. We would need to see the relevance of the snowball fight, the stubborn determination of Horace not to eat, the melodramatic plans of Horace to run away from home, or the mocking language: "Without much loss of time he decided upon California. He moved briskly as far as his mother's front gate on the road to California" (p. 517).

While Horace is still refraining from joining the fight, a "mere baby" (p. 510) pelts him with a snowball. This is more than Horace can bear—yet he does. As Horace watches, there is a dispute about snowball strategy. The Indians, the smaller boys of course, want help. All the big boys are soldiers. One of the leaders finally agrees to become an Indian, but then the smaller boys want to be Indians. Finally, the fight begins anew, and Horace joins. Then his mother arrives, to drag him away, and Horace is in disgrace: "It was already a public scandal that he could not stay out as late as other boys, and he could imagine his standing now that he had been again dragged off by his mother in sight of the whole world" (p. 513).

Event and language interweave to define the personal atmosphere of Horace. His boy's pride, when rendered into the objective accuracy of its ironic implications, reveals a world view. For Horace, his buddies are the public, his bedtime strictures a scandal, his small group of friends a world. The language and the events are thus a critique of a small boy's pride, and it is pride which is the subject of the story. The maiden aunt, who has the frustrated strength of Martha Goodwin (and is also named Martha), takes pride in being firm with Horace; the mother apparently takes a pathological pride in her widow's weeds and in her cloying vacillation between rules and indulgence. The combination has fostered in Horace a similar capacity for the melodramatic. Left alone with food, he swears, in the spirit of the dime novel, not to touch a morsel, "not to sell his vengeance for bread" (p. 515). He paints dreams of a "deadly retribution," with his mother, finally, in tears, at his feet. In fact, however, he is reduced to the mock-heroic trek to California, and his truncated adventure reveals a difference between pride (in an abstract sense) and pride in Whilomville:

All in him was conquered save the enigmatical childish ideal of form, manner. This principle still held out, and it was the only thing between him and submission. When he surrendered, he must surrender in a way that deferred to the undefined code. He longed simply to go to the kitchen and stumble in, but his unfathomable sense of fitness forbade him. (P. 518.)

A Crane character without a sense of form is a mutant, a person to make one's skin crawl, like the evil-eyed assassins who appear throughout Crane's works. A character who can try with honesty and courage to face and to embody the "ideal of form" is a hero, like Trescott. But the majority of men merely have the notion, often a sentimental version of form; and very few have luck or ability or courage when it comes to the task of embodiment.

Horace has a deep but childish pride. He is offended when his friends do not play honestly (they lie about who has been hit with a snowball, who is "dead"). He is offended by his mother, and he seeks a noble retribution; but his materials come from the dime novel and his cloying mother. Aunt Martha is hard, or tries to be; and she constantly berates the mother for not being firm. Yet when the butcher returns the run-away boy to his home, Aunt Martha screams; and it is she who has the last word:

> Aunt Martha turned defiantly upon the butcher because her face betrayed her. She was crying. She made a gesture half military, half feminine. "Won't you have a glass of our root-beer, Mr. Stickney? We make it ourselves." (P. 520).

The mother has collapsed easily, but Aunt Martha (who screams, who is crying) resists throwing herself on the boy—just as he wanted "simply to go to the kitchen and stumble in," but resisted. The irony is that Horace gets "as far as his mother's front gate on the road to California," and Aunt Martha is reduced to being—or trying to be— chatty and social, offering root-beer to hide her true feelings.

False projections come in a wide variety, but they set the tone of society; and the straight man, the man of simple honesty, is thus out of tune. He is typically the victim, the sacrifice, as shown clearly in "The Trial, Execution and Burial of Homer Phelps," one of the best of the *Whilomville Stories*.

Willie Dalzel and his gang are playing soldier. Homer Phelps approaches, refuses to give the pass-word, and is properly berated. He then responds with a direct and totally irrelevant honesty: "Oh, you knew who I was easy enough." [12] Homer does not want to play the game, just as Dr. Trescott did not want to play the game of living by the images of morality that Hagenthorpe and Twelve mistook for objective reality. Homer's honesty, like Trescott's, cannot be tolerated. He is brought before Willie Dalzel, the mighty leader, who feels, "no doubt, that he must proceed according to the books." [13]

On trial for his crime, Homer reveals a latent and animal drive for survival, as if the enigmatical "real" had touched his bones and blood; and we are reminded of Jimmie's defiance of the whole school-yard in "The Lover and the Telltale" and of the final stubbornness of Trescott before the whole town in "The Monster." Willie is forced to conciliate, and he explains that it is only a game, thus breaking temporarily the boyish suspension of disbelief he has worked so hard to establish. Reluctantly, Homer gives in and begins to play; but he has no talent for the game, and Jimmie shoulders him aside and takes his place. "Not guilty," he answers, in a manner that reminds one of Walter Mitty: "Standing there before his judge—unarmed, slim, quiet, modest—he was ideal." [14] Like good little Tom Sawyers, the boys continue the drama to the execution; again Jimmie performs magnificently. Then comes his reward, the right of condescension to lesser performers, as Jimmie "negligently" orders about the little ones who are not yet good at playing the game. Doubtless, Jimmie does not remember how Henry Johnson had lorded it over him, condescendingly, when Jimmie was caught off-base in playing the game of "engine Number 36." The penalty for failing to play the game—as Trescott and his wife learn in "The Monster"—is ostracism. For Homer, that penalty is unbearable, and he begs to be readmitted. But the next step is burial, and it is only with great reluctance and finally a "childish fatalism" (p. 155) that Homer permits himself to be buried, beneath the hemlock boughs.

The death here is in the world of pretend, but for others—like the amazingly inept Swede in "The Blue Hotel"—an inability to play or a willingness to play the wrong game can be fatal. And on the edges, always, are the "trained chorus," [15] the weak, the small, the mob—like the crowd that stones Henry Johnson, like the school children who bedevil Jimmie in "The Lover and the Telltale," Horace in "His New Mittens," Johnnie Hedge in "The Fight." And the capacity to bedevil, Crane makes clear, is in all men of all ages and ranks.

Crane's art, far from offering us only a "blurred world," is carefully structured to suit this interpretation of man as a creature caught between his real self and his play-acting self, between a personal atmosphere and an ineluctable absolute. It is in this context, also, that we can best read Crane's emphasis on motive. Those whose motives are devoted to their own personal atmospheres—like Jimmie in "Showin' Off" and Fred Collins in "A Mystery of Heroism"—are shown to be absurd. In stories like "Shame" and "The Carriage-Lamps," Jimmie's motives are, for a child, innocent; and thus the structure does not turn in the end to an ironic deflation, as it does in "A Little Pilgrimage," where his motives, even for a small boy, are reprehensible.

Crane's language is far from "fragmentary." A dishonest will calls forth the ironic judgment of the observing translator who points out the true implications of personal reactions. When a character aligns himself with an ineluctable duty, such as the duty to care for a man who is mindless and faceless, when the will of the character is an honest will, then the radical imagery is dropped. The authorial voice becomes straight, and hard, and affirmative.

NOTES

1. Warner Berthoff, *The Ferment of Realism: American Literature, 1884–1919* (New York: Macmillan, 1965), pp. 230–33.

2. Jay Martin, *Harvests of Change: American Literature 1865–1914* (Englewood Cliffs: Prentice-Hall, 1967), p. 63.

3. See Donald B. Gibson's *The Fiction of Stephen Crane* (Carbondale: Southern Illinois University Press, 1968); the introductions are J. C. Levenson's, in volume 2 of the Harcourt, Brace, and World *Major Writers of America*, pp. 383–97; and Roy Male's, in volume 2 of the Holt, Rinehart, Winston *American Literary Masters*, pp. 215–26. A convenient illustration of the "Crane problem" in general is the *Modern Fiction Studies* special Stephen Crane issue (Autumn 1959).

4. James Hafley, "*The Monster* and the Art of Stephen Crane," *Accent* (Summer 1959): 159–65.

5. The image is from Crane's "The Black Dog": "The slate-colored man moved about in a small personal atmosphere of gloom."

6. Parenthetical references are to Joseph Katz, *The Portable Stephen Crane* (New York: Viking Press, 1969).

7. Crane's statement is in a letter to John Northern Hilliard, in *Stephen Crane: Letters*, ed. R. W. Stallman and Lillian Gilkes (New York: New York University Press, 1960), p. 158.

8. I am indebted here to the prior and excellent work of James B. Colvert in his "Structure and Theme in Stephen Crane's Fiction," *Modern Fiction Studies* (Autumn 1959): 199–208. Of special relevance are pp. 200, 204, and 208.

9. See Carl Ficken, "Jimmie Trescott's Age," *Stephen Crane Newsletter* 5 (Fall 1970): 2–3.

10. Jimmie misses two turns for giving his speech to his class; the order is alphabetical with ten students per Friday. Yet, when Jimmie is made to go to school on the third Friday, Tanner is up first.

11. A common reading, but see, for example, R. W. Stallman, *Stephen Crane: An Omnibus* (New York: Alfred A. Knopf, 1952), p. 537.

12. *Whilomville Stories* (New York: Harper & Brothers, 1900), p. 142.

13. Ibid., p. 144.

14. Ibid., p. 149.

15. Ibid., p. 153.

Lillian B. Gilkes

The Third Violet, Active Service, and *The O'Ruddy:* Stephen Crane's Potboilers

Hamlin Garland: He was not born for long life and he was not born for development. His work did not change except for the worse. It remained fragmentary and severe.[1]

Joseph Conrad: He is *the only* impressionist and *only* an impressionist.[2]

Edward Garnett: His art does not include the necessity for complex arrangements; his sure instinct tells him never to quit the passing moment of life, to hold fast by simple situations, to reproduce the episodic, fragmentary nature of life in such artistic sequence that it stands in place of the architectural masses and co-ordinated structures of the great artist. . . . What he has not got he has no power of acquiring.[3]

Whether Stephen Crane, had he lived longer, might or might not have triumphed with those "architectural masses and co-ordinated structures" of the longer form, might or might not have succeeded in the desperate game of pitting his genius against best-sellerdom, are matters for soothsayers. The soothsayer's viewpoint, registered above, proliferated and prevailed from the period after Crane's death until very recently, and has become gospel.

But of more immediate interest, and contradicting Garland, whose final judgment came more and more to be influenced by moral disapproval of Crane's character and associations, is the richly diverse body of work that Crane left. Only a very few contemporary critics have since recognized the fact that in his last trio of novels Crane was experimenting, aiming at the popular market with techniques radically different from the angry realism of *Maggie: A Girl of the Streets* and the high-keyed, symbol-patterned structure of *The Red Badge of Courage*. Critical reaction in the 1960s to *The Third Violet* and *Active Service* remained in general that of the 1890s,[4] while *The O'Ruddy* had been dismissed as largely the work of Robert Barr— which we now know it was not.[5]

It was inevitable that if he was to keep his name before the public and pay his bills, Stephen Crane must sooner or later do as every writer of genius since Shakespeare, not blessed with an independent income, has had to do—adjust his creative talents to the demands of the popular market. Although the short story in America would reach its apogee in the next half century, and the old double-decker novels of Dickens's and Thackeray's time had been supplanted by the single volume, publishers nevertheless complained that collections of short stories did not sell: the public demanded their money's worth in the longer form. So the marvelous boy-author of war stories and slum tales shifted ground and returned to the romantic material of the conventional novel. So too began, in Edwin Cady's percipient phrase, "the late, desperate, and pathetic struggle of Crane's integrity with best-sellerdom"—an observation which might well be extended to include the early novel, *The Third Violet*.[6]

I

Crane began *The Third Violet* with high hopes, but two months along commenced to worry and later confessed to Curtis Brown—

who had meanwhile rejected the romance for serialization in the *New York Press* as being "of no quality"—"It's pretty rotten work. I used myself up on the accursed *Red Badge*."[7] To Ripley Hitchcock, his Appleton editor, trying to put the best face on it he said, "*The Third Violet* is a quiet little story but then it's serious work and I should say let it go."[8] At times it seemed "clever," he told Willis Hawkins, at other times "nonsensical."[9] With the second adjective American reviewers were in almost unanimous agreement, and Crane reacted characteristically with a tongue-in-cheek disclaimer, writing in a presentation copy to Frank Harris (then editor of the London *Saturday Review*), "This book is worse than any of the others."[10]

But the novel was accepted for the Chicago *Inter-Ocean*,[11] appearing there in October–November 1896, and also in the *New York World*. A notable exception to the chorus of hoots and snorts which greeted the book publication the next year was "Chelifer" (Rupert Hughes) in *Godey's Magazine* (September, 1897), who said that "Stephen Crane has given us a book wholly without flesh and blood, but which is nevertheless a remarkable exercise in technique. Its manner of treatment and its technical originality are without precedent." English reviewers were on the whole even more enthusiastic. The *Athenaeum's* critic saw a resemblance to Henry James; and Ford Madox Ford, with characteristic exaggeration, later repeatedly pronounced the work "a gem," his favorite among all of Crane's books.[12] The Jamesian motif has been argued courageously, but not wholly convincingly, by Thomas A. Gullason.[13] "Class stratification" is a subject broad enough to engage other writers of the period besides James—Howells for one—and there is no certainty that Crane had read *The Bostonians* and *The Portrait of a Lady* before writing *The Third Violet*. Another modern critic, Jean Cazemajou finds the novel of little interest aside from its technical experimentation: "In general, this little work reveals a man seeking a literary identity, who has turned from the tragic world of *Maggie* and the hallucinatory visions of the *Red Badge of Courage*, to deal with everyday middle-class banalities" (my translation).[14]

Cady sees Crane here following the example of Howells, who had "virtually invented the vacation novel, had turned it into a genre convertible for all sorts of purposes, and had made its exploitation a steady part of his career."[15] Though Crane may well have had Howells in mind when writing *The Third Violet*, the vacation setting of the first half of the story came naturally to hand from his own summers in Hartwood and Pike County—"a long, lazy time to fool away," he told Nellie Crouse. On the back of an 1896 letter he wrote, misleadingly, that the story was "really the history of the love of one of the younger and brilliant American artists for an heiress of the ancient New York family kind."[16] Very likely, he drew upon his friend Corwin Linson for certain concrete details, as he must also have drawn from the other young artists of his studio acquaintance for the delightfully realistic sketches of "Grief," "Wrinkles," "Purple" Sanderson, and the little model "Splutter" O'Connor. He gave his hero, Hawker, a variant of Willis Hawkins' name; and put his brother Edmund's dog, Chester, into the narrative as the wonderful Stanley, "a large, orange and white setter." But as for hanging the love story on Linson, in the note alluded to, this is simply one more of Crane's familiar decoys. Obviously, he himself is very much in the character of Hawker, whose painful struggle to break through with his lover's ardor the upper-class barriers surrounding Miss Fanhall closely parallels Crane's own courtship of Nellie Crouse.[17] The only important difference is that Crane's suit, conducted wholly by correspondence except for one possible visit to her home in Akron, Ohio, ended in dismissal. *The Third Violet* may justly be considered the most autobiographical of any of Crane's novels.

So much for sources. But what of the novel's "technical originality," pointed to by "Chelifer" and some other early reviewers, but never analyzed? It resides in the author's use and manipulation of dialogue which he makes the chief narrative vehicle into which almost the whole of the story action is compressed. This is both a strength and a weakness. Consider first the stronger aspect.

Crane had, on the whole, a remarkable ear for dialogue and dialect.

Only occasionally, when handling the speech of characters from a world above him, does his ear fail him and the talk become self-conscious and wooden, as in certain passages of *The Third Violet* and some of the exchanges between Coleman and the rich boy, Coke, in *Active Service*. He may have been turned toward the preferred use of dialogue in this instance by reason of his early interest in the theatre and his friendships in that period of his life with actors like Franklin Garland and James Herne—author of a Broadway hit, *Shore Acres*. The dialogue method, at any rate, was peculiarly well suited to the situation central in his story: the confrontation between a poor young artist, "nature's gentleman," struggling to make his way up in the world without surrendering his talent to a competitively organized, commercially based society, and a wealthy young woman, a "society lady" with whom he is desperately in love.

To us of this century looking back, the rigid formalities of the previous century governing intercourse between young men and women, the almost complete isolation of the sexes with little or no opportunity for male and female to know one another before getting into bed on the marriage night, seem hardly comprehensible and often not a little ridiculous today. Courtships took place on hard sofas, or at the piano, in earshot or full view of the entire family; or in the vicinity of summer hotels where the rocking-chair sitters—Crane's "feminine mules"—pronounced sovereign judgment on the speech, manners, and general comportment of the lovers. O. W. Holmes graphically summed up the earlier stages of the situation in a letter to a friend while briefly a boarding-student at the Harvard Law School:

If there was a girl in the neighborhood whose blood ever ran above the freezing point[,] who ever dreamed of such a thing as opening her lips without having her father and her mother and all her little impish brothers and sisters for an audience—nay, if there was even a cherry-cheeked kitchen girl to romance with occasionally it might possibly be endurable. Nothing but vinegar-

Stephen Crane's Potboilers

faced old maids and drawing room sentimentalists—nothing that would do to write poetry to.[18]

In the later era of the "Gibson girl," of whom Nellie Crouse and Grace Fanhall were both quite typical examples, if the young lady in one of the large cities came of a background similar to theirs, the young man, whatever his pecuniary circumstances, took her to the theatre, bought tickets for three—the chaperone, of course, went along—and paid for a horse-cab to and from the performance; and as a preliminary, not least in importance, he was expected to send her a bunch of violets costing five dollars! (One wonders whether Crane forgot to send violets to Miss Crouse before calling on her in Akron, and thus, the possible consequences to his romance.) But, needless to say, were the young man to come flat out with a simple declaration of his feelings, proposing marriage, he would be judged "crude." Instead, they conversed of moonlight and roses, who was in church and who was not, and what the minister had said in last Sunday's sermon. Feelings were masked behind trivia. "No" meant "Yes." And "Yes" meant—what did it mean? The whole thing went along much like a ceremonial dance with all of the contrapuntal twistings and turnings and side-steppings of a ballroom minuet.

Crane succeeds admirably in capturing this discursive, dancelike quality, while pursuing Hawker's shy, suffering, persistent attempts to outguess and maneuver around the obstacles placed in his way by surface trivia and the circumstance of his humiliating poverty. Ideally, the dialogue method is particularly effective to this end—in building suspense and holding back on crucial disclosures until events in the plot development have been made ready for them. We know what is happening in Hawker's feelings and keep track of developments in the whole affair only from what is registered externally, in conversation and pantomine. Hawker's various encounters with Miss Fanhall, the protracted monologues of the worldly-wise and cynical Hollanden, the malicious tongue-wagging of the porch-sitters, who approximate from the sidelines the role of a Greek chorus—this is all in the manner of good theatre on the stage. But Hollanden's presence in the story is that of a mere foil in relation to Hawker's courtship; he has no real function in the drama other than constantly pouring ice-water on the artist's hopes of winning the heart of his beloved. And in this loose, artificial capacity he overdoes it, his long-winded and inflated pronouncements after a while begin to pall, and stop the story dead. In contrast to Hawker, the artist of integrity, Hollanden is Crane's satirization of the sophisticated, overly confident, and comfortably flush pseudo-literary man; a parlor figure he despised, but whose success he no doubt envied. Some of Crane's best writing appears in the desscriptive touches which quite equal the best he was capable of—little patches of landscape and the resort background; the farm home of Hawker's parents, which bears strong likeness to the Hartwood home of Crane's brother Edmund; the dingy studio rookery in New York, a reproduction of the old Art Students League Building on West Twenty-Third Street where Stephen lived for a time with the young painters. Some critics have objected that the little silhouettes of Hawker's relatives are stereotypes, but such a judgment must rest on scant knowledge of the people of rural America, the people of the land who once were bone and sinew of the nation. Though minor figures, these Breughelian miniatures are among the most successful character portrayals in the work and belong in the category of village characters later developed and satirized in "The Monster" and the Whilomville tales. Here they are treated sympathetically.

The narrative regains momentum when the scene shifts back to New York and the rich, wonderful, elliptical, slangy talk of the studios—though here too, a contemporary critic finds the young artists lifeless mannequins, presumably because they do not sound exactly like the hippies of today's East Village. They stand in the same relation to Hawker as did Hollanden earlier, baiting and chaffing him about his relations with Miss Fanhall and the violets, about the little model and her hopeless burn for Hawker, who in turn has eyes only for the other woman. But all are more firmly integrated into the narrative structure, their light-hearted banter is certainly more interesting and more natural in tone than Hollanden's purple spoutings. Crane however revised and rewrote *The Third Violet* numerous times, with the result that the predominant note of gaiety in this section is undercut by some of the tonal quality of his own "flagons of despair"; he had by then received a stinging rebuff from Nellie Crouse.

On the negative side, counteracting the stronger features of the novel, is the fact that Crane nowhere provides a sufficient number of arrows and road signs pointing to the progressive change in Grace Fanhall's feelings toward Hawker, which causes her to accept him in the end. Hero and heroine alike are seen exclusively from the outside, recipients of no more of the author's concentrated attention and probing than are the minor characters; which amounts to seeing them in low relief only, like figures in a panoramic frieze. But it goes without saying that direct interpretation of attitudes and feelings—as in the novels of Henry James—or symbolic indirection—as in *The Red Badge of Courage*—in combination with dialogue and scenic action is the novel's great opportunity, its great strength as a form. Stripped of these accessories, dialogue alone cannot do the whole job in the novel as it can and does on the stage, where the immediacy of the visual impression and the voice and acting of the performers supplies what is missing or is barely suggested in the lines. As we shall see, Crane had learned this lesson, at least in part, by the time he got into the writing of *Active Service*.

But the illogical, too rapid, essentially theatrical reversal on which *The Third Violet* ends leaves the reader puzzled as to what actually happened in that final scene between Hawker and the hard-to-get Miss Fanhall. He must take for granted that "No" means "Yes" in this contretemps; that the lady's spoken words, "Go. Please go. I want you to go!" really translate into, "Stay, I love you! I am angry only because you have broken down all my defenses—you have seen me undressed—but I am yours!"

But more importantly, there are other than technical reasons for the failure of *The Third Violet* to realize its full dramatic potential: a failure of ideas. Thomas Beer said of the book that it was "too compressed." How true; for the immensely complex situation in which Crane has placed Hawker in relation to Grace Fanhall involves likewise a more fundamental relationship to society at large—class, convention, and sex—which is left unexplored. Such a situation calls for resolution on another level, going beyond the purely personal. But the ideas which would have given greater meaning and depth to scenes and a thematic unity to the whole are not there. We must, therefore, agree wih Cady's judgment that the real trouble with *The Third Violet* and *Active Service* is Stephen Crane's utter inability to understand women.

This lack of perception with regard to the other sex was, of course, a common failing of his time, a blind spot especially noticeable in the works of Conrad; but it is also one of the focal points whereon a great and thoroughly mature artist transcends his time. Crane, up to the day of his death at twenty-eight, had not yet outgrown his adolescent, myopic, exacerbated view of the female sex as creatures of unpredictable and often exasperating irrationality, typified in his loathing of "feminine mules" and in his portrayal of George's mother, Mrs. Kelcey—whom some critics see as a disguised representation of his own mother. At the other extreme, he like Conrad held womankind in boyish awe, as mysterious beings seen through a romantic mist not unlike Poe's "ideality." The early loves, to return to Cady again, had done nothing for his imagination where women were concerned; and he got with Cora too recently for that experience to have taken hold and permanently modified his thinking about women in general. He was as yet incapable, in more than a perfunctory sense, of entering into their feelings and aspirations, their needs and frustrations in a tightly controlled man's world, as Tolstoy had done for Anna Karenina and Hardy did for Tess. He could not look into the future and visualize a different sort of world in which the rebellions of women such as Cora, demanding for themselves sexual freedom on an equal basis with men and personal freedom to pursue their individual tastes and interests within the marriage relationship, would have become commonplace. His most complete, most imaginatively

meaningful statement of the reverential viewpoint is given near the
end of *Active Service*, in a paragraph of remarkably beautiful prose:

> In a secluded cove, in which the sea-maids once had played no
> doubt, Marjory and Coleman sat in silence. He was below her, and
> if he looked at her he had to turn his glance obliquely upward.
> She was staring at the sea with woman's mystic gaze, a gaze which
> men at once reverence and fear, since it seems to look into the
> deep, simple heart of nature, and men begin to feel that their
> petty wisdoms are futile to control these strange spirits, as way-
> ward as nature and as pure as nature, wild as the play of waves,
> sometimes as unalterable as the mountain amid the winds; and to
> measure them, man must perforce use a mathematical formula.[19]

But to return, for the moment, to *The Third Violet*: a fascinating
sidelight on that novel exists in the effect it had on Willa Cather and
the use she made of it in one of her finest though little known short
stories in which she succeeded in doing what Crane failed to accom-
plish with his romance.[20] Willa Cather's curious personal identifica-
tion with Stephen Crane, the coy interest with which she followed
developments in his career, step by step, have been traced in illumin-
ating detail by Bernice Slote.[21] At the time of her meeting with Crane
in the Nebraska *State Journal* office, Willa Cather had been writing
reviews and newspaper columns for a year and a half, and was,
says Miss Slote, "an intensely independent and opinionated young
woman." She was strongly impressed by Crane in that interview,
especially his remark about his own writing—"The detail of a thing
has to filter through my blood, and then it comes out like a native
product"—and from that moment he became a sort of lodestar-
mentor who frequently disappointed her, seeming false to his promise.
Willa Cather had already a sure sense of what she was to become,
and the technical faults of Crane's immaturity were by no means
hidden from her sharp scrutiny by any hero-worship of his genius.
(She wrote a damning review of *Active Service* for the Pittsburgh

Leader.) So, it is hardly surprising to find her, some twenty-five years after that meeting in the Nebraska *Journal* office—the only time she ever came face to face with Stephen Crane—stealing one of his plots, convinced that she could do with it something better than he had done.

Oddly enough, unlike the better known "The Diamond Mine," "The Sculptor's Funeral," and "The Gold Slipper," all of which deal with artists in a world dominated by the money-values of a competitive society, "Coming, Aphrodite!" has gone unanthologized. The situation here of Don Hedger, an impecunious and struggling young painter who has studied in France with Cèzanne, is identical with that of Hawker—who also studied abroad—except for the fact that he falls in love not with a "Gibson girl" but with a young woman of musical talent and advanced ideas, who is awaiting the delayed arrival in New York of a wealthy backer who will take her to Paris to prepare her for a career in opera. They meet in a rooming-house fronting on Washington Square, where Eden Bower installs her piano in the apartment next to Hedger's. There is even a dog to drive home the parallel: the bulldog Caesar, like Hawker's Stanley, accompanies his master everywhere and is moodily unhappy when out of his sight. Eden Bower, with her ambitions and her glorious body, is indeed a girl "whose blood runs above the freezing point." They quickly become lovers—no Victorian caperings for Miss Cather, these young people get right to it—they quarrel, and separate when the Chicago millionaire arrives in the city to take Eden to Paris.

In contrast to Crane's romance, Willa Cather's story is wholly modern in treatment and tone—although she was only two years younger than Crane—and in place of the happy ending we have a more realistic version of life's twistings and turnings. The dramatic potential is here fully explored. Eden Bower, with all of her zest for living, is nevertheless cold-hearted and utterly self-absorbed in the pursuit of her career. The immediate cause of their lover's quarrel is Hedger's scornful rejection of the values of commercial success, the only criteria of success Eden recognizes or cares about. Years later—

when Eden returns to New York a world-famous opera star—she is driven in her car past the old Washington Square neighborhood on her way uptown to visit her broker, and is touched by a flash of recollection. The business over, she inquires about Hedger's success as an artist. The man of business replies that there are many kinds of success, that Hedger is a great name with all the young men and decidedly an influence in art. "That's all I want to know," she says. "One doesn't like to have been an utter fool—even at twenty."

This touch, even the name itself, links the figure of Eden Bower with Mary Garden,[22] whom Willa Cather undoubtedly heard in her great roles, "Salomé" and "Mèlisande." Like her prototype in the story, Mary Garden too, a worldly Venus in marble, returned in triumph from abroad, with a perfume named after her and her name in the marquee lights of Oscar Hammerstein's Manhattan Opera House.

II

But in what ways does Crane's next novel, *Active Service*, show an advance over *The Third Violet*?

Crude as this novel may seem today, its author had in fact taken a big step forward toward command of the longer form. Crane broadened his canvas, with some extension as well of technical usages, although the daubed-over blanks remain; and there is still no perceptible gain in his handling of female characters. The heroine, Marjory Wainwright, is a nearly lifeless doll and the anti-heroine, Nora Black, a loud caricature of Cora Crane. Probably, Crane never really understood Cora; certainly, he was too close to her and the tensions she introduced in his personal life ever to be able to view her objectively with that "long logic" he said every story should have. So Nora Black remains, like Hollanden, a stage dummy. It is impossible to take her seriously as a *femme fatale* and the spoiler of Coleman's attachment to Marjory.

But in this novel Crane again turns inward, and technical gains may be counted by his use of interior detail in combination with dialogue and description as adjuncts of scenic action. The narrative thus takes on some of that more massive architectural structure commonly associated with the nineteenth-century novel, which Garnett, Conrad, and others found lacking in the work of Crane the impressionist. The movement also is less jerky than in *The Third Violet*, where the absence of bridge passages between scenes is sharply noticeable.

Willa Cather found the book "coarse, dull, and charmless," its protagonist, Coleman, in character nothing above the yellow journalism he represents as Sunday editor of the *New York Eclipse*.[23] It is true that Crane, having little knowledge or interest in archeology, does not bother to tell his readers why the Wainwright party had ventured across the border from Greece before they were trapped in Turkey at the outbreak of war. But Willa Cather evidently remained unimpressed by his indictment of yellow journalism, one of the book's strongest features, unable to reconcile with artistic integrity the fact of Crane's service as war correspondent to both Hearst and Pulitzer, the kings of yellow journalism. So too, his satirization of Victorian bourgeois morality and ethics in the portrayal of family relationships escapes her altogether, as it has generally escaped more recent critics, notwithstanding that satire is the heart of this book.

An anti-heroic novel, *Active Service* continues the break with the heroic tradition—begun in *Maggie* and *The Red Badge of Courage* and in the novels of Frank Norris—which in this century was to be so greatly extended under the influence of Joyce, Dreiser, Hemingway, Fitzgerald and Faulkner. Coleman has none of the attributes of the conventional hero and, though a successful and highly paid newspaperman, he is actually no better off than the lowest wage slave; with "no security in his job" he is nothing but a bondsman to "an incredible tyranny of circumstances." Crane, we know, was acutely conscious of the bind of invincible circumstances in his own situation, viz., the hounding of the New York police which had forced him into exile, and the vindictiveness of Cora's English husband in the matter of the divorce which forced them to live in "sin." The novel abounds in similar parallelisms drawn from experience.[24] "This matter," he says of Nora Black's scandalous pursuit of Coleman, "which to some people was as vital and fundamental as existence, remained to others who knew of it, only a harmless detail of life with no terrible powers, and its significance had faded greatly when it had ended the close associations of the late adventure" (*Active Service*, 1899, p. 266). Depersonalized in the characterization of Coleman and embedded in the narrative texture, these parallelisms contain some of Crane's shrewdest analysis as well as some of his best writing.

In my opinion, the defects commonly attributed to *Active Service* originated not in the circumstance of its having been undertaken as a "potboiler" when Crane was desperately short of funds, but in the paradox that a rather flimsy plot situation begun with a light touch according to the well-worn conventional love-story formula grew into a novel with a serious psychological and period thrust. Crane's own disillusionment with romantic love probably was the root cause of his hangup. But as he dug deeper—and hard going it was, for several times he had to drop the book to write short stories for "quick money"—he became more and more fascinated by the parodic possibilities he saw in the material of his love-adventure yarn. In *The O'Ruddy* he successfully combines romantic love and swashbuckling adventure within the burlesque framework; but in its predecessor, *Active Service*, the added element of realism proved an insuperable stumbling block, throwing the climactic scenes out of focus and upsetting the tonal balance of the whole. Insofar as the parodic tone is evenly maintained, about three-fourths of the way through the book—until the safe return of the Wainwright party to Athens, under Coleman's escort—the novel, in spite of blemishes noted, succeeds in the way Crane intended and suspense continues to build. But realism and parody do not mix, and at this point story and treatment break down.

If, however, one can disregard the cracks in tonal unity, the scene in which the troubled old professor kneels in guilt and pain and bewilderment at the bedside of his suffering child, trying to think what to do, comes across as one of the best in the book. There Marjory, for the first time, comes fully to life. She has saved her pride—according to the rules and forms of Victorian etiquette—but confesses, weeping, to her father, that she has lost her lover. And the professor "felt as helpless as an old grey ape";

> He did not see a possible weapon with which he could defend his child from the calamity which was upon her. There was no wall, no shield, which could turn this sorrow from the heart of his child. . . . He was potent for nothing. . . .
> He reviewed the past half in fear that he would suddenly come upon his error, which was now the cause of Marjory's tears. He dwelt long upon the fact that . . . he had refused his consent to Marjory's marriage with Coleman, but even now he could not say that his judgment was not correct. It was simply that the doom of woman's woe was upon Marjory, this ancient woe of the silent tongue and the governed will, and he could only kneel at the bedside and stare at the wall. (*Active Service*, pp. 253–54.)

If today's readers see in this and in the love scene previously cited nothing but Victorian absurdities, the failure of response must be charged not to ineptitude on the part of the author in this case, but rather to the cynicism of our age which insulates the modern reader from a just appreciation of the extent of Crane's penetration beneath the surface of Victorian society. Is not the whole preposterous sham, once glorified in the cult of "womanhood," with its reliance on "the silent tongue and the governed will," here blown sky high?

III

If Harold Frederic sponsored the genesis of *Active Service*—a supposition harped on as fact though we have only Beer's undocumented word for it—Crane owed a very real debt in the case of *The O'Ruddy* to Frederic's novel *The Return of the O'Mahony*.[25] The plot situation has little in common beyond the fact that both narratives are comic extravaganzas verging on fantasy, both strongly keyed to burlesque.

But Crane drew heavily on Frederic's schema of character relationships; his faithful Paddy, a resourceful buffoon, and the ex-highwayman Jem Bottles both stand in the same relation to the O'Ruddy as Jerry Higgins to the O'Mahony. In Crane's story, the hypocritical and evil little physician, Dr. Chord, also bears a recognizable likeness to Frederic's villain, the oily, obsequiously scheming, hereditary bard, Cormac O'Daly. The paradoxical, earthy humor in Frederic's portrayal of his impostor-hero, a Civil War army sergeant who passes for the heir to the O'Mahony estate, must have appealed strongly to Crane, who delighted in the homespun sallies of Mr. Dooley. Quite evidently, The Return of the O'Mahony served the author of The O'Ruddy as both a source and a challenge.

The characters in both novels, however, are sharply differentiated types. Notwithstanding elements in common, particularly the underlying thematic note satirizing a decadent aristocracy, The O'Ruddy should by no means be considered imitative. Crane's humor and treatment are distinctly his own; his gamey barbs are aimed at the foibles of mankind in general, whereas Frederic's commentary is quite specifically pointed toward certain perennial failings in the Irish character: the tendency to substitute talk for action, and reminiscences of ancient grandeur in the midst of present ruin.

The Return of the O'Mahony has been called Frederic's "gayest" novel, and the same may be said of Crane's The O'Ruddy, though it was conceived and written under heavy financial pressures and the lengthening shadow of death. The year of their arrival in England, at the summer's end, Stephen and Cora went on a holiday junket to Ireland with the Frederics. The party toured County Cork, the scene of Harold's Irish novel, and this first exposure to the Irish peasantry in their native villages delighted Crane, reviving his early interest in Irish characters. From this trip came also the Irish Notes, and a rewriting of an old story, "Dan Emmonds." Two years later, after beginning The O'Ruddy, the Cranes revisited County Cork, taking with them the young girl Edith Richie who had been spending the summer at Brede Place. The relaxed holiday mood pervades the writing of this novel. One feels that Crane was having fun with his story, a rich spoof of the old swashbucklers, especially *Tom Jones* and the spate of subsequent Fielding–Defoe imitations.

Influenced no doubt by Ford Madox Ford's weepy fantasies, and the impressions of Conrad and others who saw Crane when the end was near,[26] recent criticism has tended to overemphasize gloom and tragedy in the last year at Brede Place. The purely physiological symptoms of illness have been freely adorned with subjective meanings. This is a distortion, for Crane, though oscillating between extremes of depression and euphoria, apparently shared the optimism characteristic of the consumptive. "We are living very quietly devoting all out attention to my work," he wrote his brother William. "My wife is very helpful to me and feels the same interest in the stories that I feel myself. This makes it easier and if the month of March dont wipe me off the earth I hope by this time next year to be fairly rich so much confidence have I in the different life I am now leading." [27]

Too many guests there were, the Cranes never learned to live within their means, and Stephen was slogging his way through the marsh of debts incurred during the year at Ravensbrook and his absence in Cuba. But when they got to Brede Place, "this matter" of their unchurched relationship had indeed "faded" to "a harmless detail of life." Moreover, it seems probable that Crane's illness did not actually become critical until the second attack of hemorrhages in April. The great Dr. Trudeau of Saranac fame, who saw Crane there the previous summer, had diagnosed it to Cora as "a slight evidence of activity in the trouble in his lungs . . . not serious. . . ." [28] We ought to give up the drama of a death agony dragging on throughout the year 1899. At no time, up to the final crisis, was Crane ever as dangerously ill as Stevenson, who, though recurrently near death, lived fourteen years a consumptive, to die of something else. Had Crane not willfully resisted the discipline of a health routine, with the rest and nursing care essential to rebuilding blood and bone marrow after hemorrhaging, there is no doubt that Crane's life could have been prolonged. But he told someone, "I am too old to be nursed," and would not remain in bed.

The O'Ruddy is Crane's most smoothly integrated and most successful novel after *The Red Badge of Courage.* Robert Barr's portion of the book drags, lacking Crane's sparkle, and Barr puts the heroine out of character in the scene in which she aggressively dictates strategy leading to the eventual happy union of the lovers. But Crane's section, slightly under twenty-five chapters to Barr's eight, evidences no decline in his powers. The extravagances of story action are rendered acceptable by the spontaneous, continuous flow of wit in the wry philosophizing of the O'Ruddy, as Crane makes the O'Ruddy his own mouthpiece. The richness of this humor, generally warmer and mellower than is to be found in Crane's earlier writing, also relieves the episodic tedium of the usual picaresque plot. A. E. W. Mason and others asserting that romance was hardly Stevie's "cup of tea," are here disproved; though it is true that by setting the action as far back in time as the early Georgians, Crane side-steps the whole woman problem. This leaves him free to romanticize, depicting the charms of his heroine as they appeared to the captive eye of the O'Ruddy; he does not have to interpret.

The book had three printings in England, a fourth remaindered, and would probably have held on somewhat longer but for the calamitous deal in completion of the manuscript for publication after Crane's death; the interest revived in him by the tragic circumstance of early death had, three and a half years later, slacked off. This delay also put an end to David Belasco's enthusiastic interest in adapting the novel for stage production. The king of Broadway had immediately recognized in the twenty-five chapters he saw in manuscript a potential hit and was extremely anxious to obtain dramatic rights also to *The Red Badge of Courage.*[29] With two productions under such auspices, Crane's name in lights on Broadway might have made all the difference to the continued survival of his fading reputation.

Lillian B. Gilkes

The essence of Crane's permanent achievement is summed up by Eric Solomon: "Crane sliced away the traditional excrescences, and reclaimed what was of artistic value in the familiar genres by applying his own stark techniques of style and setting" to overwrought themes. He was "not simply a destructive critic but the continuer of literary tradition":[30] a judgment which perhaps applies equally well, though her influence is hardly comparable, to his captious disciple Willa Cather with her theory of the novel "demeublée."[31]

As to these three novels, flawed though the first two are, there is enough originality and creditable work in *The Third Violet* and *Active Service,* enough genius and skill in *The O'Ruddy,* to have augured well for Crane's future had he lived longer. There seems little demonstrable reason to dismiss him as "written out," or to suppose that his powers would have failed him in the trials of strength ahead.

NOTES

1. Hamlin Garland, "Stephen Crane As I Knew Him," *Yale Review* n.s. 31 (April 1914): 494–506.

2. Joseph Conrad to Edward Garnett, 5 December 1897, in *Stephen Crane: Letters,* ed. R. W. Stallman and Lillian Gilkes (New York: New York University Press, 1960; London: Peter Owen, 1960), p. 155.

3. Edward Garnett, "An Appreciation," London *Academy,* 17 December 1898.

4. For an able discussion of the critical reception of Crane's last novels, see Thomas A. Gullason, ed., *The Complete Novels of Stephen Crane* (New York: Doubleday & Co., 1967), pp. 82–97.

5. David A. Randall, *Dukedom Large Enough* (New York: Random House, 1969), p. 229. See also Gilkes and Joan H. Baum, "Stephen Crane's Last Novel: *The O'Ruddy,*" *Columbia Library Columns* 6 (February 1957): 41–48; and Matthew J. Bruccoli, "Robert Barr's Proofs of *The O'Ruddy,*" *Stephen Crane Newsletter* 4 (Spring 1970): 8–9.

6. Edwin H. Cady, *Stephen Crane* (New York: Twayne Publishers, 1962), p. 149.

7. Stallman and Gilkes, *Letters,* p. 87; and Curtis Brown, *Contacts* (New York: Cassell, 1935), p. 262.

8. Stallman and Gilkes, *Letters,* p. 107.

Stephen Crane's Potboilers

9. Stallman and Gilkes, *Letters*, p. 74.

10. Stallman and Gilkes, *Letters*, p. 198.

11. This paper was then owned by Charles T. Yerkes, the Chicago tycoon and prototype of Frank Cowperwood in Dreiser's triology: *The Financier, The Titan,* and *The Stoic.* See an important article by Philip L. Gerber, "Dreiser's Financier: A Genesis," *Journal of Modern Literature* 1 (March 1971): 354–74.

12. "American Fiction," *Athenaeum* (22 May 1897): 678. Ford Madox Ford, "Stevie and Co.," *New York Herald Tribune*, 2 January 1927, section 7, p. 6.

13. Thomas A. Gullason, "The Jamesian Motif in Stephen Crane's Last Novels," *The Personalist* 42 (Winter 1961): 71–84.

14. Jean Cazemajou, *Stephen Crane: Écrivain Journaliste* (Paris: Librairie Didier, 1969), p. 421.

15. Cady, *Stephen Crane*, p. 47.

16. Joseph Katz, "Corwin Knapp Linson on *The Third Violet*," *Stephen Crane Newsletter* 3 (Fall 1968): 5.

17. Edwin H. Cady and Lester G. Wells, eds., *Stephen Crane's Love Letters to Nellie Crouse* (Syracuse: Syracuse University Press, 1954).

18. Holmes to Phineas Barnes, 13 January 1830, The Holmes Papers, Houghton Library, Harvard University, Cambridge, Mass. Quoted by permission.

19. *Active Service* (London: William Heinemann, 1899), p. 314.

20. "Coming, Aphrodite!" in *Youth and the Bright Medusa* (New York: Alfred A. Knopf, 1920).

21. "Stephen Crane and Willa Cather," *Serif* 6 (December 1969): 3–15.

22. Mary Garden and Louis Biancolli, *Mary Garden's Story* (New York: Simon and Schuster, 1951).

23. Slote, "Stephen Crane and Willa Cather," pp. 12–13. See also Thomas A. Gullason, "Stephen Crane's Private War on Yellow Journalism," *Huntington Library Quarterly* 22 (May 1959): 201–8.

24. For a fuller discussion of this aspect and the various elements of satire in *Active Service*, see Lillian Gilkes, "Stephen Crane and the Biographical Fallacy: the Cora 'Influence,'" *Modern Fiction Studies* 17 (Winter 1970–1971). For another view of the novel see Eric Solomon, *Stephen Crane: From Parody to Realism* (Cambridge, Mass.: Harvard University Press, 1966), pp. 135–44.

25. Crane's indebtedness to Frederic is further explored in my article, "Stephen Crane and the Harold Frederics," *Serif* 6 (December 1969): 21–48.

26. Ford Madox Ford, *Portraits from Life* (Boston: Houghton Mifflin Co., 1937), pp. 21–37; A. E. W. Mason to Vincent Starrett, 4 October 1945, in Stallman and Gilkes, *Letters*, pp. 342–45; Miss M. Bothim Edwards, who met Crane at a luncheon given for him by Thomas Parkin, of Hastings, quoted in Stallman, *Stephen Crane* (New York: Braziller, 1967), p. 498.

27. Letter in the Charles Feinberg Collection, Detroit, 2 March 1899.

28. Letter in the Butler Library Collection, Columbia University, New York, 16 September [1898]. For evidence contradicting the "death agony" at Brede Place see Edith Richie Jones, "Stephen Crane at Brede," *Atlantic Monthly* 194 (July 1954): 57–61; and especially Crane's own letters and Cora's to the Frewens in the Butler Library Collection, Columbia University, and the Library of Congress, Washington, D.C.

29. See Belasco's letters to Cora in the Butler Library Collection, Columbia University.

30. Solomon, *From Parody to Realism*, p. 6. See also Marston LaFrance, *A Reading of Stephen Crane* (Oxford: The Clarendon Press, 1971).

31. Willa Cather, *Not Under Forty* (New York: Alfred A. Knopf, 1936); and *Willa Cather On Writing* (1949).

James B. Colvert

Stephen Crane:
Style as Invention

The success of *The Red Badge of Courage* in 1895–1896 firmly established Crane's literary reputation and though reviewers praised it enthusiastically for its graphic realism, it hardly represented, as Crane was uneasily aware, the kind of realism described in the theories of his "literary fathers," William Dean Howells and Hamlin Garland. Crane pledged allegiance to realism some years before, shortly after he met Garland in Asbury Park, New Jersey, in 1892, when, as he later explained, he "developed all alone a little creed of art" and later "discovered" that it was "identical with the one of Howells and Garland." [1] It was probably at Garland's suggestion that he moved to New York City that fall to study tenement life for his novels of "social realism," *Maggie: A Girl of the Streets* and *George's Mother*. Though hardly realism in Howells's sense of the term, these novels did seem—even to Crane's "literary fathers"—to honor a basic tenet of realistic theory: that "truth" in art is grounded in actual observation and experience. Howells was sure the New York fiction showed that Crane was moving in the right direction, and he advised the author, after reading *Maggie*, that he "thoroughly respected" Crane's "literary conscience."[2] But *The Red Badge of Courage* was another matter. It was a pure invention, an exercise, apparently, in the use of those "clever and witty expedients" which Crane had contemptuously denounced in 1892 when he declared himself on the side of "nature and truth" as an ally of the new realism.

Thus the novel was both a triumph and an embarrassment. In praising its realism the adulatory reviews merely advertised the author's apostasy—at least to Crane and Howells, who wrote early in 1896 to regret that Crane had chosen to abandon his career to unconventional poetry (in *The Black Riders*, 1895) and a fanciful war tale. "For me," Howells wrote, "I remain true to my first love, 'Maggie.' That is better than all the Black Riders and Red Badges."[3] Crane's reply suggests that he clearly understood the comment as a reproach for straying from the path of truth. "I am, mostly, afraid," he wrote Howells by way of explaining why he was not shouting "triumphant shouts" over the success of the novel, "afraid that some small degree of talk will turn me ever so slightly from what I believe to be the pursuit of truth."[4] As the record suggests, Howells's point had already occurred to Crane. Some months earlier, when the growing fame of the novel had begun to focus the issue, he had felt obliged to reaffirm his literary aims, though he had admitted, in effect, that his original commitment had been only "partially" fulfilled. "I decided," he had written then, referring to his beginnings in 1892, "that the nearer a writer gets to life the greater he becomes as an artist, and most of my prose writings have been toward the goal partially described by that misunderstood and abused word, realism."[5] Shortly after he received Howells's note he also reaffirmed—with a certain poignant uneasiness—his loyalty to the men whose program he officially professed. "The one thing that deeply pleases me in my literary life—brief and inglorious as it is—is the fact that men of sense believe me to be sincere. 'Maggie' . . . made me the friendship of Hamlin Garland and W. D. Howells, and the one thing that makes my life worth living . . . is the consciousness that never for an instant have these friendships at all diminished."[6] And on the same day that he assured Howells of his undiminished regard for sincerity, he wrote his editor at Appleton's, who had apparently expressed doubts about Crane's new novel, *The Third Violet*: "I dont think *The Red Badge* to be any great shakes but then the very theme of it gives it an intensity that a writer cant reach every day. The Third Violet is a quiet little story but then it is serious work and I should say let it go."[7] He might have added, judging from the evidence of his particular concern at this time, that *The Third Violet*, based on his observation of Bohemian life in the art studios he frequented in his New York City years, was "nearer . . . to life" than the anomalous war novel.

About this time he began to derogate *The Red Badge of Courage*, referring to it slightingly on various occasions as the "damned 'Red Badge,'" "that damned book," "the accursed 'Red Badge.'" He expressed the view, doubtless taking a hint from Howells, that it was overrated. "I suppose I ought to be thankful to 'The Red Badge' but I am much fonder of my little book of poems, 'The Black Riders.' My aim was to comprehend in it the thoughts I have had about life in general, while 'The Red Badge' is a mere episode in life, an amplification."[8] *The Red Badge of Courage* had not only, he seemed to think, painted him in the wrong direction, but it had also sapped his creative energy and undermined his attempt to return to realism in *The Third Violet*. "I have finished," he noted at the end of December, "my new novel—'The Third Violet'—and sent it to Appleton and Co., as per request, but I've an idea it won't be accepted. It's pretty rotten work. I used myself up in the accursed 'Red Badge'."[9]

The easy explanation for this mood of uncertainty is that the growing fame of *The Red Badge of Courage* pressed him to the challenge of producing another brilliant book on war. Under pressure from editors and an expectant public, he undertook most reluctantly the composition of *The Little Regiment*, a volume of war stories conceived as a sequel to the novel. "I am writing a story—'The Little Regiment' for McClure's," he complained. "It is awfully hard. I have invented the sum of my inventions with regard to war and this story keeps me in internal despair."[10] But the matter goes deeper than this.

James B. Colvert

Clearly the success of *The Red Badge of Courage* brought to full light the embarrassing fact that Crane, despite his claim, was no realist, and this in effect left him more or less without a theoretical conception of his literary aims and methods. He began to suspect—uneasily —that the theory of realism, as he imperfectly understood it from Howells and Garland, was largely irrelevant to his vision and aim. He apparently had little grasp of the implications of the documentary method advocated by the theory of realism, a method radically at odds with his own compositional practice. Nor did he understand fully, apparently, that Howells's equation of "truth" in art with the "authority" of first-hand knowledge of the subject matter was only indirectly and obliquely applicable to his practice. Crane was certain that his New York novels and stories correctly represented "social realism." The war stories after *The Little Regiment*, all based more or less on actual experience and observation, he would doubtless have felt also represented impeccable realism (though there is no evidence that he was much concerned after 1896 with reconciling literary theory and practice). As J. C. Levenson observes, speaking of the relation of Crane's art to real-life experience in the Whilomville tales, the citings of "particular sources . . . contribute little to an understanding of Crane's fiction. Early and late, such items furnish evidence for a negative argument: despite his own simple ideas of art as literal representation, his work is not sufficiently accounted for in that way. Whatever else it may be, his realism is not simply a matter of direct rendering of an observed object." [11]

This holds true not only for *The Red Badge of Courage* but also for the fiction drawn from experience and observation; to put it simply, what he saw in real life is rendered not as history, but as history transmuted by the resources of his imagination. These resources were the images, themes, motifs, and descriptive patterns he worked out— invented, in a manner of speaking—very early in his literary career: the compositional devices of the Sullivan County sketches of 1892. This is to say, in effect, that he observed the world from a pre-established literary point of view, a view which largely determined what was seen and what the observed event signified. "Death and the Child," a story based on his first experience of real war at Veles-tino in 1897, is a rich example of the powerful control his purely literary resources could exercise over his observation—a remarkable variation on the themes and imagery of *The Red Badge of Courage.* He adapted these resources to a variety of styles ranging from the hyperbolic, elaborately rhetorical, reflexive style of the early fiction to the lean, open, sardonically understated style of such late stories as "The Upturned Face." This style attenuates his essentially mythic sense of war so severely that it seems all but absent except in the broad context of his characteristic feeling for the ambiguous crossing of horror and humor in a dream-like suspension of the movement of time. But even at this extreme range of style and form, his composi-tion draws obliquely on resources developed essentially in the experi-mental fiction of 1892—the radical origin of all of his fiction, even of the "realistic" studies of city low life in *Maggie, George's Mother,* and other New York stories and sketches. Thus an account of his style properly begins with his earliest experiments in fiction, espe-cially with the Sullivan County sketches, written shortly before he denounced them in 1892 as merely "clever and witty expedients" and pledged his unsteady allegiance to Howells's and Garland's realism.

II

The hero of the sketches is a literary version of the naive, infinitely self-assured, middle-class vacationer Crane studied as a cub reporter in Asbury Park, New Jersey, where he worked summers in the early Nineties for his brother Townley's news agency. The vacationers were models for several satirical sketches in which he practiced the art of literary characterization. "The average summer guest," he wrote in one piece, "stands in his two shoes with American self-reliance, playing casually with his watch-chain, and looks at the world with a clear eye." He presumes a vast worldly knowledge, even as he foolishly submits to the "arrogant prices" and other practiced deceits of hotel proprietors. "However," Crane observes, "deliberately and

baldly attempt to beat him out of fifteen cents and he will put his
hands in his pockets, spread his legs apart and wrangle in a loud voice
until sundown." [12] Another passage deals with the "summer youth,"
a "rose-tint and gilt-edge" swaggerer who appears on the beach with
the "summer girl," described as "a bit of interesting tinsel flashing
near the sombre-hued waves." Also, Crane describes the millionaire
owner of the beach, a pompous gentleman who loudly advertises his
virtues and pieties and who considers it a matter of high import that
his beach lies "adjacent" to the Lord's ocean.

The recurrent motif, as these examples show, is vain human delusion, often ironically contrasted with a vast, remote, sombre nature.
The Sullivan County sketches, also written in the early Nineties, develop the theme in an elaborate metaphor of man at war against
nature. The hero is the unnamed "little man," a camper and hunter
who wanders over the haunted countryside courageously challenging
its apparently inimical spirit in ludicrous assaults on caves, bears,
mountains, and forests. The little man is fond of melodramatic, self-
assertive postures and resounding oratory celebrating his courage and
other virtues, a demeanor which masks an almost hysterical fear and
dread of what he takes to be the dark powers of the alien landscape.
What makes the landscape particularly sinister is its bewildering ambiguity, for it sometimes seems benign and sympathetic, a serene
edenic vision of a world in perfect harmony with the spirit of the
"little man's" presumed virtues. This ambiguity challenges Crane's
hero and moves him to attempt to master nature's secret meaning.
The hero's characteristic approach is to assault nature violently, as if
to overpower it and subdue it to his will.

The model for the landscape in which the "little man" pursues his
adventures was the wild country of Sullivan County, New York, which
Crane knew intimately as a hunter and fisherman. In Crane's fiction
Sullivan County country is transmuted to a dream-like symbolic evocation of the world of nature, an elusive and problematic event of the
hero's distraught fancy. Crane's metaphors and images throw over

it the weird light of heightened color and invest it with a savage animism:

> All those things which come forth at night began to make noises. Unseen animals scrambled and flopped among the weeds and sticks. Weird features masqueraded awfully in robes of shadow.[13]

It appears in contradictory moods with ironic contrasts between its vaguely sinister and idyllic aspects:

> The sun gleamed merrily upon the waters, the gaunt, towering tree-trunks and the stumps lying like spatters of wood which had dropped from the clouds. Troops of blue and silver darning-needles danced over the surface. . . . Down in the water, millions of fern branches quavered and hid mysteries.[14]

Or again, it appears as mute, stolid, indifferent, as in the ending of a story about the "little man's" assault on a supposedly malevolent hill: "The mountain under his feet was motionless." [15] There is also a recurring strain of religious imagery evoking a mournful, tender sentience in the landscape which is dramatically contrasted to the threat of demonic shadows and baleful setting suns:

> In a field of snow some green pines huddled together and sang in quavers as the wind whirled among the gullies and ridges. . . . On the ridge-top a dismal choir of hemlocks crooned over one that had fallen. The dying sun created a dim purple and flame-colored tumult on the horizon's edge and then sank. . . . As the red rays retreated, armies of shadows stole forward.[16]

The problematical nature of the landscape is suggested further in images of obscuring mists, fogs, and cloaking darkness:

James B. Colvert

The sun slid down and threw a flare upon the silence, coloring
it red. . . . Dusk came and fought a battle with the flare. . . . A
ghost-like mist came and hung upon the waters. The pond became
a graveyard.[17]

Crane's irony appears most obviously in his mocking diminishment
of the "little man" whose burlesque posturing as a hero of supreme
virtue, knowledge, and courage is constantly belied in his various encounters with nature. His swagger, noble oratory, and outrageous self-
esteem are merely hopeful shams, utterly vulnerable to the dreadful
spectres his fancy projects upon the countryside. But the "little man's"
moods are variable, and in serene, happy moments his fancy conjures
an idyllic world in perfect accord with the supposed harmony of his
soul. In these pieces, and in the later New York fiction, Crane experi-
mented with a style of composition designed to emphasize these
incongruous aspects of the hero's mind by fusing contradictory per-
ceptions in single images, often with grotesque effect. A set description in "The Mesmeric Mountain," a Sullivan County fable that
concentrates many of the motifs and images of Crane's fiction, early
and late, illustrates the point:

A lazy lake lay asleep near the foot of the mountain. In
its bed of watergrass some frogs leered at the sky and crooned.
The sun sank in red silence, and the shadows of the pines grew
formidable. The expectant hush of evening, as if something were
going to sing a hymn, fell upon the peak and the little man.[18]

A passage in George's Mother shows how Crane adapted these
images to the description of street scenes. In this example the religious
motif becomes overt in the picture of a little chapel threatened by the
lurid, mystical powers of the city:

In a dark street the little chapel sat humbly between two tower-
ing apartment-houses. A red street-lamp stood in front. It threw

a marvellous reflection upon the wet pavements. It was like the death-stain of a spirit. Farther up, the brilliant lights of an avenue made a span of gold across the black street. A roar of wheels and a clangour of bells came from this point, interwoven into a sound emblematic of the life of the city. It seemed somehow to affront this solemn and austere little edifice. It suggested an approaching barbaric invasion. The little church, pierced, would die with a fine illimitable scorn for its slayers.[19]

The "little man's" war against nature becomes to his descendants, the heroes of *Maggie* and *George's Mother*, war against the man-made world where the murky vistas of shadowy streets and looming buildings are demonic and potentially violent, like the natural objects in the Sullivan County landscape. In the city fiction Crane developed another compositional device, suggested perhaps by the technique of impressionist artists in whose studios he occasionally lived when he was writing these novels and *The Red Badge of Courage*—a method of describing scenes from odd angles of vision, deliberately distorting the conventional realistic treatment of space and time and thus intensifying the sense of a threateningly incoherent order of reality which burdens so many of his fictional heroes. A passage from "An Experiment in Misery," a description of Bowery life written in 1894, illustrates the quasi-surrealistic effect of this method:

Through the mists of the cold and storming night, the cable cars went in silent procession, great affairs shining with red and brass, moving with formidable power, calm and irresistible, dangerful and gloomy, breaking silence only by the loud fierce cry of the gong. Two rivers of people swarmed along the sidewalks, spattered with black mud, which made each shoe leave a scar-like impression. Overhead, elevated trains with a shrill grinding of the wheels stopped at the station, which upon its leg-like pillars seemed to resemble some monstrous kind of crab squatting over the street. . . . Down an alley there were somber curtains of purple and black, on which street lamps dully glittered like embroidered flowers.[20]

This strange landscape of insubstantial objects appearing in constantly shifting guises—now demonic and threatening; again hopefully idyllic, benevolent, and mystically religious; and still again sternly indifferent and neutral—is the imaginary world technically perceived by the morally disoriented hero; though it also obliquely reflects Crane's own ironic sense of half-concealed, warring powers in the worlds of man and nature, and deeper than this, the Christian sense of the fallen world as the battleground of God and the Devil— the heritage of a minister's son. He deals with the subject directly in the religious poems of *The Black Riders*, less directly in the Sullivan County fables. In the New York fiction, where his metaphor of man and nature is shifted to a social context, the theme, though vaguely omnipresent, is shadowily transformed, as in the previously cited description of the wounded little chapel, and in the following passage, which represents the hero's reflection on the mysterious city in *George's Mother:*

> He had a vast curiosity concerning this city in whose complexities he was buried. It was an impenetrable mystery, this city. It was a blend of many enticing colours. He longed to comprehend it completely, that he might walk understandingly in its greatest marvel, its mightiest march of life, sin. He dreamed of a comprehension whose pay was the admirable attitude of a man of knowledge.[21]

The immediate reference is to George's naive yearning for worldly sophistication, but in the context of the myth of the "little man" it appears as an attenuation of a metaphor which springs from Crane's deep conviction that human vanity is poignantly vulnerable to the dark, ineffable powers of the world—a conviction which is the ultimate motive of Crane's irony.

III

The Red Badge of Courage is clearly an expansion of the fable of the "little man" at war against nature. The inimical spirit of the haunted glens of Sullivan County becomes in this novel the "swollen god" of war, the ghostly manifestation of a terrible, unseen enemy concealed in the obscuring mists and smoke of battle or transformed grotesquely in the perspective of vast distances or odd angles of sight. The threatening landscape, as perceived in the hysterical fancy of Henry Fleming (an obvious elaboration of the "little man") is the abode of the mysterious enemy, the "red and green monsters" that swarm in his imagination as he flees from his first battle.

> From far off in the darkness came the trampling of feet. The youth could occasionally see dark shadows that moved like monsters. Staring once at the red eyes (the campfires of the distant enemy) he conceived them to be growing larger, as the orbs of a row of dragons advancing.[22]

Henry is bewildered by the contradictory guises in which the landscape seems to appear and reappear:

> As he gazed around him the youth felt a flash of astonishment at the blue, pure sky and the sun gleamings on the trees and fields. It was surprising that Nature had gone tranquilly on with her golden process in the midst of so much devilment.[23]

Having fled to a forest in the rear, he hopes to find consolation in what now appears to be a serene, idyllic prospect of nature:

> This landscape gave him assurance. A fair field holding life. It was the religion of peace. It would die if its timid eyes were compelled to see blood. He conceived Nature to be a woman with a deep aversion to tragedy.[24]

In a little grotto he finds a temple of worship:

> At length he reached a place where the high, arching boughs
> made a chapel. He softly pushed the green doors aside and en-
> tered. Pine needles were a gentle brown carpet. There was a
> religious half light.[25]

But in this hopeful green chapel he finds, to his horror, a decaying
corpse—a thing of terror in the very temple of nature, a corruption in
"the fair field holding life." Again he takes wild flight, pursued by
frightful visions, imagining that "some strange voice would come from
the dead throat and squawk after him in horrible menaces." From a
distance, though, the whole affair seems a puzzling mystery. "The
trees about the portal of the chapel moved soughingly in a soft wind.
A sad silence was upon the little guarding edifice."

His blind rush upon the enemy in his next battle, like the "little
man's" assault on the "hostile" peak in the early fable, is figuratively
a desperate assault on a traitorous and hostile nature. He celebrates
this event, which earns him the name of hero, not as a triumph over
enemy soldiers nor as a victory over his cowardice, but as a vengeful
subjugation of "mountains."

> He had fought like a pagan who defends his religion. Regarding
> it, he saw that it was fine, wild, and, in some ways, easy. He
> had been a tremendous figure, no doubt. By this struggle he had
> overcome obstacles which he had admitted to be mountains.
> They had fallen like paper peaks, and he was now what he called
> a hero.[26]

Henry's state of mind at this point is equivalent to the vain delusion
of his fictional ancestor, the "little man," who struts victoriously on the
brow of the motionless mountain. The logic of the metaphor requires
a resolution in terms of the hero's relations to nature, but the concluding chapters of the novel evade this central dramatic issue. The

story subtly shifts to another problem, Henry's commitment to his fellow soldiers, to the regiment as a community of men. But Henry, though a hero among men, wins no victory over nature. And the flurry of sentimental images of the landscape in the final paragraphs of the book, Henry's vision of "tranquil skies, fresh meadows, cool brooks—an existence of soft and eternal peace"—is disturbingly reminiscent of the delusionary mood in which he took temporary solace in nature's little chapel-like bower.

IV

The rhetorical and symbolic patterns of the early fiction are fully elaborated in *The Red Badge of Courage*, which—despite the assurance of a good many reviewers—demonstrated Crane's radical departure from realism. Fleming's world, hysterically perceived, is mythic, represented as a literary stylization rather than as an historical phenomenon. But neither the vision nor the style was recognized by contemporary theories of realism—one reason, most probably, for Crane's abandonment of the haunted landscape of the "little man" for a "quiet" little Howellsian comedy of courtship in *The Third Violet*. The war stories in *The Little Regiment* were undertaken grudgingly and apparently against what he took to be his true artistic conscience. Superficially considered, they appear to be simply shorter versions of the novel—as if Crane were forced, in a way, back to an imaginary world already created and abandoned—but it is only partly true, as one representative critic puts it, that they "demonstrate the themes, the conflicts, the irony and imagery of *The Red Badge of Courage* reduced to a series of fragile, synthetic miniatures." [27] What must be considered also is that Crane attempted in these tales to move closer to the realism he professed anew in the fall and winter of 1895–1896. In consequence *The Little Regiment* marks the point in the history of his style where, in a suddenly heightened concern for his identity as a realist, he begins to translate his semi-allegorical "little man" into a credible social type. The result was to alter radically the basic dramatic structure of his plots and to open the way to the development of a variant style. The poignantly alienated "little man" appears nowhere in the stories, and the animated landscape of the sketches and novels, though it appears as the characteristic setting, is merely an elaborate and largely non-functional backdrop in a different kind of story. The aims and motives of the protagonists, who are generally more rational, critical, and reflective than the heroes modeled on the "little man," are defined in terms of a social rather than a mythic world. In this respect they seem to develop a tendency shown in the closing chapters of the war novel, where Crane avoided a resolution of Henry's war against nature by subtly shifting the issue to the world of men.

The story which most closely resembles *The Red Badge of Courage* in conception and incident is "A Mystery of Heroism," and since it represents more subtly than any of the others the movement away from the fable of the "little man," it is worth examination in some detail. It describes Fred Collins's heroic charge across a field under heavy enemy fire to secure a bucket of water from a distant well, an action reminiscent of Henry's wild charges in the novel. The story opens with the familiar images ironically linking demonic war and edenic nature:

> From beyond a curtain of green woods there came the sound of some stupendous scuffle, as if two animals of the size of islands were fighting.
> The little meadow which intervened was now suffering a terrible onslaught of shells. Its green and beautiful calm had vanished utterly. Brown earth was being flung in monstrous handfuls. And there was a massacre of the young blades of grass. . . . Some curious fortune of battle had made this gentle little meadow the object of the red hate of the shells, and each one as it exploded seemed like an imprecation in the face of a maiden.[28]

The passage obviously draws upon the same source as do similar descriptions in *The Red Badge of Courage*, but there is a difference both in treatment and in dramatic significance. The image is not projected upon the landscape from the demoralized fancy of the hero; it is merely a setting constructed out of the materials of Crane's myth but adapted to a non-mythic dramatic situation. The hallucinatory sense—the violent colors, the mystical air of dread, the hyperbolic evocation of the monstrous which symbolizes the distraught moral sense of Henry Fleming—is notably subdued, though not altogether absent.

But this flattening of the metaphor is dramatically appropriate, for Collins, unlike Henry, is not similar to the "little man." Collins is aware, though vaguely, of his self-serving pride, and this awareness gives him a certain critical detachment. He can reflect, as Henry cannot in the first part of the novel, on the mystery of that pride which commits him to a senseless display of bravery. He knows, as Henry does not, that the definition of heroism as the absence of fear is incorrect, for although he has no fear he is compelled to admit that he has no heroic virtues:

No, it could not be true. He was not a hero. Heroes had no shame in their lives, and as for him he remembered borrowing fifteen dollars from a friend and promising to pay it back the next day, and then avoiding that friend for ten months.[29]

The point is that Collins argues the matter in an ethical context, in the context of the world of men and social conduct. But it is not the world of man—not even of the enemy—that exercises the consciousness of Henry when he wrestles with the same problem on the eve of his first battle:

A little panic-fear grew in his mind. As his imagination went forward to a fight, he saw hideous possibilities. He contemplated the lurking menaces of the future, and failed in an effort to see himself standing stoutly in the midst of them. He recalled his visions of broken-bladed glory, but in the shadow of the impending tumult he suspected them to be impossible pictures.[30]

Henry's adversary is the "red and green dragon," the "lurking menaces" that try the spirit in the difficult private relation of God and man. Collins's enemy is the Confederate artillery shelling the meadow he proposes to cross. The animistic manifestations of lurking menaces are in the consciousness of the narrator, not his.

The title story illustrates Crane's difficulty in adapting his rhetorical materials to a realistic revelation of character. "The Little Regiment" is about two brothers whose deep affection for one another is apparently belied by their constant bickering, and the function of the war setting, which is profusely elaborated, is merely to provide the crisis of danger which exposes unequivocally their true feelings. Though otherwise irrelevant to the dramatic issue, the war nevertheless appears as the familiar symbol of a radical violence in nature, fulsomely described in Crane's characteristic imagery and rhetoric of the haunted landscape—of lurking menace in obscure shadows, ambiguous vistas, the threatened little chapel:

> The town on the southern shore of the little river loomed spectrally, a faint etching upon the grey cloud-masses which were shifting with oily languor. A long row of guns upon the northern bank had been pitiless in their hatred, but a little battered belfry could be dimly seen still pointing with invincible resolution toward the heavens.
>
> The enclouded air vibrated with noises made by hidden colossal things. . . .
>
> Ultimately the night deepened to the tone of black velvet. . . . There was little presented to the vision, but to a sense more subtle there was discernible in the atmosphere something like a pulse; a mystic beating which would have told a stranger of the presence of a giant thing—the slumbering mass of regiments and batteries.[31]

The last phrase may indicate an unsuccessful attempt to solve a radical compositional problem by forcing symbolic evocations onto specific things, a tactic which negates both symbol and thing.

"The Little Regiment," it will be recalled, is the story that engaged Crane in a "daily battle with a tangle of facts and emotion," a difficulty which undoubtedly arose from his attempt to impose his reflexive style on an ineffectively conceived subject. However, another story, "The Veteran," a very brief sequel to *The Red Badge of Courage*, tells how old Henry Fleming bravely sacrifices his life trying to save two colts from a burning barn and points clearly toward the new style Crane was apparently seeking. The rhetorical flourishes, the studied elaboration of chiaroscuro imagery, and the startling conceits of the fables of the "little man" are here largely abandoned. The lean, open, disciplined prose of "The Veteran" moves the story rapidly and precisely from the scene in which Old Henry tells about running away from his first battle to the lucid and powerfully concentrated description of his final rush into the blazing barn, just before the roof falls in. Yet, faint as it is, there is behind the relatively circumstantial and enumerative style the ghost of Crane's metaphysical landscape. The story opens with a fleeting glimpse of "three hickory trees placed irregularly in a meadow that was resplendent in springtime green," a faint echo of that spring long ago when young Henry once found the idyllic landscape suddenly filled with "red and green dragons." Farther away, standing now invincible, is the familiar little chapel, "the old, dismal belfry of the village church. . . ." Telling the story of his flight, old Henry now appreciates "some comedy in the recital." The enemy, he recalls, appeared as a "lot of flitting figures"; and he remembers thinking at the moment of panic that "the sky was falling down" and that "the world was coming to an end." Thus he names in a serene latter-day vision the "red and green monsters."

The barn in which he meets his death is presented at first glance in "its usual appearance, solemn, rather mystic in the black night," but when he hurls aside the door, "a yellow flame leaped out at one corner and sped and wavered frantically up the old gray wall. It was glad, terrible, this single flame, like the banner of deadly and triumphant foes." The image of this satanic fire, "laden with tones of hate and death, a hymn of wonderful ferocity," crosses with the image of demonic war, and old Henry at last charges the enemy he was permitted to evade at the end of *The Red Badge of Courage.* The concluding paragraph of the story (though somewhat overwritten) extends more appropriately to the metaphor of the "little man's" redemption, which is intrinsically tragic rather than comic, than does the ambiguous resolution of the war novel:

> When the roof fell in, a great funnel of smoke swarmed toward the sky, as if the old man's mighty spirit, released from its body —a little bottle—had swelled like the genie of the fable. The smoke was tinted rose-hue from the flames, and perhaps the unutterable midnights of the universe will have no power to daunt the color of this soul.[32]

"The Veteran" is a skillful adaptation of Crane's symbolic materials to a new style, the style essentially of the fine story "The Open Boat" which bears, proudly perhaps, the subtitle "A Tale Intended to be after the Fact" but which also, like "The Veteran," is composed of elements obliquely drawn from his mythic imagination. When he wrote "The Veteran," the famous sea story was less than a year in the future, but he was now prepared for it—with a method, devised in the experimental stories of *The Little Regiment,* that seemed to atone for his apostasy from realism.

V

The author of "The Open Boat," "The Blue Hotel," "The Monster," and *Wounds in the Rain* would probably have not been much surprised by Howells's late judgment of his work, rendered a dozen years after Crane's death. "He lost himself in a whirl of wild guesses at the fact from the ground of insufficient witness," the critic wrote. *"The Red Badge of Courage,* and other things that followed it, were the throes of an art failing with material to which it could not render an absolute devotion from an absolute knowledge."[33] Crane would have known, by then, the limits of his concession to realism, for he came to realize, after he had experienced shipwreck and war, that the meaning of the real thing was even more elusive than the meaning of those imaginary wars he had described on the landscapes of Sullivan County and Chancellorsville. "But to get at the real thing," cries the narrator in Crane's reflective history of his experience in Cuba, "War Memories." "It seems impossible. It is because war is neither magnificent nor squalid, it is simply life, and an expression of life can always evade us. We can never tell life, one to another, although sometimes we think we can."[34] To "tell life," experienced or imagined (as Florida, Greece, and Cuba seem to have taught him) requires a vision of the world and a method for expressing it. The vision he had essentially from the very beginning—a view of the world invested in a version of the serpent in the edenic garden—and the method he devised by the end of 1896 as an ingenious elaboration of the compositional patterns invented in the experimental fiction of 1892.

In the sense that these patterns are common to the fiction based on imaginary as well as observed events, Crane tells the same story again and again. The vainglorious hero who makes outrageous assumptions about his place in the universe appears in "The Blue Hotel" as the mad Swede who, because he overpowers an enemy in a fist fight, assumes that he also triumphs over the world in general. The correspondent in "The Open Boat" is astonished, as his fictional forebearer the "little man" would have been, to find the meaning of the problematical seascape so elusive. It seems furiously hostile (the deadly waves, the sinister gulls, the shark); but it seems also, at times, to be nature's assurance of serenity and order (the gentle calm of the waves, the lovely pattern of the gulls in flight); like the "chapel bower" in *The Red Badge of Courage;* but then again it appears to be flatly neutral (the high cold star, the distant tower).

What Crane saw at Velestino was, in this same way, what his literary sense of war compelled him to see. John Bass, correspondent for the *New York Journal,* asked him during the battle what impressed him most about it, and Crane replied by citing precisely two radical elements of the imaginary wars described in his earlier fiction: "the attitude of the men" and the "mysterious force" which was their adversary. And he seemed also to allude to his characteristic symbolization of the mystical elements in his fictional landscapes:

> Between two great armies battling against each other the interesting thing is the mental attitude of the men. The Greeks I can see and understand, but the Turks seem unreal. They are shadows on the plain—vague figures in black, indications of a mysterious force.[35]

These are the basic elements of the one short story based on the experience, "Death and the Child," a curious elaboration in variant forms of the themes and images of *The Red Badge of Courage.* They figure largely in the composition of many of his war dispatches, as do other motifs drawn from the earlier fiction—or more precisely from the vision common to both the fiction and the dispatches. An incident reported in an article in the *Journal* on the battle of Velestino, for example, seems to cross exactly the image of war as a demon destroyer of the holy order of creation, as rendered in the passage describing the chapel in the forest in *The Red Badge of Courage.* From Greece, Crane wrote:

> The reserves coming up passed a wayside shrine. The men paused to cross themselves and pray. A shell struck the shrine and demolished it. The men in the rear of the column were obliged to pray to the spot where the shrine had been.[36]

The immediate style, though, is the spare, open, declarative manner of "The Veteran" and "The Open Boat"—the deceptively simple style Ernest Hemingway is often said to have invented.

It would be misleading, of course, to say that real-life experience had no effect on Crane's art. For one thing, his experience of war in Greece and Cuba gave him a surer knowledge of military equipment and maneuvers, and the war stories after 1897 show a heightened confidence in the description of guns, caissons, trenches, and tactics. He acquired also a practical knowledge of the politics of war, which furnished subjects for dispatches from the front and even for one of the stories in *Wounds in the Rain*, "The Second Generation." In general, the effect of this on his style was to give it a certain technical authority notably absent in *The Red Badge of Courage* and *The Little Regiment*, where the things and circumstances of military life are characteristically described, sometimes monotonously, in figurative rather than literal language. But the remarkable feature of the later war stories is the consistency with which they reflect the world of his imagination, the visionary landscapes which are the domains of ambiguously revealed spirits haunting his metaphysical sense of the world.

The vision is often severely attenuated, more severely than in "The Veteran," where the firmly restrained specifications of the pastoral setting and the satanic fire tends to give the style a feeling of realism. But it is nevertheless Crane's imagination which ultimately determines the meaning of the observed event—and often seems to select the event to be observed. The degree to which they are symbolically reduced, as one might expect, varies widely. Thus a passage in "War Memories" describing a military hospital temporarily installed in a church which Crane visited at El Caney in 1898, obviously elaborates a pattern of imagery that can be traced to a Sullivan County sketch, "Four Men in a Cave":

The interior of the church was too cave-like in its gloom for the eyes of the operating surgeons, so they had the altar-table carried to the doorway, where there was a bright light. Framed then in the black archway was the altar-table with the figure of a man upon it. He was naked save for a breech-clout, and so clear was the ecclesiastic suggestion that one's mind leaped to a

fantasy that this thin, pale figure had just been torn down from
a cross. The flash of the impression was like light, and for this instant it illumined all the dark recesses of one's remotest idea of
sacrilege, ghastly and wanton. I bring this to you merely as an
effect, an effect of mental light and shade, if you like; something
done in thought similar to that which the French impressionists
do in colour; something meaningless and at the same time
overwhelming, crushing, monstrous.[37]

The passage perhaps suggests Crane's conception of art better than
anything else he ever wrote about it, and "Four Men in a Cave"
illustrates how consistently his late writing held to a principle grasped
half-intuitively at the very beginning of his career. The sketch describes a nightmare adventure in a "haunted" cave where the "little
man" and his companions are confronted by a mystical, priest-like
creature threatening violence:

A great gray stone, cut squarely, like an altar, sat in the middle
of the floor. Over it burned three candles in swaying tin cups
hung from the ceiling. Before it, with what seemed to be a small
volume clasped in his yellow fingers, stood a man. . . . He fixed
glinting, fiery eyes upon the heap of men.[38]

The priest-like man turns out to be a half-crazed recluse who forces
the terrified men into a poker game at the point of a knife. The "small
volume" is seen later as a deck of cards. The images common to both
passages—the altar, the gloomy cave, the priest-like spectral man, the
garish lights, and the vague aura of sacrilege—are radical elements of
Crane's imagination.

More tenuous in its connection with his symbolic world is his description of a torpedo boat off the Cretan coast in 1897.

A scouting torpedo-boat as small as a gnat crawling on an enormous decorated wall came from the obscurity of the shore.

Apparently it looked us over and was satisfied, for in a few moments it was returned to obscurity.[39]

Whether the image of the animistic boat appearing in the perspective of a vast distance out of a mystic obscurity was an actual historical event rendered in casually figurative language or whether it was purely an event of the literary imagination is hard to determine, though one suspects the latter in view of the elaboration on the obscurity to which the boat returns: "It was lonely and desolate like a land of Despair. . . . Nothing lived there save the venomous torpedo-boat, which, after all, had been little more than a shadow on the water."

Circumstantial as the later stories appear to be when casually considered, they are nevertheless in one degree or another energized by Crane's mythic imagination; though they often seem, out of the context of the earlier fiction, to be merely decorated narratives of random incidents of war. An example is the comic anecdote based on a real-life war adventure, "The Lone Charge of William B. Perkins." The story is a curious adaptation of the fable of the "little man." The hero in real life was Ralph Paine, a war correspondent who foolishly wandered out of the trenches at Guantanamo to attack a Spanish sniper observed in a distant clump of mysterious trees. Paine retreated under heavy rifle fire to the safety of an abandoned sugar boiler and eventually returned unharmed to his own lines. In Crane's fictional version—and the story is fiction in the same sense "The Open Boat" is—the hero appears in the guise of the vainglorious "little man." Discovering the Spanish sniper, Perkins announces his "perception" in a "loud voice" and "declared hoarsely that if he only had a rifle he would go and possess himself of this particular enemy." When the hero finds himself in a sudden storm of bullets, it suddenly occurs to him that he is merely "an almshouse idiot plunging through hot, crackling thickets on a June morning in Cuba." Then "the beauties of rural Minnesota illumined his conscience with the gold of lazy corn, with the sleeping green of meadows, with the cathedral gloom of pine forest." He seeks refuge in the rusted sugar boiler, "a temple

149

shining resplendent with safety." When the enemy rifle fire dies down, he strolls back to his trenches "with his hat not able to fit his head for the new bumps of wisdom that were on it." Later he is observed "wearing a countenance of poignant thoughtfulness." [40]

The relation of this story to *The Red Badge of Courage* is clear enough. The vainglorious hero, the wild assault upon the concealed enemy, the mystical aspect of the adversary, the sudden panic, the yearning vision of a reassuring and idyllic nature, the retreat to the degraded temple, the reconstruction of pride to humility—all are major motifs in Crane's work, concentrated in *The Red Badge of Courage*. These figurations constantly recur in the Cuban stories and in the tales of the mythical Spitzbergan army in "The Kicking Twelfth." Though they may be more or less decorative in some of these stories, as if drawn expediently from cultivated literary resources, they also echo the portentous drama conceived in Crane's radical sense of man and his enigmatic world. Even though a story like "The Price of the Harness," based on the battle of San Juan Hill, celebrates the stoic devotion to duty of the professional soldier (an expansion, it might be noted, of the sense of character expressed in the conversion of the "loud soldier" in *The Red Badge of Courage* to a soldier of quiet, modest competency), it also obliquely defines war as the dark manifestation of a devil-corrupted world. Its realism accommodates the myth that haunted Crane's imagination from first to last. The shadows of the Cuban countryside, like those of Sullivan County and Chancellorsville, are "all grim and of ghostly shape." The setting Cuban sun throws its hostile glance upon the problematical landscape just as it does in the famous image at the end of chapter 9 in *The Red Badge of Courage*. The devoted regulars in "The Price of the Harness" perceive that their war is "not much like a battle with men" but "a battle with a bit of charming scenery, enigmatically potent for death." [41]

It may be that Crane's credo was "only to say what I saw." [42] But what he said early in 1896, when he was trying to reconcile his theoretical commitment to realism as he wrote the stories in *The Little Regi-*

ment, is also true. "I understand that a man is born into the world with his own pair of eyes, and he is not at all responsible for his vision —he is merely responsible for his quality of personal honesty. To keep close to this personal honesty is my supreme ambition." [43] The New York fiction and the fiction after 1897 tell what he saw. The essential point is the meaning he invested in what he saw, the meaning evoked by the style he invented in the Sullivan County sketches of 1892.

NOTES

1. Crane to Lily Brandon Munroe [March 1894?], in *Stephen Crane: Letters,* ed. R. W. Stallman and Lillian Gilkes (New York: New York University Press, 1960), p. 31.
2. Howells to Crane, 8 April 1893, ibid., p. 18.
3. Howells to Crane, 26 January 1896, ibid., p. 102.
4. Crane to Howells, 1896, ibid., p. 106.
5. Crane to an editor of *Leslies' Weekly* [about November 1895], ibid., p. 78.
6. Crane to John Northern Hilliard [January 1896?], ibid., p. 109.
7. Crane to Ripley Hitchcock, 27 January [1896], ibid., p. 106.
8. Crane to an editor of *Leslies' Weekly* [about November 1895], ibid., p. 79.
9. Crane to Curtis Brown, 31 December 1896 [for 1895], ibid., p. 87.
10. Crane to Willis Brooks Hawkins [about November 1895], ibid., p. 74.
11. "Introduction," *The University of Virginia Edition of the Works of Stephen Crane,* ed. Fredson Bowers (Charlottesville: University of Virginia, 1969), 7: xiii.
12. "On the Boardwalk," *New York Tribune,* 14 August 1892, part 2, p. 17.
13. "The Octopush," *Stephen Crane: Sullivan County Tales and Sketches,* ed. R. W. Stallman (Ames, Iowa: Iowa State University Press, 1968), p. 88.
14. Ibid., p. 86.
15. "The Mesmeric Mountain," ibid., p. 145.
16. "Killing His Bear," ibid., p. 67.
17. "The Octopush," ibid., p. 87.
18. "The Mesmeric Mountain," ibid., p. 144.
19. *George's Mother, The Works of Stephen Crane,* 1: 156.
20. "An Experiment in Misery," *New York Press,* 22 April 1894, part 3, p. 2.
21. *George's Mother, The Works of Stephen Crane,* 1: 135.

22. *The Red Badge of Courage* (New York, 1895), pp. 21–22.

23. Ibid., p. 63.

24. Ibid., p. 78.

25. Ibid.

26. Ibid., p. 169.

27. Thomas A. Gullason, "The Significance of *Wounds in the Rain*," *Modern Fiction Studies* 5 (Autumn 1959): 235.

28. *The Complete Short Stories and Sketches of Stephen Crane*, ed. Thomas A. Gullason (Garden City, N.Y.: Doubleday, 1963), pp. 219–20.

29. Ibid., p. 223.

30. *The Red Badge of Courage*, pp. 13–14.

31. Gullason, *Complete Short Stories*, pp. 276, 283.

32. Ibid., p. 294.

33. "Frank Norris," *North American Review* 175 (December 1902): 770.

34. Robert W. Stallman and E. R. Hagemann, eds., *The War Dispatches of Stephen Crane* (New York: New York University Press, 1964), p. 267.

35. "How Novelist Crane Acts on the Battlefield," ibid., pp. 42–43.

36. "Crane at Velestino," ibid., p. 31.

37. Ibid., p. 288.

38. Stallman, *Sullivan County Tales*, p. 74.

39. "Stephen Crane's Pen Picture of the Powers' Fleet off Crete," in Stallman and Hagemann, *War Dispatches*, p. 11.

40. Gullason, *Complete Short Stories*, pp. 554–57.

41. Ibid., pp. 507–20.

42. "Introduction," Stallman and Hagemann, *War Dispatches*, p. 107.

43. Crane to John Northern Hilliard [January 1896?], Stallman and Gilkes, *Letters*, p. 110.

Matthew J. Bruccoli

Stephen Crane as a
Collector's Item

The history of Stephen Crane as a collected author is chiefly the history of the 1893 *Maggie: A Girl of the Streets*, the Crane glamor item. No distinguished Crane collection has ever been sold at auction. There are no Wakeman or Chamberlain or Maier sales for Crane. A possible exception to this statement is the twenty-one (total: $854.25) Crane items in the 1923 John Quinn sale—including a *Maggie* ($135) and the manuscript of "The Five White Mice" ($500). But the Quinn Cranes were part of a great collection distinguished for other authors. Indeed, the surprisingly high price of $500 for the manuscript of "The Five White Mice" almost certainly resulted from the circumstance that this Crane item had a presentation inscription by Joseph Conrad, one of the star authors in the Quinn collection. Only two dealer catalogues have included a Crane collection. David Randall's first catalogue (1934) offered some ninety Crane items—including a *Maggie*—for the lot price of $1,750. This collection, which had been assembled for the occasion by Mr. Randall, did not sell.[1] Some time after 1936 the Argus Book Shop issued a mimeographed list of fifty-seven Crane items with a headnote by Vincent Starrett. This list included a *Maggie* ($350), the typescript of

"The Great Boer Trek" ($250), an autograph letter signed ($50), and twenty-one Cora Crane letters ($75).[2] Scribner catalogue number 125 (1941) listed thirteen items and noted the availability of "a complete set of the works of Stephen Crane, including all first editions in book form, pamphlets, ephemera, etc., etc., and will be glad to quote titles and prices on request."

The major private Crane collections have been transferred by private treaty or donated to libraries. The H. B. Collamore collection was sold to C. Waller Barrett and then was presented by him to the University of Virginia. The Ames W. Williams collection was sold to Syracuse University. The George Matthew Adams collection was presented to Dartmouth College.[3] A few of Vincent Starrett's Cranes were sold at auction, but most were disposed of privately. The O. L. Griffith collection has vanished, except for four lots sold at auction (American Art Association–Anderson Galleries, 30–31 October 1935). Thomas Beer's collection has vanished along with his Crane papers. The legendary—perhaps mythical—collection of John Northern Hilliard, which was reputed to include important manuscript material, has also vanished. Cora Crane's material is at Columbia University, with smaller parts at the University of Virginia. Three major collections are privately owned by Melvin Schoberlin, Joseph Katz, and Matthew J. Bruccoli.

The turning point for Crane collecting is 1923, the year of the Thomas Beer biography and the Vincent Starrett bibliography. By July 1926 *The Biblio* could rank Crane as first among authors in demand during the previous year and fourth over the past four years. In 1927 Merle Johnson offered the theory that serious Crane collecting began because Joseph Conrad wrote the preface for the Beer biography; it "followed naturally that all the Conrad collectors bought the Beer book about Crane. 'Who is this guy Crane that our Joseph thinks so wonderful? Let's look him up.' "[4] In this same article Johnson recounts forming "many years ago" an eighteen-volume Crane collection for $21.80—which included a green-ink *Black Riders* at $9.00 and a *Maggie* at $2.00. Johnson disposed of this collection at the time of World War I for "almost 100% profit." In 1929 Johnson included two Cranes in his *High Spots of American Literature*: *The Red Badge of Courage* and—surprisingly—*War Is Kind*.

I. *Maggie: A Girl of the Streets*

The story of the 1893 *Maggie* at auction begins in 1917 when the first copy brought $7.50 at an Anderson sale. Between 1917 and 1968 forty-two copies were auctioned. But not forty-two different copies. The record price was the $3,700 Dr. Rosenbach paid in 1930 for a copy inscribed to Lucius L. Button; and the record $2,100 for an uninscribed copy was set the same year. The Thirties was the great period of activity for *Maggie*: twenty-nine copies auctioned from 1930 to 1940, with at least one copy auctioned every year except 1933. On 27 October 1930, two copies were sold at the same American Art–Anderson sale ($1,125, inscribed, and $775, uninscribed). At least four more copies were offered in dealers' catalogues during the Thirties. Two factors must be considered in discussing the auctioned copies of *Maggie* during this period: the Depression and the Coughlan disclosure. To one who was not there, the Depression does not seem to have been a great depressant to the *Maggie* market. In 1930 six copies brought $500 or more, although two copies in 1932 went for $85 and $90 respectively. The 1930 prices were based on the presumption of the book's great rarity; however, too many copies of this great "rarity" turned up, and rumors began circulating about a nest of *Maggies* that were being leaked out. In 1935 the American Art–Anderson galleries disclosed that there were in fact eleven copies in the possession of Crane's niece, Mrs. Florence Crane Coughlan. It was announced that two copies per year would be sold from this group. This disclosure temporarily restored collector confidence in *Maggie*, for the copy accompanying it brought $700. Nevertheless, damage was done: the rarity of *Maggie* had been blown. Between 1936 and 1965 twenty copies were sold at auction at prices ranging from $85 to $625. The book did not bring a big price again until an uninscribed copy went for $1,900 in 1968.

THE RAREST BOOK IN MODERN AMERICAN LITERATURE
A PRESENTATION COPY
WITH A LONG INSCRIPTION BY THE AUTHOR

76 [CRANE (STEPHEN).] Maggie, A Girl of the Streets. (A Story of New York.) By Johnston Smith. N.p. [1893]

12mo, original printed yellow wrappers (small piece at bottom of backstrip wanting; front wrapper slightly frayed; hinge of front wrapper strengthened with extra leaf).

THE EXCESSIVELY RARE PRIVATELY PRINTED FIRST EDITION. PRESENTATION COPY, inscribed on the front wrapper: *"Stephen Crane to Budgon* [Lucius L. Button]. *It is inevitable that you be greatly shocked by this book but continue, please, with all possible courage, to the end. For it tries to show that environment is a tremendous thing in the world and frequently shapes lives regardless. If one proves that theory one makes room in Heaven for all sorts of souls, notably an occasional street girl, who are not confidently expected to be there by many excellent people. It is probable that the reader of this small thing may consider the author to be a bad man, but obviously that is a matter of small consequence to The Author."* At the top of the wrapper the recipient, Lucius L. Button, has written his name. The inevitable fraying of the wrapper has injured a few words in the inscription. PRESENTATION COPIES OF EVEN CRANE'S COMMON BOOKS ARE VIRTUALLY UNOBTAINABLE. Some time before the publication of "Maggie", Crane took up residence at a boarding house in Eastern Avenue where lived a group of young medical men. Here began the friendship between the young reporter and Lucius L. Button. Not long after, Crane, discouraged by the innumerable rejections of "Maggie", and having come into the possession of about a thousand dollars, determined to issue it in a cheap, paperbacked form designed to appeal to those who were dependent upon the news-stands for literary nourishment. THE FIRST COPY FROM THE BINDERY HE BROUGHT HOME AND PRESENTED TO BUTTON. Although the presentation of the book was accepted, it was not gratis, as Button insisted upon the privilege of being the first to purchase the little book and dutifully paid its author the fifty cents. Such is the history of this book as related by Mrs. Button.

The story of the reception of this, the first American ironic novel, is well known: it failed even to attain the notoriety of a news-stand circulation, and has now become THE RAREST BOOK IN MODERN AMERICAN LITERATURE. IT IS CERTAIN THAT NO MORE DESIRABLE COPY EXISTS THAN THE PRESENT ONE, WITH ITS LONG AND PERTINENT INSCRIPTION.

[SEE FRONTISPIECE]

77 —— Works.   New York, n.d.

12 vols., 12mo, cloth, uncut. One of 750 sets.

78 —— A. L. s., 3 pp., 12mo.   Pendennis Club [Dec. 15, 1892.]   To Lucius L. Button.

AN AMUSING LETTER, showing Crane's characteristic love of dogs: *"I was glad to be made aware . . . that the dragon is sad because I have escaped her. But if she be vindictive I will have my revenge. I have had a dog given me . . . a mere little fox-terrier with a nose like a black bead and a pedigree as long as your arm. It evinces a profound tendency to raise the devil on all occasions, which it does, mostly, by tearing up gloves, and wading around in any butter plate, mince pie, or cake which it may perceive. Withal it is a meek little thing when in human presence and keeps its black, white and tan coat spotlessly clean. . . . I adore dogs. . . ."*

79 —— A. L. s., 1 p., 12mo.   New York, Feb. 20, 1894.   To Lucius L. Button.

" . . . I can't have the joy of meeting you at Koster and Bials either. Nevertheless when I get all my damned books and things straightened out, we shall meet again. . . ."

Plate 1, *Sale Number 3827 . . . Valuable Books . . .*, March 11 and 12, American Art Association, Anderson Galleries, 1930.

81 Victory. *New York*: 1915. $265.00
FIRST EDITION. Presentation copy *To R(ichard) C(urle) affectionately from J. C. 1915.*

82 Victory. *London*: 1915. $15.00
FIRST ENGLISH EDITION.

83 The Warrior's Soul. *London*: 1920. $25.00
FIRST EDITION. The sheets of the pamphlet 25 copies of which were privately printed for the author.

84 Youth. *London*: 1902. $765.00
FIRST EDITION. Inscribed copy. *YOUTH and HEART OF DARKNESS are the first short stories of mine which attracted attention to my work in a wider sphere. Most critics dismissed THE END OF THE TETHER either with contempt or with a few cursory remarks. Joseph Conrad.*

CRANE, STEPHEN

85 The Red Badge of Courage. $11850.00
THE ORIGINAL MANUSCRIPT, 176 pages, folio.

86 The Red Badge of Courage. *New York*: 1895. $295.00
FIRST EDITION.

DOUGHTY, CHARLES M.

87 Adam Cast Forth. *London*: 1908. $18.00
FIRST EDITION. With the author's signature on the half title.

88 The Cliffs. *London*: 1909. $15.00
FIRST EDITION. With the author's signature on the half title.

89 The Clouds. *London*: 1912. $15.00
FIRST EDITION. With the author's signature on the half title.

90 The Dawn in Britain. *London*: 1906. $55.00
FIRST EDITION. With the author's signature on the half titles of all six volumes.

91 Hogarth's "Arabia." *London*: 1922. $60.00
FIRST EDITION, privately printed. One of 25 copies, signed by the author.

Plate 2. *A Catalogue of Original Manuscripts, Presentation Copies, First Editions, and Autograph Letters of Modern Authors,* The Rosenbach Company, 1933.

ALMOST AS FRESH AS ON THE DAY OF ISSUE

67. [COOPER (JAMES FENIMORE).] The Water Witch; or, The
Skimmer of the Seas. A Tale. 3 vols., 12mo, ORIGINAL GRAY BOARDS,
PAPER LABELS, ENTIRELY UNCUT. In a cloth folding case. London, 1830
FIRST ENGLISH EDITION, issued about two months prior to the First American Edition.
A MAGNIFICENT COPY, PROBABLY THE FINEST IN EXISTENCE, WITH THE LABELS INTACT AND
THE COVERS AND TEXT ALMOST AS FRESH AS ON THE DAY OF ISSUE. ENTIRELY UNCUT.
With 2 pp. of advertisements at the end of Vol. I.
On the front end-paper of each volume is a small library stamp.

WITH TWO FOLIO PAGES OF AUTOGRAPH MANUSCRIPT
OF THE WORK

68. [COOPER (JAMES FENIMORE).] The Headsman. 2 vols., 12mo,
original boards, paper labels; slightly rubbed, uncut; rebacked with gauze,
with the greater part of the original backs preserved. In a half brown
morocco slip case.   Philadelphia, 1833
FIRST EDITION. LAID IN THE FIRST VOLUME ARE TWO PAGES OF THE ORIGINAL MANUSCRIPT
OF THE WORK, IN THE HAND OF THE AUTHOR, folio, about TWENTY-FOUR HUNDRED WORDS.

69. [——] The Deerslayer: or, the First War-Path. 2 vols., 12mo, original
cloth; paper labels. In a half brown morocco slip case.
                                                      Philadelphia, 1841
FIRST EDITION. The first of the celebrated series "The Leatherstocking Tales". The
labels, while slightly rubbed, are more complete than usual. A copy of this rare work
much above the average in condition.
From the library of C. J. Wegner, with bookplate.

70. COWPER (WILLIAM). A. L. s., 3 pp., 4to. N.p., The Lodge, June 28,
1790. To Lady Hesketh; two or three words injured by the removal of
a seal, about 425 words.
A FINE LETTER TO COWPER'S COUSIN, beginning "My dearest Coz." It is mostly of a
personal nature.
From the collection of Richard Henry Stoddard.

THE PRIVATELY PRINTED FIRST EDITION

71. [CRANE (STEPHEN).] Maggie: A Girl of the Streets. (A Story
of New York.) By Johnston Smith. 12mo, ORIGINAL YELLOW WRAPPERS,
ENTIRELY UNCUT AND UNOPENED.   [New York, 1893]
A SUPERB COPY OF THE PRIVATELY PRINTED FIRST EDITION OF THE AUTHOR'S FIRST BOOK.
The story of the reception of this, the FIRST AMERICAN IRONIC NOVEL, is well known;
it failed even to attain the notoriety of a newsstand circulation. THIS COPY, ENTIRELY
UNCUT AND UNOPENED, IS ALMOST AS FRESH AS ON THE DAY IT LEFT THE PRINTER'S HANDS.
In view of the uncertainty that exists in the minds of collectors and dealers regarding
a so-called "large number" of copies that are supposed to have been found, we think
it advisable to make the following statement:
From March 11, 1930, to Dec. 5, 1934, 11 copies of this work appeared at public sale
in America, three of which were presentation copies; some of the volumes were in
very poor condition. Nine of the eleven were sold in these Galleries, the first (a
presentation copy) on March 11, 1930, and the last (also a presentation copy) on
Dec. 5, 1934.
Only two, however, of the nine that we have sold were the property of the owner
of the present copy, Mrs. Florence Crane Coughlan.
When Mr. Coughlan came to the Galleries to negotiate the sale of the present copy,

Plate 3. The Coughlan Disclosure. *First Editions* . . . , April 24 and 25,
American Art Association, Anderson Galleries, 1935.

MAGGIE

A Girl of the Streets

(A STORY OF NEW YORK)

By

JOHNSTON SMITH

Copyrighted

[NUMBER 71]

we gave it as our opinion that it would be unwise to offer it for sale unless a definite statement was made in the catalogue regarding the exact number of copies still held by him and his wife.

We are informed that they still hold 11 copies and that the present copy is one of the finest, being practically as fresh as on the day it left the printers' hand. The majority of the others are in more or less worn condition, some with the wrappers slightly chipped, and others torn, lightly stained, or with other slight defects.

An arrangement has been made with Mr. and Mrs. Coughlan whereby these 11 copies are to be sold in these Galleries at the rate of two copies each season hereafter until the entire number has been distributed.

In response to our request to send us in writing some statement regarding them, Mrs. Coughlan, under date of Jan. 22, 1935, has made the following statement:

"After the death of my Father, Stephen Crane's brother William, in California several years ago, two copies of 'Maggie' were sent to my sister Agnes and me by the estate. Not knowing the value, but suspecting that they would bring a few dollars at least, I took them to the Anderson Galleries, where I was congratulated on the possession of these books and they were put up at auction. The result is book history.

"Like everyone else, probably, who had ever seen or heard of 'Maggie', I racked my

[Description concluded on following page; see illustration]

Plate 3. (*continued*)

brains to remember any more possible copies in the family library. When our home in Brooklyn was broken up, most of our possessions were stored on my grandfather's farm, and I mentally repacked the books which had been sent there.

"As far back as I could remember there had always been a small pile of paper bound 'Maggies' in our storage room but when I spoke of this to my mother she said she didn't believe there were any left as my two eldest sisters had burned them, believing they were 'not nice'.

However we took a chance and went to the farm, where our books had been stored in a wagon house for twenty years, and we found the books which the American Art Association-Anderson Galleries Inc. are now handling. To my knowledge these are the only first edition 'Maggies' in our branch of the family."

(Signed) *"Florence Crane Coughlan"*

A BEAUTIFUL COPY OF
"THE RED BADGE OF COURAGE"

72. CRANE (STEPHEN). The Red Badge of Courage. 12mo, original cloth, yellow top, uncut.   New York, 1895

A BEAUTIFUL COPY OF THE FIRST ISSUE OF THE FIRST EDITION, with perfect type in the word "congratulated" on p. 225. With 4 pp. of advertisements at the end, the first page listing three of Gilbert Parker's works, the first work being the "Trail of the Sword". One of the Merle Johnson "High Spots of American Literature".

WITH TWENTY-SEVEN ORIGINAL DRAWINGS

Including the Two Original Watercolor Decorations for the Covers

73. CRANE (WALTER). Queen Summer, or, The Journey of the Lily & the Rose. *Colored illustrations by Walter Crane.* 4to, original green pictorial boards, vellum back, gilt top, with cloth protecting cover.

London, 1901

FIRST EDITION. ONE OF 250 COPIES ON LARGE PAPER. A MAGNIFICENT AND UNIQUE VOLUME, CONTAINING TWENTY-FIVE ORIGINAL WATERCOLOR DRAWINGS FOR ILLUSTRATIONS IN THE BOOK, EACH EXQUISITELY COLORED, INCLUDING A BEAUTIFULLY TINTED DRAWING WHICH WAS NOT USED IN THE WORK (illustrated on the opposite page). Each drawing is signed with Crane's initials, and the lettering in the autograph is the artist. Also inserted is a proof of one of the illustrations colored by hand and inscribed by Crane in pencil in the margin *'Hand tinted proof W. C.'* The original watercolor decorations for the covers have been pasted down on the inner side of the respective covers. Each piece is neatly inlaid to size.

APPARENTLY CRANE CONSIDERED THESE DRAWINGS HIS FINEST, as they were all framed and decorated the artist's drawing room at Kensington. After his death they were disposed of by his son, Lionel Crane.

Laid in is a L. s. by Harry Spurr, London bookdealer, to the present owner, in reference to the drawings, reading in part as follows: *"In sending you this volume with a number of the very charming exquisite. original water-colour drawings mounted and inlaid I should like to tell you that I bought them direct from Mr. Lionel Crane, son of the artist, and at the time of purchase they were all framed and hanging in Mr. Crane's drawing room at Kensington.*

"This fact appeals to me as direct evidence that Mr. Walter Crane considered them as fine examples of his own work, with which opinion I feel sure you will readily agree . . ."

Mr. Heywood Sumner, writing of Crane, has stated that ". . . Walter Crane at his best was masterly in his management of economy of means to produce a lavish result . . . his work always added distinction to the book which it adorned, and made it one to be desired and, if possible, obtained. 'If possible' is added because possession is in some instances so difficult to obtain . . ."

[See illustration]

Plate 3. (*continued*)

II. Other Crane Collector's Items

As noted above, the glamor of *Maggie* has obscured the rarity and collectability of other Crane items. For example, the *Pike County Puzzle* is probably as rare as *Maggie*; although the first copy sold at auction (in 1936) brought $210, copies brought only $25 and $50 in 1938–1939. In America, at least, *Last Words* (London, 1902) is a great rarity, but copies have attracted no special attention. The Quinn copy brought $5 in 1923 at the dawn of serious Crane collecting. The copy in the 1930 Union Square Bookshop auction brought $40 and a copy brought $50 at Swann in 1960. Two copies were offered in Scribner catalogues (Numbers 125, $5; 134, $17.50 in slipcase), and one with the Randall collection. Indeed, *Last Words* has been so underrated as a collector's item that until the publication of the Williams and Starrett bibliography in 1948, the ghost of the 1902 Philadelphia Coates edition stalked the Crane canon. *There is no known copy of a Coates edition of* Last Words.

The greatest Crane item of them all, the manuscript of *The Red Badge of Courage*, was a great flop. Dr. Rosenbach catalogued it in 1931 with no price, inviting inquiries. He recatalogued it in 1933 at $11,850. Again, nothing seems to have happened. It finally went to C. Waller Barrett in 1950 for a price reputed to be $6,000. This manuscript seems to be the clearest case of the Depression intimidating collectors.

Other Crane manuscript activity has been equally dull:
"The Snake" (5 pp.)—
Scott, 27 April 1916: $9.50
American Art–Anderson, 10 March 1924: $210.00
"The Shell and the Pine" (34 lines)—
Young, 31 March 1919: $55.00
Drake, 1920: $75.00
American Art–Anderson, 14–16 February 1927: $95.00
"A Great Mistake" (3 pp.)—
Romm, 4 March 1921: $22.50

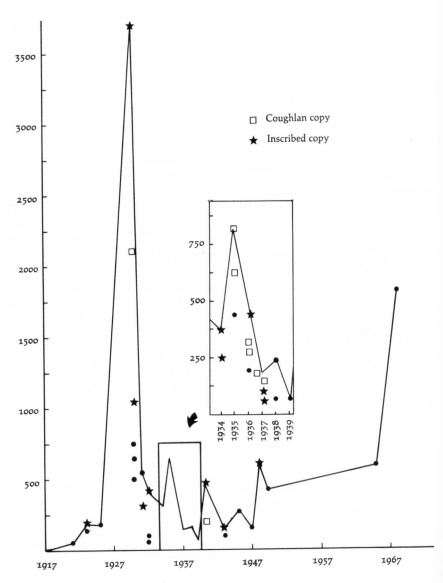

Plate 4. *Maggie* at auction.

"Raft Story"—
American Art–Anderson, March 1926: $230
The Red Badge of Courage (1½ pp.)—
American Art–Anderson, 21 October 1930: $37.50 (with book)
Rains, 21–22 April 1936: $70.00
"A Desertion" (2 pp.)—
American Art–Anderson, 23 January 1931: $17.50
Baker, 30 March 1939: $16.00
"In the Depths of a Coal Mine" (17 pp.)—
American Art–Anderson, 23 January 1931: $155.00
"An Ominous Baby" (1 p., with ALS)—
American Art–Anderson, 23 January 1931: $55.00
"The door clanged behind him"—
Ritter-Hopson, 24 March 1932: $17.50
"The Battle of Forty Fort" (3 pp.)—
American Art–Anderson, 22–23 April 1936: $130.00
"An Explosion of Seven Babies" (8 pp.)—
American Art–Anderson, 22–23 April 1936: $115.00
"The Storming of Badajos" (6 pp.)—
Scribner No. 132 (1946): $350.00
Scribner No. 136 (1950): $350.00

After *Maggie*, the best Crane item, in terms of literary value and collector appeal, is *The Black Riders and Other Lines*. In addition to the 500 trade copies, fifty copies were printed on Japan vellum in green ink—of which there were several specially bound copies, including perhaps three in goldstamped white vellum. This title has done well from the time a green ink copy brought $65 in the Quinn sale, but it has not been treated as a great collector's item. It turned up regularly between 1923 and 1948, with the top price being the $225 Goodspeed's asked for one of the three full-vellum copies. In 1968 William Young catalogued a green-ink copy at $750—and presumably offered the same copy again in 1970. The prospectus for *The Black Riders*—which preprints one poem—is a superb collector's item, but no copy seems to have been catalogued. Perhaps because it is a late book, *War Is Kind* (1899)—which is as rare as the trade copies of *The Black Riders*—has enjoyed comparatively little attention, even though it is a Johnson high spot.

Collections of Crane letters have not done well. In Scribner catalogue No. 122 (c. 1939) twenty-two autograph letters signed, three typewritten letters signed, and an autograph telegram were offered at $1,000. They were offered again in Scribner catalogue No. 125 (1941). Twenty-two Crane items were included in Goodspeed's catalogue No. 225 (1934) on the Nineties. The highlights were the manuscript of "Three little birds in a row" ($75) and three autograph letters signed to Copeland and Day about *The Black Riders* ($75, $45, $100 respectively). One of the three copies of the green-ink *Black Riders* bound in full vellum was catalogued at $225, a regular green-ink copy at $135, and a trade copy at $25. Other pieces of Crane correspondence with Copeland and Day were catalogued in *The Month at Goodspeed's* (September-October 1937), when eight autograph letters signed were offered at $350. Forty-two letters of tribute about Crane from Bennett, Conrad, Galsworthy, Lewis, etc., were sold for $60 at Parke-Bernet on 8 January 1941 and were resold there for $230 on 18 October 1955.

The Red Badge of Courage is a relatively common rare book at auction and in catalogues and is not worth tabulating here. Crane was not an active inscriber and no copy of *The Red Badge of Courage* with an important inscription has been sold. Although *The Red Badge of Courage* appears to be the first great American novel issued with a dust jacket, copies in jackets have not attracted special attention.[5] Indeed, the whole area of Crane dust jackets and even advance copies has been underemphasized. Except for *The Black Riders* and *War Is Kind,* all Crane books after *The Red Badge of Courage* were issued in jackets. The few advance copies that have turned up have not stimulated competition. In the November 1925 American Art–Anderson sale of some of Vincent Starrett's books, *The Little Regiment* in wrappers went for only $19 and *The Third Violet* in wrappers for only $25. As noted, Crane was not much of an inscriber. It is surprising then that a copy of *Active Service* with a good presentation inscription to Curtis Brown, one of Crane's agents, was catalogued five separate times at $100 by Scribner (catalogues Nos. 109, 116, 122, 125, and 130). This copy brought $30 at the Morris Parrish sale (Parke-Bernet, 13 March 1938).

It is fair to say that Crane activity in the rare book market has been routine. On the basis of catalogue evidence, dealers and collectors have concentrated on a few high spots and have overlooked or underrated some exciting items. In terms of simple rarity, *Novels and Stories. Free Number* [1896?] is a splendid collector's item, but no copy seems to have been catalogued—and the same for the program of *The Ghost.* The English editions of Crane are extremely important for bibliographical reasons. For example, the Heinemann edition of *The Open Boat and Other Stories* has nine stories not in the Doubleday and McClure edition, and the English editions of *Active Service, Wounds in the Rain, The Monster* and *Whilomville Stories* were published simultaneously with the American editions and have special textual significance. Moreover, the Colonial printings and issues of these English editions are great rarities.[6] Just try to find the Bell's Indian & Colonial Library (London and Bombay, 1901) issue of *Great Battles of the World* in wrappers.

If dealers and Crane collectors have not educated each other in the half century of Crane collecting, it may be because Crane scholars have not educated them. Apart from the interest that resulted from the 1923 publications of Beer and Starrett, there does not seem to be any correlation between Crane scholarship and Crane collecting. The 1925–1927 Wilson Follett *Work of Stephen Crane* in twelve volumes did not sell well. The Williams and Starrett bibliography (1948) and the Stallman biography (1968) did not stimulate Crane collecting. It is too early to tell what effect the University of Virginia Edition of the Works of Stephen Crane will have. The most comprehensive Crane

Matthew J. Bruccoli

exhibition ever mounted, at Columbia University in 1956—for which there was a published catalogue—had no discernible effect on Crane collecting.[7] The 1960–1965 Index volume of *American Book-Prices Current* lists eighteen books by Crane sold at auction; and volume 3 of *Bookman's Price Index* lists sixteen Crane books catalogued by dealers in 1968.

Perhaps it takes an exciting sale to excite collectors and dealers—as, for instance, the 1958 Guffey sale stimulated the Hemingway market. But the best Crane material is permanently in institutional collections, and most of the material to come will also go into institutions. It is unlikely that there will be a revival of Crane collecting.[8]

Appendixes

I. *Maggie: A Girl of the Streets* At Auction

1.	1917	Anderson; 11 April	$ 7.50
2.	1921	American Art; 4 March	40
3.	1923	Anderson; 13 February	135
		Inscribed	
4.		Anderson; 12–14 November	115
		Quinn sale	
5.	1925	American Art; 29 January	130
		Same as copy 4	
6.	1930	American Art–Anderson; 11–12 March	3,700
		Inscribed to Button	
7.		American Art–Anderson; 12–13 May	2,100
		Coughlan copy	
8.		American Art–Anderson; 21 October	500
9.		American Art–Anderson; 27 October	
		Inscribed to Hubbard	1,125
10.		Another copy	775
11.		Sotheby; 10 November	£130

166

12.	1931	Newark; 15 October	550
13.		American Art–Anderson; 19–20 November	230
		Inscribed to L. S. Linson *	
14.	1932	American Art–Anderson; 9 February	85
15.		American Art–Anderson; 19–21 April	90
16.		Ritter-Hopson; 15 December	400
		Inscribed to Tabor	
17.	1934	Union Art; 25–26 April	320
		Same as copy 13	
18.		American Art–Anderson; 5–6 December	210
		Inscribed to DeWitt Miller	
19.	1935	American Art–Anderson; 24–25 April	700
		Coughlan disclosure	
20.		American Art–Anderson; 13–14 November	475
		Coughlan copy	
21.		Rains; 12–13 December	335
22.	1936	Rains; 27–28 January	400
		Same as copy 13	
23.		Rains; 25–26 March	140
		"Coffin W. Linson" copy †	
24.		American Art–Anderson; 22–23 April	275
		Coughlan copy	
25.		American Art–Anderson; 9–10 December	280
		Coughlan copy	
26.	1937	American Art–Anderson; 28–29 January	130
		Inscribed to Arthur D. Ferguson	
27.		American Art–Anderson; 14–15 April	150
		Coughlan copy	

---

* This copy was subsequently twice catalogued by Scribner.

† Not inscribed. The catalogue notes: "This copy was presented by Crane to his friend Coffin W. Linson [Corwin K. Linson] who has written on the back strip: 'FIRST EDITION OF FIRST NOVEL OF STEPHEN CRANE—GIVEN ME BY HIM IN 1893—COFFIN W. LINSON.'"

28.		American Art–Anderson; 11–12 November	150
		Coughlan copy	
29.		American Art–Anderson; 23–24 November	95
		Same as copy 18	
30.	1938	American Art–Anderson; 22–23 March	175
31.		American Art–Anderson; 12–13 December	85
32.	1939	Parke-Bernet; 15–16 November	90
33.	1940	Parke-Bernet; 4–5 January	450
		Inscribed to Paul Lemperly	
34.		Parke-Bernet; 8–9 May	180
		One of four remaining Coughlan copies	
35.	1943	City Book; September	170
		Same as copy 23	
36.		City Book; December	195
		Presentation copy, signed twice	
37.	1945	Parke-Bernet; 23–24 January	275
38.	1947	Parke-Bernet; 13 January	170
39.	1948	Parke-Bernet; 1 March	600
		Same as copy 18(?)	
40.	1949	Parke-Bernet; 26–27 April	425
41.	1965	Parke-Bernet; 7 December	625
42.	1968	Parke-Bernet; 21–22 May	1,900

II. *Maggie* in Dealers' Catalogues

Randall #1 (1934)	part of collection
Argus #213 (1936?)	$ 350
Scribner #117 (1937)–rebound and inscribed	225
Scribner #122 (c. 1939)–same copy	225
Scribner #125 (1941)	450
Collectors' Bookshop (1942)	200
Scribner #130 (c. 1944)	450
7 Gables #23 (1947)	275
7 Gables (1954)	500
ABAA #4 (1957)	145
7 Gables (1965)	$1,000

Stephen Crane as a Collector's Item

III. *Maggie:* A Census*

1. CSmH 43715 Inscribed: "With compliments. Stephen Crane. Nov 5, 1895." In Anderson Galleries Sale 1709 (13–14 February 1923), item 61. Provenience: David G. Joyce.
2. CtW Dav. 13 Amer. C89m.
3. CtY Yale Collection of American Literature Za. C8501.893. Provenience: Thomas Beer.
4. InU Lilly PS 1449 .C85M3 1893. Inscribed: "It is inevitable that you be greatly shocked by this book but continue, please, with all possible courage to the end. For it tries to show that environment is a tremendous thing in the world and frequently shapes lives regardless. If one proves that theory, one makes room in Heaven for all sorts of souls (notably an occasional street girl) who are not confidently expected to be there by many excellent people.

   It is probable that the reader of this small thing may consider the author to be a bad man, but obviously that is a matter of small consequence to

   The Author." A note in Hamlin Garland's hand appears on the inside back wrapper: "Hamlin Garland's Book[.] MAGGIE. The first Copy Crane sent to me. probably about Oct. #92—H. G." Provenience: Hamlin Garland–Josiah K. Lilly.
5. MH*AC85 .C8507 .893. Inscribed: "My dear Tabor: I wrote this book when I was very young so if you dont like it, shut up. But my best wishes go with it. Stephen Crane." Pencil corrections of errata in an unidentified hand. Provenience: Harry P. Taber.
6. NhD Stephen Crane Collection. Unopened. Provenience: George Matthew Adams.
7. NN Berg Collection. Inscribed: "To Mr Franklin Garland from his friend." A note by Hamlin Garland appears on the back flyleaf, and a two-page holograph by him is inserted. Provenience: Franklin Garland–B. George Ulizio–W. T. H. Howe–Albert Berg.

8. NNC Special Collections B812C85 T3 1893. Unopened. Provenience: Clifton Waller Barrett.
9. NNU Fales Library, Division of Special Collections. Inscribed: "To Jim Moser from Stephen Crane. May his smile blossom like an electric light for many years. May his genial words string together like amber beads for many more years. And may he not die before he gets 'good and ready.' Gordon's Studio, New York, Nov 14, 1894" Rebound. Provenience: James Moser–John Stuart Groves.
10. NSyU Rare Book Department PS 1449 C85 M19. Inscribed: "To my friend Charles J. Pike Stephen Crane May 10th, 1896." Inserted is a note in Pike's hand: "How I came into possession of my copy of 'Maggie' (1st edition) by Stephen Crane. I knew Crane intimately. He lived for eighteen months or more with me, in my studio on the third floor front of the old building that stood just where the Sachs building now stands—on the corner of 33rd St. and 6th Ave New York. My copy of 'Maggie' was Stephen Crane's own personal signed copy, which he occasionally opened. He had promised to give me a copy of 'Maggie,' but being unable to find a new one, he ultimately gave me his own— after he had inscribed it, and drawn the two wavy lines on the front cover. The book was in about the same condition then as it is today, except that the covers were not broken away from the binding. On first reading it, I noticed (on the upper margin of one of the pages) a few small drops of ink. Evidently dropt by Crane himself. Otherwise the book is in good condition, and the inscription and signatures are as bright as when he wrote them. Although I cannot prove it, I have always believed that this copy of 'Maggie' was the last (1st edition) Stephen Crane ever owned and used personally.
    April 1st 1930. Charles J. Pike, Clinton Conn.," Provenience: Charles J. Pike–George Arents.
11. OU Rare Book Room. Provenience: Corwin Knapp Linson.
12. PBL 818.4 C891m 1893 T. Unopened.
13. PEL Stephen Crane Collection (Vault). Inscribed: "It is indeed a brave new binding and I wish the inside were braver.
    Stephen Crane
    Mr DeWitt Miller
    July 3d, 96."
American Art Association–Anderson Galleries Sale 4135 (5–6 December

1934) item 85; in Scribners Catalogue 117 (*Scribners Present The Modern Library in First Editions;* 1938), item 53. Rebound to include extra leaves by R. Clarke & Co., Cincinnati, Ohio. Clippings pasted in. Provenience: DeWitt Miller–Clifton Waller Barrett.

14. PU AC85 C8503 893m. Lacks wrappers.
15. Donald Stralem (New York, New York). Unopened. Provenience: Florence Crane Coughlan.
16. Robert H. Taylor (Princeton, New Jersey). Unopened. Provenience: Wallack–Cohn–Propper.
17. O Kent C. Unopened. Provenience: B. George Ulizio.
18. ViU C. W. Barrett Library * PS 1449 .C85M3 1893. Inscribed: " 'And the wealth of the few shall be built up on the patience of the poor.' Prophecy not made BC 1090
    Stephen Crane
    New York
    Aug. 29, 1896." Transcribed and reproduced in Baum, *Exhibition,* pp. 15–16; transcribed, with an error, in Stallman and Gilkes, *Letters,* p. 129. Provenience: Clifton Waller Barrett.
19. ViU Tracy W. McGregor Library *A 1893 .C7M3. Signature of William H. Crane. Listed in Scribner Catalogue 125. Provenience: William Howe Crane–Florence Crane Coughlan–Tracy W. McGregor.
20. Matthew J. Bruccoli (Columbia, South Carolina). Provenience: Florence Crane Coughlan–Charles E. Feinberg.
21. Unlocated. In Argus Book Shop (Chicago) List No. 213, item 1. Inscribed: "To Cortlandt St. John by William H. Crane, 'steenth cousin and brother of Stephen Crane, the author, March 31st, 1905."
22. Unlocated. Noted in John Howard Birss, "Stephen Crane: Letter and Bibliographical Note," *Notes and Queries* (7 October 1933): 243: "It is recorded in Henkel's catalogue (No. 934, item 830) for the auction sale of the William Ritter collection of autograph letters and historical documents." Accompanying the book was a letter, dated 22 March 1893, to the critic Julius F. Chambers noting that it was sent to him at the suggestion of Hamlin Garland and requesting criticism of it. Provenience: Julius F. Chambers.
23. Unlocated. Inscribed: "Stephen Crane to Budgon. It is inevitable that you be greatly shocked by this book but continue, please, with all possible courage, to the end. For it tries to show that environment is a

tremendous thing in the world and frequently shapes lives regardless. If one proves that theory, one makes room in Heaven for all sorts of souls, notably an occasional street girl, who are not confidently expected to be there by many excellent people. It is probable that the reader of this small thing may consider the author to be a bad man, but obviously that is a matter of small consequence to The Author." Reproduced and transcribed in the American Art Association-Anderson Galleries catalogue for Sale Number 3827, 11 and 12 March 1930, where it was item 76 and was described with a note that includes the following: "Some time before the publication of 'Maggie', Crane took up residence at a boarding house in Eastern Avenue where lived a group of young medical men. Here began the friendship between the young reporter and Lucius L. Button. Not long after, Crane, discouraged by the innumerable rejections of 'Maggie,' and having come into the possession of about a thousand dollars, determined to issue it in a cheap, paperbacked form designed to appeal to those who were dependent upon the newsstands for literary nourishment. THE FIRST COPY FROM THE BINDERY HE BROUGHT HOME AND PRESENTED TO BUTTON. Although the presentation of the book was accepted, it was not gratis, as Button insisted upon the privilege of being the first to purchase the little book and dutifully paid its author fifty cents. Such is the history of this book as related by Mrs. Button." Dr. Rosenbach bought this copy for $3,700—the record price for a *Maggie*. Provenience: Lucius L. Button– A. S. W. Rosenbach.

24. ICU.
25. MWiW–C
26. NN
27. TxU C85m. 1893. Inscribed: "My dear Hubbard: This tawdry thing will make you understand the full import of the words: 'It is more blessed to give than to receive.' I am very sensible of the truth of the sentence when I give book of mine I am always your friend. Stephen Crane."

NOTES

1. David Randall, *Dukedom Large Enough* (New York: Random House, 1969), pp. 220–29.

2. This typescript brought $450 at the Parke-Bernet sale, 21–23 May 1968.

3. Herbert Faulkner West, *A Stephen Crane Collection* (Hanover: Dartmouth College, Library, 1948).

4. "My Adventures with Stephen Crane," *The Bookseller's and Print Dealer's Weekly* (8 December 1927): 6.

5. In Canner catalogue #484 (1967) a copy in dust jacket was offered at $400— but with a puzzling statement that the first printing of *The Red Badge of Courage* was issued without the jacket. No evidence is supplied for this statement.

6. Matthew J. Bruccoli and Joseph Katz, "Scholarship and Mere Artifacts: The British Empire Publications of Stephen Crane," *Studies in Bibliography* 22 (1969): 277–87.

7. Joan H. Baum, *Stephen Crane (1871–1900)* (New York: Columbia University Libraries, 1956).

8. My thanks to C. E. Frazer Clark, Jr., John S. Van E. Kohn, Marcus McCorison, Charles Mann, Harold Graves, Walter Goldwater, and Roger Stoddard.

Joseph Katz

Theodore Dreiser and Stephen Crane: Studies in a Literary Relationship

A couple of weeks before "The Red Badge of Courage" made its debut as newspaper fiction, Theodore Dreiser went to New York to look for a job on a paper. To his dismay he discovered that the credentials he had developed during two years on Midwestern papers counted for little on Park Row. In November 1894 that street was a magnet attracting reporters from every part of the country, and they competed fiercely for even the bottom rung of the ladder. Luckier than most, Dreiser managed to find space-rate work on the *New York World*. That was very near the bottom, with his salary dependent on the column length of what was printed. But even there Dreiser could not hang on, and he soon found himself on the Row looking for another place. Just as he realized he probably wouldn't find one, however, another kind of opportunity opened up, and he seized it. By September 1895, when *The Red Badge of Courage* appeared in book form, Dreiser no longer was a reporter but the editor of *Ev'ry Month*, a magazine he was struggling to create for his brother's music publishing house.

Those were hard years for Dreiser, but they were important ones too, and he often thought about them afterwards. Twenty-seven years later, when he was the most controversial figure in American literature, he recalled that the decision to turn his career had been inspired by "those new arrivals in the world of letters: Kipling, Richard Harding Davis, Stephen Crane and some others, whose success fascinated me."[1] Few scholars have considered the implications of this statement. Of those who have done so, most are in general agreement with F. O. Matthiessen that although Dreiser "printed one of Crane's stories, 'A Mystery of Heroism,' in *Ev'ry Month,* he seems never to have had any feeling of close kinship with Crane's work."[2]

That judgment is wrong. The evidence points in precisely the opposite direction, indicating that Dreiser came across Crane's work almost immediately upon Dreiser's arrival in New York, and that he decided to follow it closely thereafter. Crane's work evidently stirred a number of things within him. As Dreiser's *A Book About Myself* suggests, Crane's dramatic rise because of *The Red Badge of Courage* became for Dreiser a paradigm for success, a glittering affirmation of the newspaperman's dream of the rewards that could come from writing The Great American Novel. Crane's other work demonstrated the truth in another aspect of this dream, that renowned literature might be created from journalistic materials by introducing in them only apparently slight modifications. But there is another side to Dreiser's reactions to Stephen Crane and his work, and it is a major reason Dreiser's debt to them has been unconsidered so long. Dreiser soon came to see Crane not only as an exemplar, but also as an inexplicably more successful competitor. "Something rankled," was the feeling Dorothy Dudley had from her talks with him during the Twenties and Thirties. "Perhaps it was jealousy dating from that lonely day, when he was an outcast from the World, and Crane was known as a favorite of Howells and Garland, and was being sent here and there on assignments."[3] Surely it was jealousy, or something very like it, for even while Dreiser publicly constructed a figure of Crane as the archetypical realist who suffered at the hands of the Philistines, he privately displayed reservations that colored his attitude. Certainly his reaction to Crane was complex and ambivalent, yet strong. It involved both an important set of literary borrowings and a crucial influence in his development as a writer.

I

Although Dreiser saw possibilities for his own career in the examples of those other newspapermen who struggled into the world of literature, the way he realized those possibilities was uniquely his own. As its quondam subtitle—*An Illustrated Magazine of Literature and Popular Music*—suggests, he had to make *Ev'ry Month* a magazine that would serve two distinct purposes. Howley, Haviland & Co., the music publishers in which his brother Paul Dresser was third partner and front man, wanted it to push sales of their sheet music. But evidently that was of secondary importance to Dreiser who had his own interests and wanted to learn "what a magazine was." [4] As soon as he did, this fundamental uncongeniality of aims would provoke a split that sent him away from his magazine and his brother; but for the time being it actually worked to his advantage. Since they considered it a subsidiary operation, the publishers insisted on economies that forced Dreiser to run the magazine as a one-man show. In the beginning he wrote most of the material himself, but even after he could draw regularly on outside contributors, *Ev'ry Month* remained tightly in his control, expressing his own vision of it.

He was especially slow to relinquish the literary column, perhaps because it was an opportunity to form a theory of literature through reactions to his current reading. The May 1896 "Literary Notes," the earliest of his known references to Crane, was a typical example of that technique. "Novels! Novels! A month sees no end of them, good, bad and indifferent," began his dissection of Elizabeth Stuart Phelps's *A Singular Life*, a popular novel that he thought "has no charms."

However, dismissing all this half-writing to the winds, it is pleasant to think of Stephen Crane and his splendid war story, *The Red Badge of Courage*. Here is a novelist for you, if you want an American; strong, incisive, bitter and brilliant, who has the genius which perceives and appreciates (without physical experience to any great extent) and which expresses sentiments that are nothing, if not the whisperings of an over-soul. He never could have witnessed personally what he writes of, and his heart is too young, too free and enthusiastic, to have ever raged with such wondrous fear and frantic terror as swells in the heart of his hero. This is not necessarily paradoxical for some hearts seem to grow out of graves of the anguished dead, and to throb with all the griefs and passions that went to the soil with the body when it ceased its toil and cares. It is not strange nor inconceivable, that in a land so torn by discord and battle as has been this union of ours; so haunted with memories of the many who went and never came back, who loved and fought, struggled and fell and now lie in lone, uncared for graves, that there should rise a heart made up of the memories and bitterness of the past, and throbbing with a deep, innate sentiment for all the old woes and old terrors. It is not strange, but rather to be expected, and Stephen Crane, the first, is not necessarily the greatest nor last, for the mighty woes of the rebellion have not yet dwindled into a song nor a story, either. Crane is brilliant, *The Red Badge of Courage*, a proud effort, but it is only one novel after all, and this earth has had its battles by scores and multi-scores, while the human heart has been wrung as only the dead know or could tell, were they permitted to live again and speak.[5]

Illustrating these remarks was a photograph of Crane reproduced from the *Bookman*. Dreiser's caption for it was: "This is the author of the now famous *Red Badge of Courage*, who is not quite twenty-four years of age. He seems to possess a complete knowledge of the sentiments which actuate men in battle."

The pages of *Ev'ry Month* reflect Dreiser's preoccupation with defining the place of fiction in the scheme of literature. A few months after he reviewed *The Red Badge of Courage* he urged his readers to postpone their attention to novels until they had undergone a course of study that would stretch intellect and sensibility. First read popular works on science to gain facts of the world, then history for perspective on it, then evolutionary philosophers to refine judgment of it—and afterwards all literature would hold much more meaning.[6] Dreiser was here pursuing the speculations that would develop into the philosophy underlying his fiction later. Essentially, this philosophy was based on the evolutionary Utilitarianism of Herbert Spencer, whose work he had discovered just before moving to New York. Spencer's emphasis on a dynamic universe in which individualism and science were the keys is reflected quietly in a column Dreiser published in *Ev'ry Month* a few issues before he reviewed *The Red Badge of Courage*. Speaking of historical fiction, he expressed the view that it was valuable because it could translate history into terms that would interest the common reader. Too many historical writings are dull, and most people follow the path of least resistance. Historical fiction "is fine—it is making us understand all that has ever happened in the world. . . . We are nearing the time when every sentiment will have been portrayed and every period and every event will have been told simply and colorfully, so that all may understand."[7]

That is perspective on his review of Crane's novel. The emphasis on the writer's youth in the photograph caption was, of course, a common note struck by most reviewers and encouraged by Crane. For Dreiser its significance may have been in making him think of his own status. But most significant of all is that although Dreiser displayed reservations about the novel's achievement, in the context of the review he linked its author with his literary idol, Balzac. "*There* was a novelist, for you! There was a man who knew the human heart, proud, foolish, self-glorifying, self-abasing, and one who never ridiculed it nor traduced it, but simply presented its trials and contentions, how it developed, loved, hated and died. Grand, gorgeous, self-conscious Balzac, the Alexander of literature, in whom romance and realism blend and become one! Oh, what a school are his novels to the well-balanced heart!"

From this time on, Crane was much on Dreiser's mind. By the fall of 1896 *Ev'ry Month* was producing enough revenue from subscriptions and advertising for him to begin buying an occasional story from syndicate backlists. The first of these was "A Mystery of Heroism," Crane's ironic war tale that had been distributed by the Bacheller Syndicate the year before, which went into two full pages in September. But just as there was an undercurrent of restraint in his praise of *The Red Badge of Courage*, Dreiser's endorsement now was tempered when, a few pages later, he remarked of Mary E. Wilkins that "unlike Stephen Crane . . . she has refrained from writing night and day, which accounts for the fact that the public knows comparatively less about her."[8] This ambivalent attitude is a feature of most comments by Dreiser on Crane. In November, for example, his piece on The Yellow Kid cartoonist R. F. Outcault implied that Crane was a literary meteor who soon might burn out: "Every once in a while there is some one who rises above the crowd, someone who makes what is termed 'a metropolitan success.' One time it is an unheard of dramatist whose despairing effort succeeds and then all New York flocks to see his play, and buys all the papers to read what is said of him, and he is—famous. . . . Again it is the writer, like Stephen Crane. . . ."[9]

Dreiser had become concerned with the problem of artistic recognition during the same period in which he became interested in Stephen Crane, so perhaps it was inevitable that the two became linked in his mind. Recognition is a major theme in *Ev'ry Month* from its earliest issues. He had begun by lamenting the propensity of American heiresses for titled European husbands, then came to argue against the uncritical admiration Americans gave Europe's art. From these seeds blossomed Dreiser's belief that the dominant American culture was materialistic and that this worked the defeat of the native artist. Although privately he seems to have felt that Crane had skyrocketed into prominence above his merits, in May 1897 he made Crane the first protagonist in this conflict. "It is high time America developed an opinion of its own, and ceased following after the opinion of Europe," he insisted. "If a book is 'out' in America that is nothing much toward

its popularity, however fascinating, with Americans. It may drift unnoticed for months, as did Stephen Crane's 'Red Badge of Courage,'
until some English literary paper of recognized standing discovers it,
and gives it a sendoff." [10] Dreiser retained Crane in this role for a
quarter-century, publicly making Crane a surrogate of his own problems with recognition when he wrote a letter to be read at Ceremonies
honoring Crane in 1921.

In October 1896, however, Dreiser had surrendered the literary
column of *Ev'ry Month* to George C. Jenks, a free-lance writer. Jenks
shared Dreiser's mixed fascination with Crane. In his first piece for
the magazine he ended by comparing Crane with Clinton Ross,
another young former newspaperman making a stir with his stories:
"The only thing that puzzles me in his fiction is whether he is an imi-
tator of Stephen Crane, or vice versa." [11] So literary talk in the *Ev'ry
Month* office must have often touched on Crane. If Dreiser's remarks
show general trends in those conversations, Jenks's give something
of their specifics. Although Dreiser wrote of Crane only as the author
of war stories, Jenks revealed a wider knowledge that must have been
shared by his editor. Reviewing the recent book collection of six Crane
war stories, including "A Mystery of Heroism," he showed his ground-
ing in Crane's slum novels:

> Looking over Stephen Crane's last new book, *The Little Regi-
> ment*, I see that it is full of the martial fire and noise that we
> found in his *Red Badge of Courage*. This is well. Crane can shoot
> a gun and lead a bayonet charge in a book with the best writers
> that I know. He heads a forlorn hope with the dashing chivalry
> of a Balaklava charge, and, like our greatest general, "he never
> counts his dead." All this is delightful in a book. No one is hurt,
> and our savage instincts for bloodshed are indulged to the point of
> satiety. But I am still of the opinion that Stephen Crane is equally
> strong when he produces a melodrama of the streets as he is amid
> the carnage of the battlefield. Therefore, I am pleased to see that
> his *Maggie: A Girl of the Streets* is in its fourth edition. I have

maintained, with scores of critics opposing me, that this book is one of the most moving pictures of a certain phase of city life that has ever been painted in letter-press. And Crane's other work on the same lines, *George's Mother*, is equally good, if not better.[12]

Jenks explained that position in his ambitious three-part series, "Some Views of Fiction." The first part, "The Perfervid Type," appeared in February 1897, and discussed Crane's slum writing as the exemplar of current literary style and interests.

In the feverish battle for new effects in literature, there has sprung up a class of writers who invest the utterly commonplace with romanticism by sheer force of oddity of expression. One of the prominent exemplars of the perfervid in every day narrative is Stephen Crane. Setting aside his "Red Badge of Courage," in which the clash of arms and the fierce scent of gunpowder are *sui generis*, we find in his sketches of the squalid life of the city, where the beings he introduces are sordidly miserable, that he lets his pen burst forth into explosive battle-pieces of description that some critics have declared to be out of all proportion to the subject. That is a matter of opinion. It is not apparent that a writer violates any of the canons of taste or literary facility in using the most dramatic language at his command to tell his story.

The importance of his work is largely defined by his manner of doing it. We may tell of an old woman sweeping her one poor room, of her washing dishes and teacups, of her shaking out a tablecloth and taking the ashes out of her stove, and tell it in such a way that it is tedious and uninteresting. Or we may, as does Mr. Crane, tell of the thunderous charge of that old woman with her broom couched for strenuous strife, of her clashing her dishes and teacups martially, flaunting the tablecloth to the breeze banner-wise, and sending up clouds of rolling smoke from her stove.

Mr. Crane does this in his much-discussed book, "George's

Mother." The poor old woman lives her life in her tenement room, and to her the daily labor she performs is as fateful as the movement of armies by a commander-in-chief. Why should she not do it with a free swing, and why should not Mr. Crane invest it with a halo of adventure that accords with the spirit of warlike determination with which she manages her household?

Probably the old woman is only dimly conscious of the clarion note she strikes. She only knows that she is energetic, and that physical striving is part of her being. She expends her vitality in the only way of which she is cognizant, and pushes her campaign against her sworn enemies, dirt and disorder, because she has no others. If Mr. Crane can see that there is such a campaign, and that it is worthy of his most flamboyant colors in painting the picture of it, then he is all the greater artist.

A graphic example of the latent poetry in the most commonplace of conditions is afforded by Mr. Crane in one of his latest sketches, "The Men in the Storm," in the January "Philistine." He begins by saying:

"The blizzard began to swirl great clouds of snow along the streets, sweeping it down from the roofs and up from the pavements, until the faces of pedestrians tingled and burned as from a thousand needle-prickings."

After showing, in a turmoil of imagery, what rampant discomfort comes with a heavy snowstorm, he takes up the more interesting element of human nature, beginning thus: "There was an absolute expression of hot dinners in the pace of the people. If one dared to speculate upon the destination of those who came trooping, he lost himself in a maze of social calculations; he might fling a handful of sand and attempt to follow the flight of each particular grain. But as to the suggestion of hot dinners, he was in firm lines of thought, for it was upon every hurrying face. It is a matter of tradition; it is from the tales of childhood. It comes forth with every storm." [13]

It is not surprising, then, that in the concluding part of the series, "Authors Old and New," Jenks concluded that "Stephen Crane, with his wild stories of battle afield and griping poverty at home," is in the mainstream of literature.[14] Dreiser probably agreed.

II

Tension between the aims Dreiser had for *Ev'ry Month* and those of its publisher became irreconcilable by the second anniversary of the magazine's birth. Dreiser wanted more money and more control; Howley, Haviland & Co. disagreed. The result was a split. Although Dreiser evidently edited the October 1897 issue before he left, his name for the first time does not appear on its masthead. His career had entered a new phase. From the fall of 1897 until the time in 1904 when he took a minor editorial job on the *New York Daily News*, he was a freelance writer, hacking out hundreds of things, often appropriating material along the way. In his constant and largely successful effort to keep the pot boiling, he did not forget Stephen Crane.

It is odd that although both men moved through the same world, even along the same streets, there is no evidence that they ever met. But there is evidence that they knew the same people. Three of the people Dreiser knew also had been in contact with Crane. Charles Michelson, a reporter for the *New York Journal*, was in Jacksonville, Florida, with Crane when *Ev'ry Month* published Michelson's "A Romance of Feathers" in January 1897. Michelson was one of those New York newspapermen on whom Dreiser depended for contributions to his magazine, and later, at least, when the Cuban insurrection burst into the Spanish-American War, Michelson knew Crane well. William Louis Sonntag, Jr. was an artist whom Dreiser sought out in the fall of 1896 for a color illustration in *Ev'ry Month* that December, and whose career Dreiser followed closely during the following months in which their acquaintance deepened. He must have known that early in July 1897 Sonntag rode the London & North Western and the Caledonian railroads with Crane to illustrate "The Scotch

Express." It might have been lapse of memory that made him write that Sonntag's drawings were for "one of Kipling's fast express stories which one of the magazines published," because they weren't.[15] Mary Annabel Fanton, an editor of *Demorest's Family Magazine*, published both Crane and Dreiser. When *Ev'ry Month* was reviewing *The Red Badge of Courage*, *Demorest's* was publishing a long letter it had solicited from Crane on his life and art; and while *Ev'ry Month* published "A Mystery of Heroism," *Demorest's* did "A Gray Sleeve."[16] In its last two years of publication, 1898–1899, the ladies' magazine also published nineteen of Dreiser's free-lanced pieces. Among them was "Curious Shifts of the Poor" which appeared in November 1899.[17]

"Curious Shifts of the Poor" is one of the seminal works in the Dreiser canon. Subtitled "Strange Ways of Relieving Desperate Poverty.—Last Resources of New York's Most Pitiful Mendicants," the piece is a series of four interrelated sketches. In the first, the subject is the Captain who nightly begs the price of paupers' beds from passersby in the theatre district; the second describes the luncheon charity of the Sisters of Mercy mission on Fifteenth Street; the third depicts a group of men formed in front of a Bowery lodging house, pelted by snow while they wait to rent a cheap bed for the night; and the fourth tells of the midnight bread distribution at Fleischmann's Vienna Model Bakery on Broadway and Tenth Street. "Curious Shifts of the Poor" is seminal in part because Dreiser drew on these sketches again and again for later work. As late as 1923, in *The Color of a Great City*, he had revised the bakery and Bowery house scenes into "The Bread-Line" and "The Men in the Storm." And he had used "The Men in the Storm" at least twice before then: once as one of "Three Sketches of the Poor" for a 1913 newspaper feature and once in *Sister Carrie*.[18]

But Dreiser had not created "The Men in the Storm." He had borrowed it from Crane. After one of Crane's prowls through New York's demimonde in February 1894 he set down his description of the defeated, and he called it "The Men in the Storm." First published in the *Arena* that October, then reprinted in the January 1897 *Philistine*, it finally was collected in the London edition of *The Open Boat and Other Stories* in 1898. Dreiser could have seen its first appearance very easily. When he arrived in New York he studied the magazines to learn what New Yorkers bought. B. O. Flower's crusades were much-discussed then; and if Dreiser had not already seen the latest issue of his *Arena* before his train arrived in New York, there were copies on waiting-room tables once he reached there. Certainly, however, once the *Philistine* published Crane's sketch again, Dreiser knew about it: George C. Jenks had lavished praise upon it in *Ev'ry Month* that February 1897.

The internal evidence of a source relationship between Dreiser's sketch and Crane's is conclusive. Both can be summarized the same way. Each begins on a winter afternoon with a heavy snowfall layering the streets, hurrying respectable pedestrians along their way while homeless men drift towards a bed-house. The snow takes on greater force as the crowd of derelicts increases, trying the men to keep warm until they are admitted to the house. With no other aim they mill about—jostling each other, commenting on things outside their world, and occasionally giving false notice that the door is about to open. When it finally does, they stampede through it like cattle. The scene ends with that. The two sketches differ only slightly in details: Crane's men are in front of a West Side charitable house, Dreiser's in front of a Bowery flophouse; Crane's are contrasted with an affluent shopkeeper across the street, Dreiser's with a man passing comfortably in a vehicle; Crane's men are rewarded small, with a meager breakfast and a bed, Dreiser's even smaller, with just the bed. The relationship between the two sketches is obvious: [19]

DREISER

It was a winter evening. Already, at four o'clock, the sombre hue of night was thickening the air. A heavy snow was falling— a fine, picking, whipping snow, borne forward by a swift wind in long, thin lines. The street was bedded with it, six inches of cold, soft carpet, churned brown by the crush of teams and the feet of men. Along the Bowery, men slouched through it with collars up and hats pulled over their ears.

Before a dirty four-story building gathered a crowd of men. It began with the approach of two or three, who hung about the closed wooden doors, and beat their feet to keep them warm. They made no effort to go in, but shifted ruefully about digging their hands deep in their pockets, and leering at the crowd and the increasing lamps. There were old men with grizzled beards and sunken eyes; men who were comparatively young, but shrunken by disease; men who were middle-aged.

With the growth of the crowd about the door came a murmur. It was not conversation, but a running comment directed at anyone in general. It contained oaths and slang phrases.

"I wisht they'd hurry up."

"Look at the copper watchin'."

"Maybe it ain't winter, nuther."

"I wisht I was with Otis."

Now a sharper lash of wind cut down, and they huddled closer. There was no anger, no threatening words. It was all sullen endurance, unlightened by either wit or good fellowship.

A carriage went jingling by with some reclining figure in it. One of the members nearest the door saw it.

"Look at the bloke ridin'."

"He ain't so cold."

"Eh! Eh! Eh!" yelled another, the carriage having long since passed out of hearing.

Little by little the night crept on. Along the walk a crowd turned out on its way home. Still the men hung around the door, unwavering.

"Ain't they ever goin' to open up?" queried a hoarse voice suggestively.

This seemed to renew general interest in the closed door, and many gazed in that direction. They looked at it as dumb brutes look, as dogs paw and whine and study the knob. They shifted and blinked and muttered, now a curse, now a comment. Still they waited, and still the snow whirled and cut them.

A glimmer appeared through the transom overhead, where someone was lighting the gas. It sent a thrill of possibility through the watcher. On the old hats and peaked shoulders snow was piling. It gathered in little heaps and curves, and no one brushed it off. In the center of the crowd the warmth and steam melted it, and water trickled off hat-rims and down noses which the owners could not reach to scratch. On the outer rim the piles remained unmelted. Those who could not get in the center lowered their heads to the weather and bent their forms.

At last the bars grated inside and the crowd pricked up its ears. There was someone who called, "Slow up there now!" and then the door opened. It was push and jam for a minute, with grim, beast silence to prove its quality, and then the crowd lessened. It melted inward like logs floating, and disappeared. There were wet hats and shoulders, a cold, shrunken, disgruntled mass, pouring in between bleak walls. It was just six o'clock, and there was supper in every hurrying pedestrian's face.

"Do you sell anything to eat here?" questioned one of the grizzled old carpet-slippers who opened the door.

"No; nothin' but beds."

The waiting throng had been housed.

CRANE

At about three o'clock of the February afternoon, the blizzard began to swirl great clouds of snow along the streets, sweeping it down from the roofs and up from the pavements until the faces of pedestrians tingled and burned as from a thousand needle-prickings. Those on the walks huddled their necks closely in the

collars of their coats and went along stooping like a race of aged
people. The drivers of vehicles hurried their horses furiously on
their way. They were made more cruel by the exposure of their
positions, aloft on high seats. The street cars, bound up-town,
went slowly, the horses slipping and straining in the spongy brown
mass that lay between the rails. The drivers, muffled to the eyes,
stood erect and facing the wind, models of grim philosophy.
Overhead the trains rumbled and roared, and the dark structure
of the elevated railroad, stretching over the avenue, dripped little
streams and drops of water upon the mud and snow beneath it.

All the clatter of the street was softened by the masses that lay
upon the cobbles until, even to one who looked from a window, it
became important music, a melody of life made necessary to the
ear by the dreariness of the pitiless beat and sweep of the storm.
Occasionally one could see black figures of men busily shovelling
the white drifts from the walks. The sounds from their labor
created new recollections of rural experiences which every man
manages to have in a measure. Later, the immense windows of the
shops became aglow with light, throwing great beams of orange
and yellow upon the pavement. They were infinitely cheerful, yet
in a way they accented the force and discomfort of the storm, and
gave a meaning to the pace of the people and the vehicles, scores
of pedestrians and drivers, wretched with cold faces, necks and
feet, speeding for scores of unknown doors and entrances, scatter-
ing to an infinite variety of shelters, to places which the imagination made warm with the familiar colors of home.

There was an absolute expression of hot dinners in the pace of
the people. If one dared to speculate upon the destination of those
who came trooping, he lost himself in a maze of social calculations;
he might fling a handful of sand and attempt to follow
the flight of each particular grain. But as to the suggestion of hot
dinners, he was in firm lines of thought, for it was upon every
hurrying face. It is a matter of tradition; it is from the tales of
childhood. It comes forth with every storm. . . .

In this half-darkness, the men began to come from their shelter
places and mass in front of the doors of charity. They were of
all types, but the nationalities were mostly American, German
and Irish. Many were strong, healthy, clear-skinned fellows with
that stamp of countenance which is not frequently seen upon
seekers after charity. There were men of undoubted patience,
industry and temperance, who in time of ill-fortune, do not
habitually turn to rail at the state of society, snarling at the arro-
gance of the rich and bemoaning the cowardice of the poor, but
who at these times are apt to wear a sudden and singular meekness
as if they saw the world's progress marching from them and were
trying to perceive where they had failed, what they had lacked, to
be thus vanquished in the race. Then there were others of the
shifting, Bowery lodging-house element who were used to paying
ten cents for a place to sleep, but who now came here because it
was cheaper.

But they were all mixed in one mass so thoroughly that one
could not have discerned the different elements but for the fact
that the laboring men, for the most part, remained silent and
impassive in the blizzard, their eyes fixed on the windows of the
house, statues of patience.

The sidewalk soon became completely blocked by the bodies of
the men. They pressed close to one another like sheep in a winter's
gale, keeping one another warm by the heat of their bodies. The
snow came down upon this compressed group of men until, directly
from above, it might have appeared like a heap of snow-covered
merchandise, if it were not for the fact that the crowd swayed
gently with a unanimous, rhythmical motion. It was wonderful to
see how the snow lay upon the heads and shoulders of these men,
in little ridges an inch thick perhaps in places, the flakes steadily
adding drop and drop, precisely as they fall upon the unresisting
grass of the fields. The feet of the men were all wet and cold and
the wish to warm them accounted for the slow, gentle, rhythmical
motion. Occasionally some man whose ears or nose tingled acutely

from the cold winds would wriggle down until his head was protected by the shoulders of his companions.

There was a continuous murmuring discussion as to the proba-
bility of the doors being speedily opened. They persistently lifted
their eyes toward the windows. One could hear little combats of
opinion.

"There's a light in th' winder!"

"Naw; it's a reflection f'm across th' way."

"Well, didn't I see 'em lite it?"

"You did?"

"I did!"

"Well, then, that settles it!"

As the time approached when they expected to be allowed to
enter, the men crowded to the doors in an unspeakable crush,
jamming and wedging in a way that it seemed would crack bones.
They surged heavily against the building in a powerful wave of
pushing shoulders. Once a rumor flitted among all the tossing
heads.

"They can't open th' doors! Th' fellers er smack up ag'in 'em."

Then a dull roar of rage came from the men on the outskirts;
but all the time they strained and pushed until it appeared to be
impossible for those that they cried out against to do anything but
be crushed to pulp.

"Ah, git away f'm the' door!"

"Git outa that!"

"Throw 'em out!"

"Kill 'em!"

"Say, fellers, now, what th' 'ell? Give 'em a chanct t' open th'
door!"

"Yeh, damned pigs, give 'em a chanct t' open th' door!"

Men in the outskirts of the crowd occasionally yelled when a
boot-heel of one of the frantic trampling feet crushed on their
freezing extremities.

"Git off me feet, yeh clumsy tarrier!"

"Say, don't stand on me feet! Walk on th' ground!"

A man near the doors suddenly shouted: "O-o-oh! Le' me out—
le' me out!" And another, a man of infinite valor, once twisted his
head so as to half face those who were pushing behind him. "Quit
yer shovin', yeh"—and he delivered a volley of the most powerful
and singular invective straight into the faces of the men behind
him. It was as if he was hammering the noses of them with curses
of triple brass. His face, red with rage, could be seen; upon it,
an expression of sublime disregard of consequences. But nobody
cared to reply to his imprecations; it was too cold. Many of them
snickered and all continued to push.

In occasional pauses of the crowd's movement the men had
opportunity to make jokes; usually grim things, and no doubt very
uncouth. Nevertheless, they are notable—one does not expect to
find the quality of humor in a heap of old clothes under a snowdrift.

The winds seemed to grow fiercer as time wore on. Some of the
gusts of snow that came down on the close collection of heads cut
like knives and needles, and the men huddled, and swore, not like
dark assassins, but in a sort of an American fashion, grimly and
desperately, it is true, but yet with a wondrous under-effect, inde-
finable and mystic, as if there was some kind of humor in this
catastrophe, in this situation in a night of snow-laden winds.

Once, the window of the huge dry-goods shop across the street
furnished material for a few moments of forgetfulness. In the
brilliantly-lighted space appeared the figure of a man. He was
rather stout and very well clothed. His whiskers were fashioned
charmingly after those of the Prince of Wales. He stood in an attitude of magnificent reflection. He slowly stroked his moustache
with a certain grandeur of manner, and looked down at the snow-
encrusted mob. From below, there was denoted a supreme com-
placence in him. It seemed that the sight operated inversely, and
enabled him to more clearly regard his own environment,
delightful relatively.

One of the mob chanced to turn his head and perceive the figure
in the window. "Hello, lookit 'is whiskers," he said genially.

Many of the men turned then, and a shout went up. They called to him in all strange keys. They addressed him in every manner, from familiar and cordial greetings to carefully-worded advice concerning changes in his personal appearance. The man presently fled, and the mob chuckled ferociously like ogres who had just devoured something.

They turned then to serious business. Often they addressed the stolid front of the house.

"Oh, let us in fer Gawd's sake!"

"Let us in or we'll all drop dead!"

"Say, what's th' use o' keepin' all us poor Indians out in th' cold?"

And always some one was saying, "Keep off me feet."

The crushing of the crowd grew terrific toward the last. The men, in keen pain from the blasts, began almost to fight. With the pitiless whirl of snow upon them, the battle for shelter was going to the strong. It became known that the basement door at the foot of a little steep flight of stairs was the one to be opened, and they jostled and heaved in this direction like laboring fiends. One could hear them panting and groaning in their fierce exertion.

Usually some one in the front ranks was protesting to those in the rear: "O—o—ow! Oh, say, now, fellers, let up, will yeh? Do yeh wanta kill somebody?"

A policeman arrived and went into the midst of them, scolding and berating, occasionally threatening, but using no force but that of his hands and shoulders against these men who were only struggling to get in out of the storm. His decisive tones rang out sharply: "Stop that pushin' back there! Come, boys, don't push! Stop that! Here, you, quit yer shovin'! Cheese that!"

When the door below was opened, a thick stream of men forced a way down the stairs, which were of an extraordinary narrowness and seemed only wide enough for one at a time. Yet they somehow went down almost three abreast. It was a difficult and painful operation. The crowd was like a turbulent water forcing itself through one tiny outlet. The men in the rear, excited by the success of the others, made frantic exertions, for it seemed that this large band would more than fill the quarters and that many would be left upon the pavements. It would be disastrous to be of the last, and accordingly men with the snow biting their faces, writhed and twisted with their might. One expected that from the tremendous pressure, the narrow passage to the basement door would be so choked and clogged with human limbs and bodies that movement would be impossible. Once indeed the crowd was forced to stop, and a cry went along that a man had been injured at the foot of the stairs. But presently the slow movement began again, and the policeman fought at the top of the flight to ease the pressure on those who were going down.

A reddish light from a window fell upon the faces of the men when they, in turn, arrived at the last three steps and were about to enter. One could then note a change of expression that had come over their features. As they thus stood upon the threshold of their hopes, they looked suddenly content and complacent. The fire had passed from their eyes and the snarl had vanished from their lips. The very force of the crowd in the rear, which had previously vexed them, was regarded from another point of view, for it now made it inevitable that they should go through the little doors into the place that was cheery and warm with light.

The tossing crowd on the sidewalk grew smaller and smaller. The snow beat with merciless persistence upon the bowed heads of those who waited. The wind drove it up from the pavements in frantic forms of winding white, and it seethed in circles about the huddled forms, passing in, one by one, three by three, out of the storm.

It is no coincidence that Dreiser published "Curious Shifts of the Poor" while he was writing *Sister Carrie*, for it became the paradigm for George Hurstwood's last decline. Fallen to the level of "New York's Most Pitiful Mendicants" by the middle of chapter 45, entitled "Curious Shifts of the Poor" in the first printing of the novel, he joins the Captain's ragged line to have a bed begged for him.[20] Then, in the last chapter, he continues to drop along the way outlined in the interlocking sketches: first he leans on the Sisters of Mercy, then on the baker, and at last he becomes one of the men in the storm. There he ends. In Dreiser's world, a man like Hurstwood, brought low to dereliction, must destroy himself. Once through the opened lodging house door he finds a cubicle and turns on the gas.

But "Curious Shifts of the Poor" is seminal not only because Dreiser returned to it so often. It is seed work also because it marks the beginning of Dreiser's major career. Donald Pizer has identified more than two hundred of Dreiser's fugitive writings prior to this one.[21] Most of those are undistinguished hack jobs, indistinguishable from the stuff that filled most of the magazines and newspapers during the Nineties. None of them seems to show a hint of the author who announced himself with *Sister Carrie*, but in "Curious Shifts of the Poor" he is all there. The inescapable conclusion is that his reading of Crane's sketch in some way helped him discover himself.

So while it is significant that he responded strongly enough to Crane's sketch to adopt it, it is even more significant that as he did he made it his own. "The Men in the Storm," therefore, is a way of defining how Dreiser's vision differed from Crane's. Those differences begin in stylistic devices. In "The Men in the Storm," as in most of Crane's other writings, narrative distance is a primary technique. It serves not only to direct the reader's attention but also to guide his reactions. With a quiet skill matched only by Hawthorne's, Crane manipulates the gap between the narrator and his observations so as to permit infinite variation in degrees of engagement and disengagement while the reader shares the narrative platform. In this sketch, distance is varied by means of discursive narration and replicating dialogue, and these in turn also play upon the reader's sense of society. The result is the reader's involvement in a complex of ironies. When Dreiser took over "The Men in the Storm" he slimmed it according to his own insights into life and art. Narrative distance is much more constant in his version, and the narration is direct, terse, and relatively reportorial. His dialogue, too, is more economically used, serving more to characterize the men as isolates than to suggest the world in which they are isolated. Generally speaking, Dreiser's suppression of elements that Crane had stressed tend to reduce the reverberations of the sketch. While Crane's irony, for example, is self-reflexive, Dreiser's is directed exclusively at the men. The result is that where Crane involves the reader in the implications of their plight, Dreiser displays it to him. The root of all this is a difference in vision. Crane reveals a heterogeneous group of men temporarily assembled by a common need. The depression that had begun in the fall of 1893, he suggests, had leveled those who were made jobless with those who would never look for work. Dreiser projects a homogeneous group: as the title of the last chapter in *Sister Carrie* indicates, this is "The Way of the Beaten." There is, therefore, a note of possibilities struck by Crane that Dreiser ignored when he borrowed the sketch. In the bovine rush of the men towards the opened doors, Crane implies that the energy expended now might prove irresistible were it properly harnessed. For Dreiser, however, that surge simply is the final throe of degenerated man. It is the expression in art of "a literary credo which would insist that the main battle of man is with his fate, that human character is ever pitted against ultimately destructive circumstances, and that the battle, if not lost in the full tide of action, is most certainly lost later through the natural waning of youth and strength and all the ambitions and successes that accompany man's best years." [22] Dreiser suggested, in "The Great American Novel," that Crane shared this creed. But he did not. Crane's was a more hopeful view of the human condition.

III

Despite his obvious debts to Crane, despite his early acquaintance with a spectrum of Crane's work, and despite the intimacy of his response to it, Dreiser came to deny any significant relationship between his career and Crane's. The revisionary process was gradual, and it seems to be tied in some way to both Dreiser's struggle for recognition and Crane's posthumous reputation. Dreiser mentioned Crane fairly frequently in his correspondence as well as in his public work. At first he is laudatory, then he tends to reverse that impression. On 15 October 1911, for example, he wrote William C. Lengel that "few American books if any interest me," but among the twelve books that "are quite the sum total of my American literary admirations" is *The Red Badge of Courage*. And on 22 March 1915, when he asked H. L. Mencken for a list of "fugitive realistic works of import," Crane was among the eleven writers whose works Mencken did not have to bother to list.[23] Even more important is a letter Dreiser wrote for publication.

In 1921, with Crane's reputation in almost total eclipse, the Schoolmen's Club of Newark, New Jersey, decided to mark the fiftieth anniversary of his birth. Throughout that city elaborate ceremonies were scheduled for 7 November—six days after the actual anniversary—with the major event set for the steps of the Newark Public Library. Its principal feature was to be the unveiling of a plaque in Crane's memory amidst the reading of tributes to him from a number of absent writers of note. When Dreiser, then in California, received a request for something appropriate from the chairman of the committee on arrangements, he replied at length.

Dear Mr. Herzberg:

Your letter of October 24 asking for an appropriate word in connection with the unveiling of a bronze tablet to Stephen Crane in Newark on Nov. 7th., reaches me today. It pleases me no little to learn that the Schoolmen's Club is to honor Stephen Crane with a bronze tablet. He was among the very earliest of my purely literary admirations and one of a very few writers who stood forward intellectually and artistically at a time when this nation was as thoroughly submerged in romance and sentimentality and business as it is today. At that time, in so far as America was concerned, there were but James and Howells and Mark Twain among the elder realists and Garland and Fuller and Crane as beginners. Of this younger group Crane was a peer. And he certainly had more of directness and force and daring than most of his elders. *Maggie* and *George's Mother*, while little more than sketches in the best sense, bear all the marks of a keen and unbiassed sympathy with life as well as a high level of literary perception. At this time when realism, on the one hand, stands in danger of becoming a trivial fad and pastime, a task to which every seeker after a little notoriety seeks to set his hand and, on the other hand, can only be written with a vice-crusader leaning over one's shoulder to see whether the American home and school however dull or ignorant, are being properly preserved in their dullness and ignorance, it is just as well that an organization somewhere should take it upon itself to honor a genius like Crane and so to write itself down as not entirely submissive to the American program of business first and sweetness and light afterwards.

The little Crane did, as you will note, was done with fire and a conscious or unconscious independence of our strawy and smothering notions and theories in regard to letters. Also it boded well for American letters. He took our hampering hurdles without a thought or care. *The Red Badge of Courage* is a fine picture of war. And, it is not pleasant. There is not much sweetness about it and very little uplift. It ends as it begins, grimly, and without any solution, moral or spiritual. This in itself is wrong, according to our moral and hence our spiritual standards. If you doubt it study our current books and magazines. But let that be.

You are putting in its place a bronze tablet which commemorates what he did. I hope that the sight of it will inspire at least an occasional literary aspirant to be fearless in his interpretations of life. If so, it will not have been put in place in vain. And we may pray then that the Gods will endow him with divine fire. If so, our American vice societies and their associate dullards can be safely trusted to do the rest, i.e. make his life a burden and his name anathema.[24]

There are at least four reasons why that letter is important. First, it acknowledges publicly that Dreiser had read Crane's work early. Second, it includes with the work Dreiser knew, the two most important writings in Crane's slum group, *Maggie* and *George's Mother*. *The Red Badge of Courage* alone, which everyone knew he had read, could have been of only minimal importance as an influence on his own work; and "A Mystery of Heroism," the war story he printed in *Ev'ry Month*, does little to reinforce a claim to influence by Crane's war fiction. The Crane who would most likely have affected Dreiser was the Crane of the slum stories that George C. Jenks had praised in February 1897, and Dreiser evidently had read Jenks. Third, it makes explicit the attitudes that implicitly lay behind Dreiser's letters to Lengel and Mencken, i.e., respect for the work and acknowledgement of the author for noteworthy contributions to American literary realism. And, fourth, it shows that Dreiser had identified Crane as a surrogate in his own troubles with critics and purity forces. By 1921 those difficulties had included the defeat of *Sister Carrie*, denunciations by leading critics, and turmoil over *The "Genius"* that led to its banning. The terms with which he praised Crane project him as Dreiser saw himself, a great writer bravely and honestly working his art in defiance of the powerful forces of a society that had misplaced its values.

But a short time later Dreiser began to reverse himself sharply. In 1927, for example, the Russian critic Sergei Dinamov asked if he had been "inspired" either by Stephen Crane or Frank Norris. To this natural question Dreiser made an evasive reply:

To say that any writer is influenced or inspired by another is, I believe, hardly ever a conscious process. Certainly there are temperaments which think and see in compatible terms—with the same understanding and sympathy for life, and when two or more such temperaments set their thoughts on paper, people immediately suspect or imagine that one is influenced by the other. But in many cases it has so happened that they were not even familiar with each other's work. In the case of Frank Norris, I first became acquainted with him and his work, when he was a reader for Doubleday-Page and Company, and I took *Sister Carrie* to them to be published.[25]

The implication, of course, is that just as he owed no literary debt to Norris, so too he owed none to Crane—because he had read neither man before announcing himself their peer with *Sister Carrie*. But, of course, that evidently was not true.

The turn in his statements on Crane continued thereafter. In 1928, Doubleday, Doran & Company published the third and most lavish of the collected editions of Frank Norris. Ten volumes bound in simulated vellum stamped in gold, top edges gilded, and a page of the *McTeague* manuscript inserted into the first volume of each of the two hundred and forty-five sets. The Argonaut Manuscript Edition was probably the most flossy of the manufactured collector's items that publishers poured into the affluent Twenties. In the established tradition of its kind, each volume contained an introductory essay by a literary notable: Kathleen Norris, Rupert Hughes, Charles G. Norris, H. L. Mencken, Christopher Morley, and others of the well-known writers of that day. Dreiser introduced *McTeague*. His brief essay set Norris alongside Crane, concluding that Norris was "the far more distinguished luminary of the two. For where *The Red Badge of Courage* concerns the psychology of war in general, this work of Norris's concerns San Francisco and the everyday life of a certain element of that city." In contrast with his statement to the Newark Schoolmen's Club a few years before, this one continues on to refuse Crane significance as a pioneering American realist of the second generation. Henry Blake Fuller's *The Cliff-Dwellers* and *With the Procession*—published respectively in 1886 and 1891, according to Dreiser—earn their author supremacy. Dreiser of course was wrong in his dating: *The Cliff-Dwellers* appeared in 1893, coincidentally with the first edition of *Maggie*, and *With the Procession* came out in 1896, after *The Red Badge of Courage*. But Dreiser's mangling of the facts is not the point. What is the point is that he had publicly taken a new stand on Crane. To him facts always were established subjectively, according to his position at the time in which he cited them. An example of that is in his next public comment on Crane in "The Great American Novel," his contribution to the second issue of *The American Spectator*, the literary newspaper he edited in collaboration with George Jean Nathan, Ernest Boyd, James Branch Cabell, and Eugene O'Neill. It is a survey of American realism from a starting point in Fuller's work, with Crane given but passing remarks. One is in connection with a jab at H. L. Mencken for "complete ignorance not only of the work of Norris but of these other contemporaries of mine. Also as to who the true pioneers in this field were. In proof of this I suggest that anyone interested examine Mencken's introduction to 'McTeague' in the collected edition of Norris's work published in 1929, where he will find him referring to Norris as the pioneer of American realism, ignoring Melville, James, Wharton, Fuller and Crane. H. G. Wells is still sure that it was Stephen Crane who led the van." Two years later, in 1934, when *The American Spectator Year Book* republished his essay, nobody seems to have reminded Dreiser that anyone interested would find that the notorious introduction was not Mencken's but his own.[26]

IV

Why did Dreiser come to deny claims on him that he once acknowledged and that now have been proven? One can only speculate on the reasons. It is not likely that they include a relatively late discovery of Henry Blake Fuller that led him to devalue Crane's importance. Dreiser knew Fuller as early as 1907, when he tried to get from Fuller a blurb when *Sister Carrie* was being republished; and he was corresponding with Fuller in 1911, at about the time Dreiser began writing admiringly of Crane.[27] Possibly the passage of time alone caused a change in attitude, and there was no other isolatable reason for it. Then again, there may be something to Dorothy Dudley's impression that jealousy had some part in Dreiser's feelings about Crane during the Thirties. It is worth looking at the situation of the two men around that time.

Crane, of course, had been dead since 1900. But Dreiser was still striving for recognition. A man of his temperament might well have envied Crane's apparently easy rise while he himself was making a feverish attempt to support himself and develop a career by over-working on a small woman's magazine. If so, his envy might well have multiplied because of subsequent events. Crane's reputation among the general reading public died with him. Sales of his most popular book, *The Red Badge of Courage*, tell the story: for the eleven years between January 1911 and the end of December 1922, the period during which Dreiser was boosting Crane, sales averaged only 406 copies a year.[28] When Dreiser was writing so strongly to the Newark Schoolmen's Club, in November 1921, that the public had forgotten Crane, he was absolutely right: only 191 copies were sold during that accounting period. Almost certainly he would not have known these confidential figures, but evidently he was well aware of the situation they represented. No one was reading Stephen Crane.

But the Newark testimonial was a sign that something was happening. That same year saw not only testimonials but also the publication of Vincent Starrett's *Men, Women and Boats*—a collection of some of Crane's short writings—by Dreiser's own publishers, Boni & Live-right. It was followed in 1923 by more Starrett on Crane: the first *Stephen Crane: A Bibliography*, and an enthusiastic essay in *Buried Caesars*. Starrett pushed Crane again in 1924, with two uncollected pieces in *Et Cetera*. Largely through his missionary work with these books, several things in magazines and newspapers, and his urging of Crane to the Chicago Renaissance circle, the first revival of interest in that buried Caesar was under way. It was more apparent than real, that indication of mass devotion to Crane, but it was effective. Be-fore Ralph Paine dedicated *Roads of Adventure* in part to Crane's memory in 1922, he wrote his publisher: "As a publicity suggestion for 'Roads of Adventure', there is a strong revival of interest in Stephen Crane and his works. . . . There is more about him in my book than is found anywhere else, I am quite sure."[29] Starrett and a little band of similarly-minded people had succeeded in giving the effect of being a premonitory ripple of a tidal wave.

One prominent result of their efforts was another of those pretentious uniform editions that delighted the twenties, *The Work of Stephen Crane*, published in twelve boxed volumes at $90 by Alfred A. Knopf in 1925–1927. The revival was not based solidly enough to save the well-advertised set from being remaindered, just sufficiently vocal to warrant its production. Soon afterwards, Dreiser wrote his cool response to Dinamov's letter asking whether Crane had influenced him.

From the time in 1917 that Horace Liveright spoke with Dreiser about publishing a uniform edition of his works, Dreiser increasingly dwelled on the prestige such a project would bring him. In 1921, according to W. A. Swanberg, "He was dickering with several houses in an effort to unsnarl his publishing muddle and to achieve the end that had become an obsession—a collected edition of Dreiser books, uniformly bound, published and promoted by one publisher." [30] But he never was able to manage that. The obsession remained with him, unsatisfied, until he died. When that early rival, Stephen Crane, was so honored, the blow must have been heavy. He could be generous to Frank Norris at the time of a Norris set; but then he had neither borrowed from his work as he had from Crane's nor had he been in competition with Norris as he had been with Crane.

NOTES

1. *A Book About Myself* (New York: Boni & Liveright, 1922), p. 490.

2. *Theodore Dreiser* (New York: William Sloane Associates, 1951), p. 58. Among the remarkable few who have discussed the possibility of Crane's having influenced Dreiser are Dorothy Dudley, *Forgotten Frontiers* (New York: Harrison Smith and Robert Haas, 1932), pp. 125–28; Claude Simpson, ed., *Sister Carrie* (Boston: Houghton Mifflin Company, 1959), p. xiii; Jay Martin, *Harvests of Change* (Englewood Cliffs, New Jersey: Prentice-Hall, Inc., 1967), p. 61; and

Theodore Dreiser and Stephen Crane: Studies in a Literary Relationship

Ellen Moers, *Two Dreisers* (New York: The Viking Press, 1969), passim. At several points in this essay I am much indebted to Miss Moers's remarkable book.
3. Dudley, *Forgotten Frontiers*, p. 125.
4. Ibid. Perhaps the single most serious lacuna in Dreiser studies is the apparent absence of a complete file of *Ev'ry Month* for the term of Dreiser's editorship. Dudley, the first critic to discuss Dreiser's connection with the magazine, seems not to have seen any copies of it. The copyright deposit set at the Library of Congress disappeared over forty years ago, and no copies are known to survive in any other library. Five years after publication of *Forgotten Frontiers*, John F. Huth, Jr. discussed issues he had found from September 1896 to July 1897 in the pioneering "Theodore Dreiser: 'The Prophet,' " *American Literature* 9 (May 1937): 347–54. Thirty years later, in *Two Dreisers* (p. 324), Miss Moers noted that five more issues, beginning with June 1896, have been recovered. By sheer luck I have been able to acquire the most complete file known so far, missing only the first two issues Dreiser edited. This run will be republished as *Theodore Dreiser's "Ev'ry Month"* in 1973 by the University of South Carolina Press. I discuss this phase of Dreiser's career in "Theodore Dreiser's *Ev'ry Month*," *Library Chronicle*.
5. "Literary Notes," *Ev'ry Month* 2 (1 May 1896): 11–12. This review confirms Ellen Moers's guess (*Two Dreisers*, p. 37): "As this remarkable burst of Crane's publications coincided with the first year of *Ev'ry Month*, there is reason to assume that Dreiser reviewed one or more of them—but assume, alas, is all that the extant files of *Ev'ry Month* permit us to do."
6. "Reflections," *Ev'ry Month* 2 (1 September 1896): 4.
7. "Reflections," *Ev'ry Month* [1] (1 February 1896): 4—5.
8. "A Mystery of Heroism" and "The Literary Shower," *Ev'ry Month* 2 (1 September 1896): 10–11, 23.
9. "A Metropolitan Favorite," *Ev'ry Month* 3 (1 November 1896): 22.
10. *Ev'ry Month* 4 (1 May 1897): 20.
11. "The Literary Shower," *Ev'ry Month* 3 (1 October 1896): 24.
12. "Things Literary," *Ev'ry Month* 3 (1 January 1897): 31.
13. *Ev'ry Month* 3 (1 February 1897): 22.
14. *Ev'ry Month* 4 (1 May 1897): 5.
15. Theodore Dreiser, "W. L. S.," *Twelve Men* (New York: Boni & Liveright, 1929), p. 356. Sonntag had indeed illustrated Kipling. One book of Kipling's which has a "fast express" story and illustrations by Sonntag is *The Day's Work* (New York: Doubleday & McClure Co., 1898). But ".007" is illustrated by W. D. Stevens; Sonntag did "The Ship that Found Herself." Crane's "The Scotch Express" was published in *McClure's Magazine* 12 (January 1899): 273–83. In addition to Sonntag's drawings, his railroad passes were used as illustrations to that sketch. The magazine noted that "the illustrations are from drawings made by the late W. L. Sonntag, Jr., who made the journey in company with Mr. Crane, expressly for McCLURE'S MAGAZINE. It was only a short time after these draw-

ings were completed that Mr. Sonntag died—in the very prime of his fine powers and to deep regret of all who knew him or his work." Sonntag had died on 11 May 1898.

16. Crane's letter is reprinted in Joseph Katz, *The Portable Stephen Crane* (New York: The Viking Press, 1969), pp. 534–35, from its appearance in *Demorest's Family Magazine*, 33 (September 1896): 628–32.

17. *Demorest's Family Magazine*, 36 (November 1899): 22–26.

18. *The Color of a Great City* (New York: Boni & Liveright, 1923), pp. 228–30; *New York Call*, 23 November 1913, p. 10.

19. Quotations from Crane's "The Men in the Storm" are from the text in *Arena*, 10 (October 1894): 662—67. It differs from the text in the *Philistine*, 2 (January 1897): 37–48, in numerous small ways, chief of which is the opening eight words ("At about three o'clock of the February afternoon,") which are omitted in the later appearance. Ellen Moers (*Two Dreisers*, p. 61) argues that "Dreiser did not read Crane's piece when it appeared in the *Arena*. At the time he was still in Pittsburgh; he had probably never heard of the *Arena*, and he had not then heard of Stephen Crane." Perhaps. But Dreiser's version seems closer to the *Arena* text, in part because it echoes its opening—including those eight words at the beginning. This may, however, be coincidental.

20. *Sister Carrie* (New York: Doubleday, Page & Co., 1900).

21. Pizer, "A Checklist of Theodore Dreiser's Publications," *Proof* 1 (1971): 247–92.

22. Dreiser, "The Great American Novel," *American Spectator*, 1 (December 1932): 1–2.

23. Robert H. Elias, ed., *Letters of Theodore Dreiser* (Philadelphia: University of Pennsylvania Press, 1959), 2: 121, 185.

24. Dreiser to Max J. Herzberg, 2 November 1921, Alderman Library, University of Virginia. The letter was first published with minor editing in *The Michigan Daily Sunday Magazine*, 27 November 1921, entitled "A Letter About Stephen Crane."

25. 5 January [1927], Elias, *Letters of Theodore Dreiser*, 2: 449–50.

26. George Jean Nathan, et al., eds. *The American Spectator Year Book* (New York: Frederick A. Stokes Company, 1934), pp. 16–25.

27. W. A. Swanberg, *Dreiser* (New York: Charles Scribner's Sons, 1965), p. 116. Dreiser to Fuller, 7 November 1911, Henry Blake Fuller Papers, The Newberry Library.

28. Joseph Katz, "*The Red Badge of Courage* from 1911–1923," *Stephen Crane Newsletter*, 5 (Winter 1970): 1–2.

29. George Monteiro, "Ralph Paine and 'The Memory of Stephen Crane,'" *Stephen Crane Newsletter*, 2 (Fall 1967): 6–7.

30. Swanberg, *Dreiser*, pp. 222, 257.

Joseph Katz

Afterword: Resources for the Study of Stephen Crane

One reason for the transition in Stephen Crane studies at the close of his centenary year is that serious students are learning to cope with the flawed abundance of available resources. There are several research collections and a number of bibliographies, checklists, editions, and biographies, even a specialized journal. Yet in all this plenty there are faults that define the limitations of Crane scholarship and criticism. As they are established, these limitations reveal its challenges as well. The simple truth is that very little of the work done on Crane so far is definitive. So a detailed view of resources available for the study of his life and work can provide insights not only into the past and present of Crane studies but also into what must come in the future.

Although primary material is scattered, much of it can be found in institutional libraries. The most splendid of the Stephen Crane collections are at Columbia University and the University of Virginia. Their holdings have been used as the bases of nearly all work on Crane in the past twenty-five years. These collections deserve their eminence: after repeated minings during a quarter century they barely have been stripped, much less exhausted. An indication of their treasures is the important exhibition described in Joan H. Baum's *Stephen Crane (1871–1900): An Exhibition of His Writings Held in the Columbia University Libraries September 17–November 30, 1956* (New York, 1956), itself an important bibliographical tool.

The more striking of these star collections is the one in the Butler Library of Columbia University. It contains the bulk of the Cranes' own papers, Cora's as well as Stephen's. Cora left them to Ernest C. Budd when she died in September 1910, but they never reached him. Budd, a failed businessman who was Cora's intimate during her last years in Jacksonville, Florida, was diddled out of the benefits of her estate, including a legendary trunk containing these papers. Somehow it disappeared from her rooms before her will was proved; and somehow it soon turned up in the possession of Henry W. Walters, a meter reader for the Jacksonville Gas Company, Norman W. Hill, a businessman, and Carl Bohnenberger, assistant librarian of the Jacksonville Free Public Library. It held the material referred to as the Bohnenberger-Hill Collection in writings about Crane through 1952, when it was bought by Columbia University for a price reputed to have been $8,500.

Lillian Gilkes's *Cora Crane: A Biography of Mrs. Stephen Crane* (Bloomington, 1960) details the curious story of the trunk's travels, which is worth knowing at least in outline because it is an alert to look for some of the Cranes' things in places other than Columbia. And some of those things have turned up in other places: Cora's copy of the Methuen *Wounds in the Rain*, with notes by Moreton Frewen, Rudyard Kipling, and Stephen tipped into it (in a private collection, described in George W. Hallam's "Some New Stephen Crane Items," *Studies in Bibliography*, 1967); a copy of Kipling's *The Seven Seas* which Stephen had given to Cora (in a private collection, described in Matthew J. Bruccoli's "Cora's Mouse," *Papers of the Bibliographical Society of America*, 1965); a copy of *Jude the Obscure* from The Court, Cora's last Jacksonville establishment (at the University of Virginia, recorded in James E. Kibler, Jr.'s "The Library of Stephen and Cora Crane," *Proof*, 1971); and Cora's Brede Place scrapbook (at the University of Virginia). Presumably these things drifted away from Bohnenberger, Hill, and Walters before the lot was put up for sale. More things are probably around.

But even though it is not complete, the Stephen and Cora Crane Collection at Columbia University is a superb resource. It contains approximately 1,300 items including manuscripts, scrapbooks, and memorabilia, as well as most of the known letters to Stephen and Cora, most of the books from their library at Brede Place, and most of the documents relating to their life together. Scholars from Daniel G. Hoffman on have worked over the collection, but it continues to reward the imaginative researcher. Because there is no adequate guide to the collection and because Crane scholarship is not yet notable for its thoroughness, an informed scholar with the time and patience to turn over every leaf in this lot will discover important new information. The Cranes often used the clean side of a discarded draft for a different attempt.

The collection in the Alderman Library of the University of Virginia does not have either the coherence or the aura lent the one at Columbia by its provenance, and it is only one-third as large—but it is important. Formed by Clifton Waller Barrett as part of his remarkable library of American literary materials, the 400 items in this holding include about 150 letters by and about Crane, Copeland & Day's materials relating to the production of *The Black Riders and Other Lines*, the script for the aborted American publication of *Last Words* by Henry T. Coates and Company, and the major part of the manuscript of *The Red Badge of Courage* (scattered pages are also at Columbia University, Harvard University, and the New York Public Library's Berg Collection). Additional material that would seem as spectacular as all this in a more humble setting is a quantity of Crane's books in variant copies, scripts for much of his short work, and items like Cora's Brede Place scrapbook and Stephen's 1894 notebook (published as *The Notebook of Stephen Crane*, ed. Donald J. Greiner and Ellen B. Greiner [Charlottesville, 1969]).

Four other institutional libraries have Crane collections worthy of notice. Less often talked about and probably less often used than the collections at Columbia and Virginia, they nevertheless are major holdings. The best of them is the George Arents Stephen Crane collection at Syracuse University. It began building in 1927 as a marker of Crane's token attendance at the university in 1890–1891, but the acquisition of a group of manuscripts, the Nellie Crouse letters, and the books gathered by Ames W. Williams and used for the bibliography he did with Vincent Starrett made it into a fine working collection. Its contents are described in Edwin H. Cady and Lester G. Wells's edition of *Stephen Crane's Love Letters to Nellie Crouse* (Syracuse, 1954) which published most of Crane's letters and photographs at Syracuse. Not to be overlooked at Syracuse is Crane material in the Mayfield Library, the Lillian Gilkes papers, and the substantial collection of materials relating to Crane's ancestors. His maternal line, the Pecks, is of special interest to the university for their participation in the school's founding. Another good working collection was formed by George Matthew Adams and donated to the Baker Library of Dartmouth College. Its strengths are books, letters, and Willis Brooks Hawkins's file on his service as Crane's agent with Amy Leslie prior to her embezzlement suit against Crane (discussed in Joseph Katz, "Some Light on the Stephen Crane–Amy Leslie Affair," *Mad River Review*, 1964–1965). Herbert Faulkner West's *A Stephen Crane Collection* (Hanover, 1948) describes the Dartmouth holdings.

Still another good collection is in the Lilly Library of Indiana University. In addition to its explicit Crane material—books, manuscripts, and letters—are the papers of D. Appleton & Co., publishers of *The Red Badge of Courage, Maggie: A Girl of the Streets, The Third Violet*, and *The Little Regiment*, and those of S. S. McClure whose book house published *The Open Boat* and whose syndicate distributed much of Crane's other writings. Corollary material of that kind makes the collections at the New York Public Library of major interest in Crane studies. The Berg Collection has Crane's letters to Ripley Hitchcock, editor of D. Appleton & Co., a page of *The Red Badge of Cour-*

age manuscript, fragments of *The Ghost* (see John D. Gordan's "*The Ghost* at Brede Place," *Bulletin of the New York Public Library*, 1952, written before the manuscript was acquired), and other things including some books owned by Crane; but the real adventures in the library are to be found in exploring such other resources as the files of the *Century*, which hold Crane material.

There are important things scattered among several other institutions. The Henry E. Huntington Library has letters and the manuscript of "The Five White Mice"; the Houghton Library of Harvard University has Crane's letters to William Dean Howells and two pages of *The Red Badge of Courage* manuscript; the H. G. Wells Collection at the University of Illinois has letters to Wells; the University of Southern California has letters to Hamlin Garland; other Garland letters about Crane are at the Ohio State University which also holds the papers of Louis Zara containing notes he gathered for *Dark Rider: A Novel Based on the Life of Stephen Crane* (Cleveland and New York, 1961). Still other libraries have smaller amounts of material, sometimes only a letter or two. Among these are the Boston Public Library, St. John's Seminary of Camarillo, California, St. Lawrence University, Newark Public Library, New Jersey Historical Society, Historical Society of Pennsylvania, Fales Library of New York University, University of California at Los Angeles, Yale University, the Rare Books Division of the Library of Congress, and Delta Upsilon fraternity at Syracuse University. There doubtless are other libraries that have no Crane "collection" but that hold fugitive items of interest and importance; certainly there are good things held by a number of private collectors. Auction catalogues record much that emerged into the brief spotlight of the sales room only to submerge again once the hammer fell; while other items, such as the Thomas Beer materials discussed in connection with his Crane biography, should have existed, almost certainly did exist, and probably still do. But where?

That is the continuing challenge of Crane studies: the need to seek out and record all available material. Handlists of the collections at Columbia and Virginia are available from their curators, but most things have gone unregistered. A calendar of Crane manuscripts, documents and letters promised by the series Calendars of American Literary Manuscripts (CALM) will help to meet that need.

Another challenge of Crane studies is the need for a good Crane bibliography. Stephen Crane bibliography suffers from the general complaint troubling the study of most American authors. It formed under the misconception that collectors and scholars needed different kinds of information, at a time when academics were uninterested in American bibliography. So the earliest Crane bibliographers were book collectors who wrote for each other. Their concern was to establish priorities in publication; their method was to study what came to hand in order to establish "points" for distinguishing early printings, states, and issues; and their focus was almost exclusively on American appearances. That stance seems unsophisticated today, when bibliographers are becoming aware of those concepts and techniques needed for understanding a period in the book trade for which the earlier position is irrelevant and when their aims are to connect bibliography with larger areas of scholarship and criticism.

It is for these reasons that the Crane bibliographies done to date are mainly of historical interest. They began with O. L. Griffith's "Stephen Crane" (*Publishers' Weekly*, 1922), the basis of the Crane section in Merle Johnson's *American First Editions* (New York, 1929; fourth edition, 1942). It essentially is a simple listing of titles with place and date of publication, sometimes accompanied by a brief note on related information. The first separately published bibliography came the following year: Vincent Starrett's *Stephen Crane: A Bibliography* (Philadelphia, 1923). More ambitious, it included simple descriptions, notes, and an introductory essay "On Collecting Stephen Crane" that still is valuable for its discussion of lost works. Usefulness of *Stephen Crane: A List of His Writings and Articles About Him* (Newark, 1930) is negligible, now interesting only as a sign of activity from the Stephen Crane Association, born in the Twenties and dead in the Forties. But its preparation brought Benjamin John Reeman Stolper, a Columbia University education professor, useful letters about Crane which are housed in a small collection of his papers at the Butler Library. Eighteen years later, the second revival of interest in Crane began with the appearance of Ames W. Williams's and Vincent Starrett's *Stephen Crane: A Bibliography* (Glendale, California, 1948). Fuller descriptions, expanded notes, and information drawn from trade advertisements, deposit copies, publishers' records, and more specimens of Crane's books than had been seen by earlier bibliographers make this the standard bibliography. Jacob Blanck's second volume in the *Bibliography of American Literature* (New Haven, 1957) is a useful supplement to it.

Nevertheless, there is no bibliography adequate to the needs of Crane studies. By focusing on first publications of the books, the existing bibliographies neglect information that is essential to studies of Crane's texts, their reception, and his life. And by assuming that the periodical writings had "first" publications, when in fact the large number of syndicated pieces bore a different relationship to one another, those bibliographies actually distort Crane's situation as a professional writer. Unfortunately, they also suffer sins of commission by injecting legends and ghosts into Crane studies. There are two keys to understanding that situation. One is Augustus De Morgan's rhyme about fleas. Although nearly every succeeding bibliography advanced knowledge, all of them accepted some mistakes that had been made earlier, taking them as facts and passing them along with renewed authority. The result is a kind of tradition in Crane bibliography, aspects of which make fascinating study. Complicating this transmission is the fact that provides the second key: Crane bibliographies came out of one group. Merle Johnson, O. L. Griffith, and Vincent Starrett swapped information and gossip freely, exchanging what they knew with people like Thomas Beer, Crane's first biographer, and A. J. Marks, a collector. While their apparent disregard for preserving their own claims is admirable in the light of far different circumstances today, too often it was coupled with an easy acceptance of rumor as fact. What seems to have happened was that one man would mention a hunch and have it circulate around the group, the hunch gaining weight as it was discussed. When the cycle was completed, he had something that looked very like a fact.

One of the many legends created in this way is a story that concerns *The Lanthorn Book*, to which Crane contributed "The Wise Men." Each member of the Lantern Club contributing to the anthology was to have signed his piece in each of the 125 copies published, but somehow a story began that Crane signed only a few copies—variously ten, twelve, or fifteen. Griffith's 1922 list seems to have been this rumor's first appearance in print, from where it has been repeated by bibliographers, collectors, and especially booksellers ever since. This small bibliographical question has great biographical implications because it reinforces the picture of Crane's returning to New York after the Spanish-American War tired and drained by illness, only to be hounded out of the city by police. He had more things on his mind than signing a club publication, the story about *The Lanthorn Book* implies. Perhaps. But the number of signed copies that have survived makes the legend look like a myth, a conclusion reinforced by the apparent absence of even one unsigned copy. One or more may have gone unsigned, but there is bibliographical evidence to make that a doubtful possibility (Katz, *"The Lanthorn Book: A Census"* [*Stephen Crane Newsletter*, 1970]). Legends like that one and ghosts of many kinds surround nearly every Crane book. They need closer scrutiny than they were given by his early bibliographers.

To some extent this is being done incrementally, in articles and notes published in *Stephen Crane Newsletter, Studies in Bibliography, Papers of the Bibliographical Society of America*, and the textual introductions to the University of Virginia Edition of The Works of Stephen Crane. The chief effort is being placed on untangling the histories of individual books and on locating new periodical appearances. A more interesting secondary direction is the use of bibliographical information to clarify the biography, as in James Stronks's "Stephen Crane's English Years: The Legend Corrected" (*Papers of the Bibliographical Society of America*, 1963) and Matthew J. Bruccoli and Katz's "Scholarship and Mere Artifacts: The British and Empire Publications of Stephen Crane" (*Studies in Bibliography*, 1969), both repudiations of the notion that Crane in England was a Gatsbyesque figure. Such work, however, depends on more information, and information of a different kind, than is available in any of the bibliographies done so far. The editor has promised a full-dress descriptive bibliography that will attempt to do what is needed.

The available checklists of writings about Stephen Crane are superior to the bibliographies of his own work—as they ought to be. There are a number of checklists; while none is perfect, all are good. The most useful are Maurice Beebe and Thomas A. Gullason's "Criticism of Stephen Crane" (*Modern Fiction Studies*, 1959), Robert N. Hudspeth's et al., "A Bibliography of Stephen Crane Scholarship" (*Thoth*, 1970), and Katz's *The Merrill Checklist of Stephen Crane* (Columbus, 1969). Following the general rule that the best checklist is the most recent, the one done by the Hudspeth group is indispensible. However, despite its age, Beebe and Gullason is still valuable for its index to work done on individual titles. *The Merrill Checklist* is selective in an attempt at giving the beginning student a list of the essential work. All of these lists are marred by annoying errors which fortunately do not seriously impede the user. Checklists date rapidly, so the continuing lists available annually in *Thoth* and quarterly in *Stephen Crane Newsletter* are important supplements to any basic checklist.

Two surveys of Crane studies are interesting complements to the checklists. Wertheim's section on Crane in Theodore L. Gross and Stanley Wertheim's *Hawthorne, Melville, Stephen Crane: A Critical Bibliography* (New York, 1971) is selective, with husky abstracts and evaluations of slightly more than 100 works, emphasizing those that have been published since 1950. Donald Pizer's section in *Fifteen American Authors Before 1900* (Madison, 1971) opted for scope over detail, covering the spectrum of secondary work with dashing brevity. Of course all such surveys—not excepting this one—must be read with the awareness that they reveal as much about the writer as about his material. Robert W. Stallman, whose frenetic activity in Crane studies since the early Fifties contributed to its growth, has promised a survey of his own in an annotated checklist coupled with a reprinting of the 1948 Williams and Starrett bibliography. Perpetuation of that quarter-century-old bibliography is to be deplored, but this colorful critic's opinions of the secondary work should prove interesting.

Crane has been edited and re-edited so many times that observers have taken to speaking about an "industry." With a number of pieces reappearing in two collected editions and about twenty scholarly and semi-scholarly editions of particular groups of writings, it appears that Crane studies has trapped itself in an exercise in redundancy. To some extent this is true: a few of the editions are practically unjustifiable. Most of them, however, were attempts to remedy certain serious inadequacies. As a professional writer in the Nineties, Crane had to spend most of his time turning out short pieces for newspapers and magazines. These outlets had become the primary market for nearly everyone who used his pen to make a living. That is why Crane, who wrote only six novels, produced hundreds of short stories, sketches, reports, and other short work. To know Crane means to know this body of writings. But although he himself wanted to collect much of it, when he died most of it lay buried in the periodicals. *Last Words* (London, 1902) was Cora's attempt to resurrect some of it. Unfortunately, neither her timing nor her selections were right.

Then, some twenty years later, the time seemed to come for a collected edition. Wilson Follett's *The Work of Stephen Crane* (12 vols., New York, 1925–1927; reprinted, 6 vols., New York, 1963), was a bibliopolic venture typical of the Twenties. It combined an implication of completeness with big name introductions, a lavish format, and a limited edition in an attempt at catching some of the easy money that had created book collectors out of the newly rich. The attempt failed, and the set was remaindered quickly. It was not a good job of editing either. Follett had not included all of the works, not even all of the good works. Those that were presented were subjected to heavy editorial tampering of sources that often lacked authority. And they were arranged in a thematic order that falsely patterns Crane's work.

Despite some interesting introductions—those by Robert H. Davis, Willa Cather, and Charles Michelson are especially important because they had known Crane—Follett has long been judged inadequate as the standard edition. So one of the chief occupations of Crane studies has been filling the gaps left by *The Work of Stephen Crane*.

The most obvious of these gaps is formed by holes in the canon. Crane began writing in his early teens, turning professional before he was seventeen. While he was in prep school he helped out during vacation periods in his brother Townley's press bureau, and he continued doing that in summers while he was at college. During college semesters he worked as a newspaper stringer. After he quit college he returned to work for Townley full time; then he went to New York as a leg man and space rate writer for papers there until *The Red Badge of Courage* thrust him into his major career. But in all those seven years of his apprenticeship period, fewer than fifty periodical publications have been discovered. His major period is represented better, but by no means completely. Work after mid-1895, when Crane's by-line was saleable, is concealed by distribution methods rather than by anonymity. While his Civil War novel was awaiting its first publication in the newspapers, Crane was taken up by Irving Bacheller's syndicate. Afterwards, early in 1896, he contracted with S. S. McClure's too. Although these two organizations were responsible for distributing the work of nearly every worthwhile American writer during the Nineties, so little has been done on these organizations that the details of their operations are only dimly understood. Evidently, however, they sent out broadcast announcements of upcoming material, among which potential buyers could pick and choose according to their immediate needs. No one newspaper necessarily bought everything, not even everything by Stephen Crane. According to census figures, there were 12,652 newspapers in 1889, 15,904 in 1899; nearly any of them could be harboring an unknown work by Crane—or by any other writer of the period—and some of them are. People turning pages of old newspapers continue to reap new things.

For the earlier period, through the fall of 1894, the major problem in their discovery is attribution. Literary scholarship has no indisputable means for determining authorship on stylistic grounds alone. Inevitably, unsigned work dredged up as Crane's cannot always be proven his. "Great Bugs in Onondaga," a tongue-in-cheek report in the *New York Tribune* in 1891, was submitted as a possibility by John S. Mayfield to a number of scholars who delivered their opinions in the *Courier* (1963), with the piece and the opinions being reprinted separately as *Great Bugs in Onondaga* (Syracuse, 1964). Although there is no way of proving it was by Crane, it is offered as definitely his in two editions. The case is not unique.

Textual authority replaces attribution as the major problem for work published after Crane began writing for the syndicates. They would edit his copy, sometimes supplying such appurtenances as titles, dates, subheadings, and illustrations, then put it into a form suitable for distribution to their clients. Both the Bacheller Syndicate and the S. S. McClure Syndicate sent out material as releases in the form of proofs. Subscribing newspapers then did as they pleased with the material: cutting, revising, retitling, and redating it at will. There are, therefore, multiple texts for every one of Crane's syndicated things, many distorted in one way or another. It is impossible to determine Crane's own text for most of them. The best that can be done for some is to recover the text that the syndicate released. That is no problem when their proofs survived; when those releases are missing, however, the problem is enormous. The pioneering works in the area are Katz's *"The Red Badge of Courage"* (Gainesville, 1967), a study of the newspaper version sponsored by Bacheller, and *Stephen Crane in the West and Mexico* (Kent, 1970), a study of the pieces Crane wrote for Bacheller during the 1895 trip.

Textual problems surround Crane's non-syndicated work as well. All of his books except *Last Words* appeared on both sides of the Atlantic, several in one version for England and another for America. The solution hit upon by some editors—presenting the American text because Crane was an American—has simplicity as its only virtue. Crane in fact prepared two typewritten versions of *Active Service*;

intentionally or not, England was given one and America the other. Scholarship rather than flag following is the more fruitful way of determining whether the book should be presented in a text based on the English version, the American version, or in a version drawn from the two eclectically. Not all of the editorial turmoil in Crane studies is caused by transatlantic publications, however. *Maggie, The Red Badge of Courage,* and *The O'Ruddy* each present distinct difficulties of their own, which will be discussed later.

Because Follett's edition ignored most of these complex questions, recent scholars have tried to answer them in editions of their own. They have directed their main efforts to filling out the canon, to presenting a complete Crane. "Complete" in this usage is understood best when one recalls Humpty Dumpty's rule that "When *I* use a word . . . it means just what I choose it to mean—neither more nor less." Invoking that rule, most of Crane's editors imply completeness within areas established by principles of exclusion and selection that vary from one edition to another.

These editions have supplanted Follett's by providing the general reader with the majority of Crane's known writings. One can have the bulk of Crane's public prose in three volumes: Olov W. Fryckstedt's *Stephen Crane: Uncollected Writings* (Uppsala, 1963) and Thomas A. Gullason's companion books, *The Complete Short Stories and Sketches of Stephen Crane* (Garden City, 1963) and *The Complete Novels of Stephen Crane* (Garden City, 1967). All three, of course, omit discoveries made while they were in press. The scope of Fryckstedt's collection is restricted further by the following exclusions: poems, letters, prose in unpublished manuscripts at press time, and work that had been "(1) put into a volume by Crane himself, (2) included in Cora Crane's posthumous gathering of his writings, *Last Words,* London 1902, (3) later collected in the Knopf twelve-volume edition of *The Work of Stephen Crane,* New York 1925–27, or (4) printed by Melvin H. Schoberlin in his edition of *The Sullivan County Sketches,* Syracuse 1949." All three books are, however, textually naive.

Joseph Katz

Textual sophistication is the exception and not the rule in a number of specialized editions too. Usually these collections take each text from the handiest source, ignoring the complexities of transmitting periodical publications during the Nineties, and often present them in less than scrupulously accurate transcriptions. A useful way of looking at these books is as casebooks rather than as editions. They present a neglected version of a work or bring together a related group of works, mainly as documentation of the thesis espoused in their introductions. This is not to deride their value. To the contrary, these special editions offer the serious student information, judgments, and works that are difficult to obtain elsewhere. Most of the volumes lumped together as editions of Crane's work provide something of value as they traverse the major periods in his career.

Appropriately, they began in earnest with Melvin H. Schoberlin's *The Sullivan County Sketches of Stephen Crane* (Syracuse, 1949), a collection of ten sketches Crane wrote during 1892 when he was eager to leave his brother's press bureau for the New York papers. Crane repudiated the sketches four years later, but they had been important apprentice work and are worth more study than they have received. Schoberlin did not discover them; they had been known before he collected them. By bringing them together, however, he provided necessary illumination on their coherence as a group. R. W. Stallman's *Stephen Crane: Sullivan County Tales and Sketches* (Ames, 1968) dims the light Schoberlin had kindled. It seems that before Crane could write successful fiction he had to circle his subjects first in other pieces. Apparently he did this with Sullivan County in a group of hunting sketches he drew from local legends and wrote up for the *Tribune* shortly before doing the *Sketches*. Stallman dug out seven of these predecessors, unsigned but almost certainly by Crane, and added them to nine of Schoberlin's collection of the ten to form the first section of his book, "The Tales and Sketches." Immediately he obscured the distinctions between the two groups. The Sullivan County Sketches result from Crane's decision to personalize in fiction some of what he had been treating reportorially a few months earlier.

218

They differ from the former group in sharing a consistent cast of characters, narrative stance, and peculiar bizarrerie. "The Fables," the second section of the book, continues the distortion: "The Mesmeric Mountain," rightly considered a Sullivan County Sketch by Schoberlin, is by no means a fable; "How the Donkey Lifted the Hills" is indeed a fable, but it has nothing at all to do with Sullivan County, being one product of Crane's 1895 trip to the West and Mexico. Ten months before this book was published, Thomas A. Gullason's "A Stephen Crane Find: Nine Newspaper Sketches" (*Southern Humanities Review*, 1968) did its job effectively by publishing three more of the *Tribune* sketches with a useful introduction.

This same incoherence is apparent in Stallman and E. R. Hagemann's collection of the writings Crane turned out during the next phase of his apprenticeship, once he decided to go to Park Row. Actually, *The New York City Sketches of Stephen Crane and Related Pieces* (New York, 1966) has some earlier and later things too. That is its trouble. The book divides into four sections that share no principle of selection or unity. "New York City Sketches" has things Crane wrote while he was in the city, although some of them were written before he got there or after he left. Pieces he wrote about the city are included, although some of the works included were written about such other places as Mexico. One thing, Howells's introduction to the English *Maggie*, is not by Crane. Not everything ascribed to him necessarily is his, such as " 'Youse Wants "Petey," Youse Do'," a few paragraphs from the 1892 *Herald* which John Berryman suggested might be by Crane. Nor is everything by him about New York, written while he was there—such as his interview with Howells, a sketch. "Stephen Crane, Dora Clark, and the Police," the second section, contains newspaper reports by and about Crane documenting his contretemps with the police—but it does not contain all of the things known. So much for New York City. "On the New Jersey Coast," the third section, has some pieces Crane probably wrote while he was working for his brother in Asbury Park, and something he wrote about the Methodist resort town years later—but not everything of either time. And "Excursions" has two pieces, one on a coal mine in Scranton, Pennsylvania, and one on Sing Sing prison in Ossining, New York—by no means all that came from reportorial jaunts away from Manhattan. Crane's four years in that city are crucial to understanding how he came to write *Maggie*, but this book is not the way to approach them.

Crane's first novel has itself become the subject of diverse editorial interest, in part because scholars have begun to pay attention to the biographical, critical, and textual questions it raises. In America *Maggie* appeared in two different versions: first in an 1893 edition Crane published on his own because no commercial firm would take it; then in an edition bowdlerized by D. Appleton & Co. in 1896 as a way of cashing in on the fame of *The Red Badge of Courage*. As Katz explained in "The *Maggie* Nobody Knows" (*Modern Fiction Studies*, 1966), the two texts represent Crane's bargain for success. He participated in changes that modified the novel's original angry attack on the inhumanity of man's traditions, and he did it because he wanted something that would sell. The 1896 *Maggie* has been available ever since; but, until Katz's facsimile of the 1893 edition (Gainsville, 1966), that crucial text was practically inaccessible. Once it was recognized that the 1893 edition was important, more republications quickly took place. Maurice Bassan's *Maggie Text and Context* (Belmont, 1966), a controlled research textbook good enough to transcend the limitations of that species of book, gave it wider circulation together with useful material for its study. And two more facsimiles enable the student to see roughly how *Maggie* looked to its first readers, from two different viewpoints suggested by contemporary scholars; Donald Pizer's (San Francisco, 1968) reconciles legends about the novel's birth; Philip D. Jordan's (Lexington, 1970) sets it, somewhat superficially, as social history. Where knowledge of *Maggie's* existence used to be the mark of the Crane buff, today the novel is being read and studied as it deserves. Even the unauthoritative 1896 English text has been reprinted (London, 1966), with an introduction by William Sansom that is interesting mainly for its enthusiastic inaccuracies.

Coincidentally, the textual situation of *Maggie* has revealed the need to modify current theories of critical editing. That branch of textual scholarship is concerned with restoring the texts of literary works to a state that most nearly represents the author's intentions by purging corruptions introduced during the publishing process by such factors as printer's error, editorial tampering, and coerced revision. As currently practiced, the discipline commonly operates on theories based on the study of books produced in Renaissance England. At that time the situation seems to have been one in which works had a relatively uncomplicated development from initial draft through the processes of printing and publishing. The author apparently brought his text from one stage to another until he was satisfied—or until circumstances forced him to be satisfied—that the work was fit for publication. The job of the critical editor is to identify that stage, to choose a copy-text closest to it, and then to emend the copy-text so that it more nearly reflects that stage.

Maggie, however, reveals that works published in nineteenth-century America reflect a situation in which greater complication was possible. Certainly Crane brought this novel through stages of development very like those of the earlier day; and certainly when it was published in 1893 he, like most authors of that time, let its text alone. But then, after three years which changed him, circumstances made him turn to the book again. D. Appleton & Co. forced him to rework it, giving him the opportunity to revise but really forcing the lines along which revision had to proceed. Unlike other authors of his time, he seems not to have relished the opportunity to go back over earlier work with a fresh eye. In fact *Maggie* seems to have been the only thing he revised after a significant period had elapsed since initial publication. It does not, therefore, represent the end product of a continuing developmental process in quite the same way, for example, as a correct copy of the first folio of Shakespeare's plays. The editorial treatment it receives ought to take into account the difference. One implication of the divergent situation is that although it might be possible to do a so-called definitive text of *Hamlet,*

that is not possible for *Maggie*. The two versions of Crane's novel
reflect such different authorial concepts that actually there are two
Maggies. Therefore the sensible editorial goal would be the preparation of two critical editions: one of the 1893 text, another of the 1896.
So far this has not been done. The general discomfort provoked by
one attempt to create a definitive text by blending the two versions
of the novel is considered below, in connection with the University of
Virginia Edition of the Work of Stephen Crane.

There has been controversy over the text of *The Red Badge of
Courage*, but its terms have been retrogressive. Crane worked this
novel through several draft stages, many of which are preserved in
surviving manuscripts, before he was satisfied that it was ready for
publication. But when he tried to sell his book the country was in the
midst of an economic depression; he had to settle for serialization in
newspapers served by the Bacheller Syndicate. Because syndication
demanded the cutting of the story into six short installments for Bacheller's "Six Day Serial Service," Crane had to prepare still another
manuscript with still another version of the text. This abbreviation
turned the novel into a fast-paced adventure tale which was not what
Crane had in mind as the ultimate direction of his book, but it gave
him the opportunity to continue certain patterns of revision which he
had established earlier. So the syndication is important critically and
textually: it gives the reader perspective on how the subtle qualities of
the book were achieved, by displaying a version of the plot without
them; and it provides still another document in the history of the
novel's text. William L. Howarth tells part of the story in *"The Red
Badge of Courage* Manuscript: New Evidence for a Critical Edition"
(*Studies in Bibliography*, 1965); Katz added to it, in *"The Red Badge
of Courage"* (Gainesville, 1967), a study of the syndicate appearances
including a facsimile of the one in the *New York Press*. Eventually
Crane used clippings of the newspaper appearances to catch the interest of D. Appleton & Co., who published the book in 1895. Since
the book incorporates revisions in the syndication not present in the

surviving manuscripts, it is evident that Crane had prepared for it still another script, now missing.

This situation is a relatively straighforward case of linear development in the text of *The Red Badge of Courage*, but it has been distorted by a well-meaning decision to produce a collector's item. In 1952 The Folio Society of London published an edition of *The Red Badge of Courage* in which John T. Winterich introduced uncancelled manuscript passages that had been omitted from the book. His explicit intention was to produce a bibliophilic curiosity rather than a critical edition in which these passages were being sanctioned. He understood correctly that the manuscript at Virginia, from which they were taken, was not printer's copy for the book. Nevertheless, he had begun a trend in texts of the novel. Later in the same year of the Winterich publication, R. W. Stallman's *Stephen Crane: An Omnibus* (New York, 1952) supplied a text of *The Red Badge of Courage* with the omitted passages plugged in, and a few years after that came such paperback editions as William M. Gibson's *The Red Badge of Courage and Selected Prose and Poetry* (New York, 1956; revised, New York, 1968) which did the same unfortunate thing. The result is that Crane's attempt to work his novel carefully into the way he wanted it read has been thwarted by a number of editions that in effect revoked several stages of his revision. This blundering, along with deficiencies in texts of the novel published for the general reader, is discussed in Katz's "Practical Editions: *The Red Badge of Courage*, by Stephen Crane" (*Proof*, 1972).

The O'Ruddy has been exempted from the maltreatment received by Crane's earlier novels because today almost nobody reads it. It is worth reading if for no other reason than it is the rollicking good story that Frederick A. Stokes advertised it to be in 1903. A major problem that had plagued Crane scholarship earlier has been solved recently, so it has been possible to produce a good text of the novel Crane actually wrote. Crane was dying as he wrote *The O'Ruddy*, bringing it to a certain point in manuscript himself and then dictating notes for the rest as he was being carried to the sanitorium where he died. After much negotiation, Robert Barr, a popular novelist who was widely read at the time, took on the job of completing the novel. It was first published in variant form in *The Idler*, a magazine he edited. The longstanding problem was that nobody knew which portions of *The O'Ruddy* were Crane's and which were Barr's. Then, in one of those odd chains of coincidence common in Crane scholarship, the links of the solution of the problem were quickly discovered one after another: Bernard O'Donnell's *An Analysis of Prose Style to Determine Authorship* (The Hague, 1971) argued by statistical evidence that chapter 26 was the first Barr wrote on his own; the argument was given further weight by the discovery of a set of galley proofs on which Barr noted that he wrote the part beginning with that chapter; and the note in turn was confirmed by the discovery of Crane's original manuscript for his section of *The O'Ruddy*.

Less spectacular but equally significant findings reward the scholar who turns his attention to Crane's poetry and correspondence. Crane wrote 135 poems which span the period from his move to New York to the time of his death. He collected sixty-eight poems in *The Black Riders and Other Lines* (1895), the book that followed the 1893 *Maggie*, and thirty-seven in *War Is Kind* (1899)—both showpieces of book publishing in the Nineties. When he died, he left seven poems which had appeared in magazines uncollected and twenty-three other poems unpublished. All have been collected in Katz's *The Poems of Stephen Crane: A Critical Edition* (New York, 1966; revised, New York, 1971), available in paperback without the textual apparatus as *The Complete Poems of Stephen Crane* (Ithaca, 1972). His suggestion in these volumes that *The Black Riders and Other Lines* is not a miscellany but a coherent cycle of poems that express Crane's world view has been taken in interesting directions by Yoshie Itabashi's "The Modern Pilgrimage of *The Black Riders*: An Interpretation" (*Tsuda Review*, 1967).

Editorially Crane's correspondence is in somewhat worse condition. R. W. Stallman and Lillian Gilkes's *Stephen Crane: Letters* (New

York, 1960) is inadequate on most counts. Its texts, datings, and annotations are often wrong, and its contents are seriously incomplete. This book omits nearly as many letters by Crane as it includes, with an important group of letters to his agent Paul Revere Reynolds being perhaps the most astonishing gap. But other omissions are almost equally significant. Cora served as Stephen's amanuensis and business manager while they lived together and continued to correspond about his life and work after he died, but only a few of her letters about his affairs are available in this edition. It also overlooks the need to publish as many as possible of the letters written to Crane, because without them his side of the correspondence has little context. *Stephen Crane Newsletter* has published supplements and corrections to *Stephen Crane: Letters* in nearly every issue; these will be incorporated into the edition of the Cranes' correspondence being prepared by Katz and Gilkes for publication by the University of South Carolina Press.

Material of that kind has been explicitly excluded from the University of Virginia Edition of the Works of Stephen Crane, the second attempt at a complete edition and the first at a critical edition of the public prose. An edition of this kind was called for as early as 1963, in William M. Gibson and Edwin H. Cady's "Editions of American Writers, 1963: A Preliminary Survey" (*PMLA*, 1963), the manifesto for what became the Center for Editions of American Authors. The University of Virginia Edition began to appear in 1969 under the editorship of Fredson Bowers and with the blessing of the CEAA. Projected for completion in ten volumes (Charlottesville, 1969–   ), the edition is announced as intending to contain "every known piece of Crane's creative writing and journalism except his letters and memoranda." So far, six volumes have appeared: I. *Bowery Tales: Maggie and George's Mother* (1969), IV. *The O'Ruddy* (1971), V. *Tales of Adventure* (1970), VI. *Tales of War* (1970), VII. *Tales of Whilomville* (1969), IX. *Reports of War* (1971). Promised are II. *The Red Badge of Courage* and III. *On Active Service* [sic]; *The Third Violet*, the remaining two volumes to be announced.

Because editing on this level requires satisfactory resolution of as yet unanswered questions about the transmission of nineteenth-century American texts as well as those about Crane's own practices, it is not surprising that publication of the first two volumes (that is Volumes I and VII) resulted in immediate outcries against the edition, especially against the editorial methods used on *Maggie*. The sharpest and most frequent critic has been Donald Pizer. Beginning with a review in *Modern Philology* (1970), he went on in the *Bulletin of the New York Public Library* (1971) to argue against the principles on which the edition has been based. Rebuttals in that journal soon came from Norman Grabo and Hershel Parker, members of the Center for Editions of American Authors executive committee, and they were given a reply by Pizer. At major contention was the implication of Bowers's decision to create an "ideal" text of *Maggie* by choosing the 1893 edition as copy-text and emending it liberally from the 1896 edition. He declared:

> On the evidence of Crane's recorded literary convictions . . . backed by the solid evidence of the limited nature of the actual literary and stylistic alterations that he chose to make in 1896 when he had the chance, a synthesis of the two editions is possible to create a form of the text that will represent his final artistic intentions divorced from the censorship alterations that were alien to him. This may properly be called the 'ideal' text of *Maggie* as a literary fact, not a limited 'ideal' text either of the 1893 or of the 1896 edition. It is the text presented in this edition. (P. xcv)

Pizer objected that such a method makes the text reflect Bowers's own critical reading of the novel: "The 1893 *Maggie* is one kind of book, the 1896 another, and Bowers's a third." Although many of Pizer's more general opinions on the proper performance of textual scholarship represent a position that is open to serious criticism, in the specific judgment of *Maggie* he seems to be right. Subsequent volumes in the University of Virginia Edition have drawn little more than mildly approving notices of publication, possibly because reviewers have decided that since Bowers is wrestling with complicated questions in virtually unexplored territory his work ought to be judged in its entirety, when the edition is completed.

There have been three full-scale biographies of Stephen Crane: Thomas Beer's *Stephen Crane: A Study in American Letters* (New York, 1923), John Berryman's *Stephen Crane* (New York, 1950), and R. W. Stallman's *Stephen Crane: A Biography* (New York, 1968). Although the first two make good reading, none of them is particularly accurate, competently documented, convincing in portraying Crane as either man or writer, or reasonable in setting his work in the context of his life. The broad outlines of Stephen Crane's existence are well established, but Crane biography to date consists mainly of rough chronology fleshed out by a disproportionate number of unverified stories and obvious legends.

Crane himself caused part of the problem. Secretive, he seemed to have guarded his privacy from even his close friends; careless, he did not trouble to keep the facts straight even for his own use; youthful, he delighted in striking whatever pose served his immediate purpose. A fair number of people who thought they knew Crane tried to write about him after he died, but the quality that comes through their memoirs most strikingly is his elusiveness. "I spent ten years planning a study of Crane," remarked a friend quoted by Williams and Starrett in the introduction to their 1948 bibliography, "and ended by deciding there was no such animal, although I knew him for eleven years." Nevertheless, these divergent accounts have been used as biographical sources. Because they offer the potential of approaching closer to the elusive Stephen Crane, they ought to be collected soon with a view to reconciling as many of their differences as possible.

Other difficulties have been created by Thomas Beer, Crane's first biographer. Beer apparently did a great deal of research for his book, interviewing people who had known Crane and gathering documentary material from them. He was in an enviable position to do this: twenty years after Crane's death there were many who would come forward to talk about their reasonably fresh recollections and to turn up the letters he had sent them, and Beer had a wide circle of notable friends who gave his attempt credibility and luster. Unfortunately, no one seems to know what happened to the material Beer gathered for his life of Crane. So unhappy is their disappearance that R. W. Stallman fabricated a story that Beer must have burned them all. Embarrassing to that theory is the survival, unnoticed until recently, of a couple of letters Beer quotes in his book. The fire must have been apocryphal; if some material survives, others may too. But where?

All that is known of them now is what Beer quoted, paraphrased, or interpreted in his biography. The two surviving letters suggest not so much that he was inaccurate as that, consciously or unconsciously, he selected facts that would represent Crane in a certain way. Youthful, brilliant, gentlemanly, moral, but hag-ridden by fears he was driven to master and oppressed by the hypocrisies of a philistine age he could not overcome, this Stephen Crane is the one everyone knows. A compelling figure of the heroic artist torn between the demands of his art and those of his society, the image results more from the vision of the Twenties than from the reality of the Seventies, Eighties, and Nineties. It is the view of the artist's situation propounded by H. L. Mencken and others in the set to which Beer belonged, and it is faithful to the strains Beer placed on the protagonist of *The Fair Rewards*, the novel that he published the year before his *Stephen Crane*. He seems to have lived the artist's life much as he wrote it; small wonder that he, like another of his circle, Theodore Dreiser, saw Crane as having done so too. The dilemma created by Beer's book, then, is that it is basic to Crane biography because it is based on information for which no other sources survive, but at the same time it cannot be trusted as reliable in any sense. Some day it will be possible to regard it as exclusively of value in its appropriate place—as splendid reading that illuminates by its style and its theses the Twenties' view of the Nineties—but now it must be recommended, with cautions, as the first book about Crane to be read by serious students and general readers.

John Berryman's biography was based on Beer's and benefited from the spate of memoirs evoked by the earlier book. Like Beer, Berryman had done his homework: he corresponded with those friends and relatives of Crane who had survived both Crane and Beer; he saw Crane's letters to Nellie Crouse; he read the unedited script for Corwin Knapp Linson's long memoir subsequently edited by E. H. Cady as *My Stephen Crane* (Syracuse, 1958); and he evidently studied relevant articles in the academic journals. Like Beer too, Berryman had his thesis, and like Beer's, Berryman's shaped his book. Berryman saw Crane's life as charged with continuing and uncontrollable excitement created by self-fulfilling frustrations generated by Oedipal drives. Where Beer saw fear and philistinism as Crane's mistresses, Berryman sees Freud as his master. And, like Beer, Berryman's theory of Crane influences at least his interpretation and selection of facts. This is understandable: every biographer, try as he might to be objective, must eventually arrive at a thesis which will be at once his strength and his weakness. Attempting to interpret his subject, he is bound in some ways to distort it. Unfortunately, Berryman's theory of Crane seems to be untenable. As Edwin H. Cady's masterful "Essay on Basic Books" points out (in his *Stephen Crane* [New York, 1962], an essential work for the student's bookshelf), the facts on which the theory is based are wrong, and the theory itself is strained. Berryman is nevertheless required reading because he is in advance of Beer on facts, because he has influenced such critics as Daniel G. Hoffman (in *The Poetry of Stephen Crane* [New York, 1957]), and because—despite his apologies in a paperbound reissue of the biography (Cleveland and New York, 1962)—his critical readings of Crane's work are rewarding. In addition, like Beer's book, Berryman's has the considerable advantage of being good reading.

R. W. Stallman's biography is another matter entirely. Almost immediately after publication it received nearly unanimous praise from reviewers for being the long awaited "definitive" work. The handful of Crane scholars who pointed out quietly that the book was a regression rather than an advance were for the most part ignored, but the passage of time sees the truth of their position. Even the laudatory reviewers did not argue either that Stallman's biography was well written or that it produced an acceptable portrait of Crane: many of them recognized that it was more a collection of notes toward a biography than a finished work. Now it is becoming increasingly clear that this *Stephen Crane* is not really even a useful set of notes: its "facts" often are just wrong; its interpretations of incidents and writings are unconvincing; it is oblivious to obvious contradictions in the testimony it presents; and it transposes incidents from Crane's work into his life. Worst of all, it adds further confusion to what it should have tried to set right. The next full scale biography after Berryman's had the obligation to establish a base for Crane biography by evaluating its sources, documenting the recoverable facts, and reconciling the conflicting stories. Had it achieved that goal it would have earned exemption from most other tests of good biography and deserved an enduring place in Crane scholarship. Sadly, Stallman evaded this primary obligation. Twelve appendices and hundreds of notes give the show but not the substance of the research on which his book should have been built, for their dominant function is to carry on quarrels with the people who have been steadily contributing the information on which Stallman has drawn, instead of to verify, analyze, and document the material it presents. The result is that it is next to impossible to know now whether new material here is based on fact or surmise, and so additional elements of uncertainty have been introduced into an area that has long had enough.

Although Stephen Crane biography is therefore largely traditionary, with stories passed on from biographer to biographer for further embroidery in the process, the alert student can piece together from it some temporary version of Crane's life until the necessary has been done. To the primary materials and the biographies by Beer and Berryman he can add a few books and a number of articles as basic sources. All Crane checklists provide access to the essential articles, with writings by Thomas A. Gullason, Lillian Gilkes, and William Randel being among the more significant academic pieces, and those in the *Stephen Crane Newsletter* adding significant quanta of primary information. Cady's *Stephen Crane* has sections that offer admirable insights making it one of the first books to read. Lillian Gilkes's *Cora Crane: A Biography of Mrs. Stephen Crane* (Bloomington, 1960) is authoritative on that period of Crane's life. And Louis Zara's *Dark Rider: A Novel Based on the Life of Stephen Crane* provides many rewards for the student who has read everything else, because it was based on the kind of research that could have produced the scholarly biography that some day will come.

These are the resources fundamental to the serious study of Stephen Crane. Many of them are flawed, but Crane studies is in transition today because it has learned to recognize those flaws and to try to remedy them. It is, therefore, in transition from worshipful amateurism to respectful professionalism. At the close of the Crane centenary year, its significant features are continuing affirmation of his importance to the modern reader, new dedication to discovering the facts on which a proper assessment of that importance must draw, and a positive reevaluation of the work itself. Crane has provided a specially colorful case of the artist in advance of his students, but the process of their maturation is one to which other writers have been subjected and to which still others must submit. It is a process in which that part of their audience which prizes their work sufficiently to give it close study is making the attempt to approach it more satisfactorily by refining its tools to a lesser degree of imperfection.

Index

Index

Index

tion at Syracuse, 208; edits Linson
memoir, 229; importance of, 231; on
Crane and Howells, 109; on Crane's
relations with women, 114; on *The
Third Violet* and *Active Service*, 114;
quoted on Crane, 107; writes mani-
festo for Center for Editions of
American Authors, 225
"Caged with a Wild Man," 27
Calendars of American Literary Manu-
scripts (CALM), 210
Cather, Willa: as continuer of literary
tradition, 124; introduction of, in
collected edition, 215; on *Active Ser-
vice*, 115–16, 118; relationship with
Crane, 115–16; story by, contrasted
with Crane's, 116–17
Cazemajou, Jean, 108
Center for Editions of American Au-
thors, 225
Century, 209
"Chelifer" (Rupert Hughes), 108, 109
Chicago *Inter-Ocean*, 108
Chicago Renaissance Circle, 201
Clark, Dora, 4, 9
Cliff-Dwellers, The (Fuller), 199
Coates, Henry T. and Company, 161,
207
Collamoro, H. B., 154
Color of a Great City, The (Dreiser),
184
Columbia University: Crane collection
at, 154, 166, 205, 206, 207, 211
Colvert, James B., 46
"Coming Aphrodite" (Cather), 116
Commodore, S. S.: account of sinking
of, quoted, 66; and United States
neutrality laws, 83–84n; charges
made on, 83n; Crane sails on, 5;
Crane's experience on the, and fic-
tion, 16, 27; mentioned, 28, 69, 70,
80, 82; on the sinking of, 5, 84n;
scholarship on the sinking of, 67–68;
sketch on the, explained, 23
Complete Short Stories and Sketches

of Stephen Crane, The (Gullason),
217
*Complete Novels of Stephen Crane,
The* (Gullason), 217
Complete Poems of Stephen Crane, The
(Katz), 224
"Coney Island's Failing Days," 15
Conrad, Joseph: critical of Crane's
work, 118; effect of impressions of,
on Crane criticism, 122; inscription
by, in Crane work, 153; letter of,
sold, 164; on Crane as an impres-
sionist, 106; on women, 114; preface
by, for Crane biography, 154
Copeland and Day, 164, 207
*Cora Crane: A Biography of Mrs.
Stephen Crane* (Gilkes), 206, 231
"Cora's Mouse" (Bruccoli), 206
Corbett, James, 13
Coughlan, Florence Crane, 155
Courier, 216
"Crane at Velestino," 16
Crane, Cora Taylor: as Crane's common-law wife, 5; authoritative biography of, 231; caricature of, in Crane
novel, 117; Crane material of, 154;
failure of attempts of, in *Last Words*,
214, 217; holidays with Crane, 121;
letters by, on collection list, 154;
mentioned, 122; missing letters of,
225; papers of, 205, 207; role of, 225;
trouble with husband of, 118
Crane, Edmund (brother), 111
Crane, Rev. Jonathan Townley (father),
32n
Crane, Stephen (1871–1900):
His IDEAS: and his vision of the
world, 136, 145; and skepticism, 14;
changes in, 19; cynicism in, 14, 15;
difference between, and Dreiser's,
194–95; discussed, 26, 28; fatalism
in, 14, 16; impact of schools of
thought on, 12–13; in *Maggie*, 45;
lack of philosophic determinism in,
35, 37, 51; on existence, 82; on man

235

Crane, Stephen (*continued*)
88; his New York City works and
social realism in, 26, 127, 130; illness and criticism of, 122; imagery
in, 37, 86, 88–93, 95–99, 104; importance of Crane's mythic imagination in, 149, 151; importance of
motivation in, 90; influence of, on
Dreiser, 175, 194–96, 198, 199; influences on, 26, 27, 109; irony in,
104, 179; irreverence in, 13; "little
man" fable in, 132, 134–41 *passim*,
143, 145, 148, 149; major private
collections of, 154; man and nature
metaphor in, 136; moral responsibility in, 41–42; motivations of, 12;
naturalism in, 37–38, 93; naturalistic
criticism and sociological theory on,
51; Nature in, 22, 23, 70, 71, 77, 80,
91, 132, 135, 137, 138, 145; need for
bibliographies of, 210–13; New York
fiction shows experiments in, 11,
135, 145; note to William Crane
quoted from, 122; on Asbury Park,
9, 13–14; on coal mines, 8, 22, 32–
33n, 163, 220; on studies of, 209–10,
213–15, 231; on the Boer War, 19,
154; on the S. S. Commodore, 5, 16,
23, 27, 66, 67, 68–69; origins of style
of, in experimental fiction, 131; over-
view of scholarship of, 205, 231;
parallelisms with experience in, 118–
19; peace in, 54–58 *passim*, 62, 64;
penetration beneath Victorian society in, 118, 120; poetry in, 128;
possible stage productions of, 123;
preference for West in, 15, 16; problems of collections of, 217; problems
of scholarship regarding correspondence, 225; quote on hell in, 59–60;
quote on literary aims of, 128;
realism and war stories in, 130; realism in, 196, 197, 200; recurring
motifs of, 132, 134–35, 150; return
to the conventional novel in, 107;

revival of interest in, 211; sale of,
after Crane's death, 201; similarities
in, 36, 37, 40, 45–47, 50, 90–104
passim; similarity of, to Melville,
60, 62; stylistic development of, 19–
26 *passim*; "The Men in the Storm,"
compared with Dreiser, 184, 185–93;
theme of endurance in, 16; theme
of escape in, 15; *The Red Badge of
Courage* as an exercise, 128; Vincent
Starrett pushes, 201–2; war against
nature and man-made world in, 132,
135, 136–40, 142; war and death in,
54–64 *passim*, 146, 149; war fiction
in, 5, 9–10, 28, 30, 129; war journalism and, 16, 17, 18, 19, 22–25, 28–29;
Whitman's style and, 57
"Crane Tells the Story of the Disembarkment," 18–19
Crane, Townley (brother), 3, 7, 131,
215
Crane, Wilbur (brother), 3
Crane, William (brother), 122
"Criticism of Stephen Crane" (Gullason and Beebe), 213
Crouse, Nellie: as "Gibson girl," 111;
Crane's courtship of, 113; Crane's
courtship of and *The Third Violet*,
109; Crane's letters to, 109; letters
of, at Syracuse University, 208; letters to, and Crane biography, 229
"Crowding into Asbury Park," 13
"Curious Shifts of the Poor" (Dreiser),
184, 193–94

"Dan Emmonds," 121
*Dark Rider: A Novel Based on the Life
of Stephen Crane* (Zara), 209, 231
Dartmouth College, 154, 208
Davis, Richard Harding, 11, 175
Davis, Robert H., 215
"Death and the Child": and Crane's de-
velopment of style, 28–29; basic ele-
ments of, 146; shows Crane's control

over his observation, 131; snipes at yellow journalism, 9–10
Defoe, Daniel, 122
Demorest's Family Magazine, 184. See also Mary Annabel Fanton
"Denies Mutilation of Bodies," 10
"Desertion, A," 163
"Devil's Acre, The," 40
"Diamond Mine, The" (Cather), 116
Dickens, Charles, 107
Dinamov, Sergei (Russian critic), 198–99, 202
"door clanged behind him, The," 163
Doubleday, Doran and Company, 199
Doubleday-Page and Company, 199
"Down in a Coal Mine," 32–33n
Dreiser, Theodore: and Frank Norris, 199; and Henry Blake Fuller, 200; and *Sister Carrie*, 184, 193, 194, 195, 198, 199, 200; and the "Crane problem," 86; and "The Men in the Storm," 184–93; anti-heroism in, 118; careers of, 174, 183, 194; complex attitudes of, toward Crane, 175-79, 183, 195–98, 199, 200–202, 228; difficulties of, with critics, 198; influence of Crane on, 175, 193–94, 198, 199; *McTeague*, 199; seminal work of, 184; shares acquaintances with Crane, 183; thought of, 178; vision of, differs from Crane's, 194–95; works of, published, 184, and
Dresser, Paul (brother of Theodore Dreiser), 176
Dudley, Dorothy, 175, 200–201

"Editions of American Authors, 1963: A Preliminary Survey" (Gibson and Cady), 225
"Encantadas, The" (Melville), 60
Et Cetera, 201
Ev'ry Month: Crane works reviewed in, 180–81, 184; Crane's works printed in, 175, 184, 198; Dreiser leaves, 183; George C. Jenks and,

180; moderate success of, 179; publishes Michelson story, 183; Spencer's article published in, 178; under Dreiser's direction, 174, 176, 177–78, 179
"Experiment in Luxury, An": published, 4, 11, 14, 15; quoted, 22; version of war in, 55
"Experiment in Misery, An": and *George's Mother*, 36, 47; and *Maggie*, 36; Bowery life in, 45, 135; implication of moral guilt in, 50; mentioned, 21; pauperism in, 40, 46; published, 4, 11, 14; reality in, 135
"Explosion of Seven Babies, An," 163

Fair Rewards, The (Beer), 228
Fanton, Mary Annabel, 184. See also *Demorest's Family Magazine*
Faulkner, William, 94, 118
Fielding, Henry, 122
Fifteen American Authors Before 1900 (Pizer), 213
"Fight, The," 94, 104. See also *Whilomville Stories*
Fitzgerald, F. Scott, 118
"Five White Mice, The," 26, 153, 208
"Flanagan and his Short Filibustering Adventure," 27
Folio Society of London, The, 223
Follett, Wilson, 165, 214, 217
Ford, Ford Madox, 108, 122
"Four Men in a Cave," 147. See also *Sullivan County Sketches*
"Fragment of Velestino, A," 23
Frederic, Harold, 120–22
Frewen, Moreton, 206
Frost, Robert, 76
Fryckstedt, Olov W., 217
Fuller, Henry Blake, 197, 199, 200

Galsworthy, John, 164
Garland, Franklin, 110
Garland, Hamlin: and *Maggie*, 128; contradicted, 107; Crane letters to,

Index

Garland, Hamlin *(continued)*
in collection, 209; Dreiser on, 197;
influences Crane, 6, 26, 127; on
Stephen Crane, 106, 175; realism of,
and Crane, 30, 130, 131
Garnett, Edward, 106, 118
"Genius, The" (Dreiser), 198
George Arents Stephen Crane Collection, 208
George's Mother: as novel of social realism, 127, 131, 134; Dreiser praises,
197; lack of philosophic determinism
in, 37, 51; mentioned, 198; pauperism in, 40, 45, 47, 49, 50; review of,
181–82; similarity of, to other works,
26, 45; symbolism in, 47; war in, 56,
135, 136
Ghost, The, 165, 209
"Ghost at Brede Place, The" (Gordan),
209
Gibson, William M., 223, 225
Gilkes, Lillian: details travels of Crane
papers, 206; future work of, 225; im-
portance of Crane writings of, 230,
231; on book of Crane letters by,
224–25; papers of, at Syracuse, 208
"God Rest Ye Merry Gentlemen," 29–
30. *See also Wounds in the Rain*
Godey's Magazine, 108
"Gold Slipper, The" (Cather), 116
Goodspeed's, 163, 164
Gordan, John D., 209
Grabo, Norman, 226
"Gray Sleeve, A," 184
"Great American Novel, The" (Dreiser),
195, 200
Great Battles of the World, 165
"Great Boer Trek, The," 154
"Great Bugs in Onondaga," 20, 216
Great Bugs in Onondaga, 216
Great Gatsby, The (Fitzgerald), 91
"Great Mistake, A," 161
Greiner, Donald and Ellen, 207
Griffith, O. L., 154, 210, 211
Gross, Theodore L., 213

Gullason, Thomas A.: and *George's
Mother,* 49; argues Jamesian motif
in Crane's work, 108; on Crane's social novel, 26; writings of, concerning Crane, 213, 216, 219, 230

Hafley, James, 87–88
Hagemann, E. R., 219
Hallam, George W., 206
Hardy, Thomas, 114
Harris, Frank, 108. *See also Saturday
Review* (British periodical)
Harvard University, 207, 209
Hawkins, Willis Brooks, 108, 208
Hawthorne, Julian, 9
*Hawthorne, Melville, Stephen Crane:
A Critical Bibliography* (Gross and
Wertheim), 213
Hawthorne, Nathaniel, 92, 194
Hearst, William Randolph, 5, 8, 9, 11,
118
Heine, James, 110
Heinemann, William, Ltd., 165
Hemingway, Ernest: anti-heroism in,
118; market on works of, stimulated,
166; style of, similar to Crane's, 24,
88, 91, 146
Henry E. Huntington Library, 209
Herzberg, Max J., 196–97
Higgins, William, 16, 66; as character,
68, 70, 80, 82
High Spots of American Literature, 155
Hill, Norman W., 206, 207
Hilliard, John Northern, 6, 154
"His New Mittens," 100, 104. *See also
Whilomville Stories*
Hitchcock, Ripley, 108, 208
Hoffman, Daniel G., 207, 229
Holmes, O. W., 110–11
"Horses—One Dash," 26
House of the Seven Gables, The (Haw-
thorne), 92
Howarth, William, 222
"Howells Discussed at Avon-by-the-
Sea," 6

240

Index

Howells, William Dean: and nine-teenth-century values, 12; class strat-ification in writings of, 108; Crane as a favorite of, 175; Crane's inter-view with, 219; Crane's letters to, at Harvard, 209; Dreiser on, 196; influ-ences Crane, 6, 26, 127, 128; on Crane's works, 127, 128, 144; realism of, 30, 130, 131; writes introduction to *Maggie*, 219

Howley, Haviland and Co., 176, 183

"How Novelist Crane Acts on the Battlefield," 11–12

"How the Donkey Lifted the Hills," 219

Hudspeth, Robert N., 213

Hughes, Rupert, 199

Idler, The, 224

"I Have Seen a Battle," 25

Illinois, University of, 209

"In a Park Row Restaurant," 20

"In the Depths of a Coal Mine," 8, 22, 163

Indiana University, 208

Irish Notes, 121

Itabashi, Yoshie, 224

Jacksonville Free Public Library, 206

James, Henry: Crane's resemblance to, 108; Dreiser on, 196, 200; technical device of, 113; way of thinking, 12

Jenks, George C., 180–81, 185, 198

Johnson, Merle: Crane bibliography by, 210, 211; mentioned, 164; on Crane collecting, 154–55

Johnson, Willis Fletcher, 3, 7

Jordan, Philip D., 220

Joyce, James, 118

Jude the Obscure (Hardy), 206

Jung, Carl Gustav, 59

Junior Order of United American Me-chanics, 3–4, 7

Katz, Joseph: Crane collection of, 154; Crane works by, 208, 212, 213, 216,

220, 222, 223, 224; future work of, 225

Kibler, James E., Jr., 206–7

"Kicking Twelfth, The," 150

"King's Favor, The," 20

Kipling, Rudyard, 175, 184, 206

"Knife, The," 100. *See also Whilom-ville Stories*

Knopf, Alfred A., 202

Langel, William C., 196, 198

Lantern Club, The, 11, 212

Lanthorn Book, The, 212

"The Lanthorn Book: A Census" (Katz), 212

Lanthorne Club, The. *See* Lantern Club

Last Words: and Cora Crane, 214, 217; lack of a Coates edition of, 161; men-tioned, 216; rarity of, 161; script of, at University of Virginia, 207

Leslie, Amy, 208

Levenson, J. C., 130

Lewis, Alfred Henry, 9

Lewis, Sinclair, 164

"Library of Stephen and Cora Crane, The" (Kibler), 206

Linson, Corwin Knapp, 8, 109, 167*n*, 229

"Little Pilgrimage, A," 104

Little Regiment And Other Episodes of the American Civil War, The: ab-sence of technical authority in, 147; and Crane's realism, 142, 150–51; Crane quoted on, 129; publisher of, 208; reviewed, 180–81; Starrett's copy of, sold, 164–65; style and method in, 139–40, 143, 144; under-taken reluctantly, 139; war stories after, and realism, 130

Liveright, Horace, 202

"Lone Charge of William B. Perkins, The," 10, 29–30, 149. *See also Wounds in the Rain*

"Lover and the Telltale, The," 103, 104. *See also Whilomville Stories*

Index

McClure, S. S. (Book House and Syndicate), 208, 215, 216
McClure's Magazine, 8, 129
McTeague (Norris), 199, 200
Mad River Review, 208
Maggie: A Girl of the Streets: and Crane's friendship with Garland and Howells, 128; and naturalism, 37–38; and The Cliff-Dwellers, 199; anti-heroic motif in, 118; as collector's item, 153, 154, 155, 161, 163, 166–72 passim; as novel of social realism, 26, 45, 107, 127, 131, 220; Bowery world of, 46, 108; church in, 50; destructiveness in, 38, 39, 40, 41, 43, 44; different versions of, 220–22; difficulties of, 217, 220–22; Dreiser on, 197; Howells's introduction to, 219; Howells on, 127, 128; in Crane collected edition, 225, 226; lack of philosophic determinism in, 35, 37, 51; mentioned, 198, 224; moral responsibility in, 41, 42, 43, 44; pauperism in, 40–41; promise of, unfulfilled, 12; psychological progression in, 36, 37; published, 180, 208; similarity of, to other works, 26; war against man-made world in, 135
"Maggie Nobody Knows, The" (Katz), 220
Maggie Text and Context (Bassan), 220
"Making an Orator," 100. See also Whilomville Stories
"Man and Some Others, A," 26
Marks, A. J., 212
Marshall, Edward, 4, 10–11
Martin, Jay, 87, 88
Mason, A. E. W., 123
Matthiessen, F. O., 175
Mayfield, John S., 216
Melville, Herman, 60, 62, 94, 200
"Men in the Storm, The" (Crane): analyzed, 14; and differences be-

tween Crane and Dreiser, 194–95; compared with Dreiser's version, 185–93; Dreiser borrows, 184–85; implication of moral guilt in, 50; pauperism in, 40; praised, 185; published, 184–85; quoted, 182. See also "Curious Shifts of the Poor"
Men, Women and Boats (Starrett), 201
Mencken, H. L.: and Crane, 13, 228; and Dreiser, 196, 198, 200; and McTeague, 200; essay of, in Norris collected edition, 199
Merrill Checklist of Stephen Crane, The (Katz), 213
"Mesmeric Mountain, The," 36, 134, 219
Michelson, Charles, 183, 215
"Minetta Lane," 40
Modern Fiction Studies, 213, 220
Modern Philology, 226
"Modern Pilgrimage of The Black Riders: An Interpretation, The" (Itabashi), 224
"Monster, The": and the Whilomville Stories, 99, 100, 101; and yellow journalism, 9; characters satirized in, 112; clarity of, 94; criticism of, 87; drive for survival in, 103; editions of, in collecting, 165; images in, 86; mentioned, 144; similarity of, to other Crane works, 94; structure of, 89, 96–97, 98; style changes in, 88
Montgomery, Charles R., 83n; as character, 68
Month at Goodspeed's, The, 164
Morley, Christopher, 199
"Mr. Stephen Crane on the New America," 18
Munroe, Lily Brandon, 19
Murphy, Captain Edward: blamed, 83n; Crane praises, 16, 66; leader on life boat, 28; quoted, 68; as character, 71, 72, 73, 78, 79, 82

Index

Index

Index

Stephen Crane Newsletter: and the Lantern Club rumor, 212; importance of Crane writings in, 230–31; quarterly checklist in, 213; supplements of, and letter collections, 225

"Stephen Crane's English Years: The Legend Corrected" (Stronks), 212

Stephen Crane's Love Letters to Nellie Crouse (Cady and Wells), 208

"Stephen Crane's Own Story": explained, 28; mentioned, 27; published, 5, 16; quoted, 66

Stephen Crane: Sullivan County Tales and Sketches (Stallman), 218–19

"Stephen Crane's Vivid Story of the Battle of San Juan," 18, 23

"Stephen Crane Tells of War's Horrors," 9, 16

Stephen Crane: Uncollected Writings (Fryckstedt), 217

Stevenson, Robert Louis, 122

Stokes, Frederick A., 223

Stolper, Benjamin John Reeman, 210–11

"Storming of Badajos," 163

Stronks, James, 212

Studies in Bibliography, 206, 212–13, 222

Sullivan County Sketches: as early experiment in fiction, 131, 151; compositional devices in the, 130; imagery in the, 134, 147; irony in the, 20–21; published, 14; religious subject in the, 136; similar structure of the, to other Crane works, 94; theme in the, 132

Sullivan County Sketches of Stephen Crane, The (Schoberlin), 217, 218

Swanberg, W. A., 202

Syracuse University, 154, 207, 208

Syracuse University *Herald,* 20

"Talk of London, The," 19

Taylor, Cora. *See* Crane, Cora Taylor

Tenderloin, 4, 15, 16

Thackeray, William Makepeace, 107

Third Violet, The: Active Service and, 117, 118; as autobiographical novel, 109; as best-seller, 107; as Howellsian comedy, 139; Crane quoted on, 129; effect of, on Willa Cather, 115; failure of, 113, 114; in collected edition, 225; mixed reviews of, 107, 108; published, 108, 208; realism and, 129; Starrett's copy of, sold, 165; "technical originality" of, 109, 110, 111, 112, 113, 124

"This Majestic Lie," 30, 54

Thoth, 213

"Three little birds in a row," 164

"Three Sketches of the Poor" (Dreiser), 184

Tolstoy, Leo, 114

Tom Jones (Fielding), 122

Townsend, Edward, 9

"Trial, Execution and Burial of Homer Phelps, The," 102. *See also Whilomville Stories*

Tsuda Review, 224

Twain, Mark (Samuel Clemens), 12, 196

Union Square Bookshop, 161

"Upturned Face, The," 36, 131

"Veteran, The": as sequel to *The Red Badge of Courage,* 143; dualism in, 92; new style and method appears in, 143, 144, 146; realism in, 147

Virginia, University of: collected edition published by the, 165; Crane collection at the, 154, 205, 206, 207, 209

"Virtue in War," 29–30. *See also Wounds in the Rain*

Walters, Henry W., 206, 207

War Is Kind, 155, 163, 164, 224

"War Memories": imagery in the, 147–48; quoted, 33n; realism in the, 145; temperate character of the, 17

Wells, H. G., 200, 209

Wells, H. G., Collection, 209

Index

Wells, Lester G., 208
Wertheim, Stanley, 213
West, Herbert Faulkner, 208
Westbrook, Max R., 46
Westminster Gazette, 5, 9
Wharton, Edith, 200
"When Everyone is Panic Stricken," 22
Whilomville Stories: best of the, 102; characters satirized in the, 112; companion to "The Monster," 99, 100; Crane's art and experience in the, 130; critique of the, 99–100; editions of the, in collecting, 165; in collected edition, 225; similarities among the, 104; stories in the, 94, 100, 102, 103, 104
Whitman, Walt, 57
Wilkins, Mary E., 179
Williams, Ames W.: Crane bibliography by, 161, 165, 208, 211, 214, 227; Crane collection of, sold, 154
Winterich, John T., 223

"Wise Men, The," 212. *See also The Lanthorn Book*
Wister, Owen, 17, 30
With the Procession (Dreiser), 199
Work of Stephen Crane, The (ed., Follett, 12 vols., 1925–1927), 165, 202, 214–15, 217
Works of Stephen Crane, The (Univ. of Va., 10 vols., 1969–   ), 165, 222, 225, 226
Wounds in the Rain: as collection of Cuban stories, 29; Cora's copy of the, 206; editions of, in collecting, 165; mentioned, 144; stories in, 29–30, 54, 147, 149; war in the, 147

Yerkes, Charles T., 125n
Young, William, 163
"Youse Wants Petey, Youse Do," 6, 219

Zara, Louis, 209, 231
Zoo Story, The (Albee), 55